English Reprints

ROGER ASCHAM

Toxophilus

1545

EDITED BY

EDWARD ARBER

F.S.A. ETC. LATE EXAMINER IN ENGLISH
LANGUAGE AND LITERATURE
TO THE UNIVERSITY OF
LONDON

WESTMINSTER
A. CONSTABLE AND CO.
1895

CONTENTS

CHRONICLE

of

foine of the principal events

in the

LIFE, WORKS, and TIMES

of

ROGER ASCHAM,

Fellow of St. John's College, Cambridge. Author. Tutor to Princess, afterwards Queen Elizabeth. Secretary of Embassy under Edward VI. Latin Secretary to Queens Mary and Elizabeth. Friend of Queen Elizabeth, &c.

---

* Probable or approximate dates.

THE chief contemporary authorities for the life of Ascham are his own works, particularly his Letters, and a Latin oration *De vitâ et obitu Rogeri Aschami*, written by Rev. Dr. Edward Graunt or Grant, Headmaster of Westminster School, and 'the most noted Latiniste and Grecian of his time.' This oration is affixed to the first collection of Ascham's Letters : the date of Grant's dedication to which is 16. Feb. 1576.

The figures in brackets, as (40), in the present work, refer to Ascham's letters as arranged in Dr. Giles' edition.

1509. April 22. Henry VIII. succeeds to the throne.

1511-12. 3. Hen. VIII. c. 3. required—under penalty on default of 12d per month—all subjects under 60, not lame, decrepid, or maimed, or having any other lawful Impediment; the Clergy Judges &c excepted : to use shooting in the long bow. Parents were to provide every boy from 7 to 17 years, with a bow and two arrows : after 17, he was to find himself a bow and four arrows. Every Bower for every Ewe bow he made was to make 'at the lest ij Bowes of Elme Wiche or other Wode of mean price,' under penalty of Imprisonment for 8 days. Butts were to be provided in every town. Aliens were not to shoot with the long bow without licence.

3 Hen. VIII. c. 13. confirms 19. Hen. VII. c 4 'against shooting in Cross-bowes &c,' which enacted that no one with less than 200 marks a year should use. This act increased the qualification from 200 to 300 marks.—*Statutes of the Realm. iii. 25. 32.*

*1515.

ROGER ASCHAM was born in the year 1515, at Kirby Wiske, (or Kirby Wicke,) a village near North Allerton in Yorkshire, of a family above the vulgar. His father, John Ascham, was house-steward in the family of Lord Scroop, and is said to have borne an unblemished reputation for honesty and uprightness of life. Margaret, wife of John Ascham, was allied to many considerable families, but her maiden name is not known. She had three sons, Thomas, Antony, and Roger, besides some daughters ; and we learn from a letter (21) written by her son Roger, in the year 1544, that she and her husband having lived together forty-seven years, at last died on the same day and almost at the same hour.

Roger's first years were spent under his father's roof, but he was received at a very youthful age into the family of Sir Antony Wingfield, who furnished money for his education, and placed Roger, together with his own sons, under a tutor, whose name was R. Bond. The boy had by nature a taste for books, and showed his good taste by reading English in preference to Latin, with

Childhood.

wonderful eagernes. . . . —*Grant. Condensed trans-*
lation by Dr. Giles in Life: see p. 10, *No* 9.

"This communication of teaching youthe, maketh me
to remembre the right worshipfull and my singuler good
maynter, Sir Humfrey Wingfelde, to whom nexte God,
I ought to refer for his manifolde benefites bestowed on
me, the poore talent of learnyng, whiche god hath lent
me : and for his sake do I owe my seruice to all other
of the name and noble house of the Wyngfeldes, bothe
in woord and dede. Thys worshypfull man hath euer
loued and vsed, to haue many children brought vp in
learnynge in his house amonges whome I my selfe was
one. For whom at terme tymes he woulde bryng downe
from London bothe bowe and shaftes. And when they
shuld playe he woulde go with them him selfe in to the
fyelde, and se them shoote, and he that shot fayrest,
shulde haue the best bowe and shaftes. and he that shot
ilfauouredlye, shulde be mocked of his felowes, til he shot
better."—*p.* 140.

In or about the year 1530, Mr. Bond . . . resigned the
charge of young Roger, who was now about fifteen
years old, and, by the advice and pecuniary aid of his
kind patron Sir Antony, he was enabled to enter St.
John's College, Cambridge, at that time the most famous
seminary of learning in all England. His tutor was Hugh
Fitzherbert, fellow of St. John's, whose intimate friend,
George Pember, took the most lively interest in the
young student. George Day, afterwards Bishop of
Chichester, Sir John Cheke, Sir Thomas Smith, Dr.
Redman, one of the compilers of the Book of Common
Prayer, Nicholas Ridley the Martyr, T. Watson Bishop
of Lincoln, Pilkington Bishop of Durham, Walter Had-
don, John Christopherson, Thomas Wilson, John Seton,
and many others, were the distinguished contemporaries
of Ascham at Cambridge.—*Grant and Giles, idem.*

He takes his B.A. "Being a boy, new Bacheler of arte,
I chanced amonges my companions to speake against the
Pope : which matter was than in euery mans mouth, bycause *Dr. Haines* and *Dr. Skippe* were cum from the
Court, to debate the same matter, by preaching and dis-
putation in the vniuersitie. This hapned the same tyme,
when I stoode to be felow there : my taulke came to *Dr.
Medcalfes* [Master of St. John's Coll.] eare : I was called
before him and the Seniores : and after greuous rebuke,
and some punishment, open warning was geuen to all the
felowes, none to be so hardie to geue me his voice at that
election. And yet for all those open threates, the good
father himselfe priuilie procured, that I should euen than
be chosen felow. But, the election being done, he made
countinance of great discontentation thereat. This good
mans goodnes, and fatherlie discretion, vsed towardes me
that one day, shall neuer out of my remembrance all the
dayes of my life. And for the same cause, haue I put
it here, in this small record of learning. For next Gods
prouidence, surely that day, was by that good fathers
meanes, *Dies natalis*, to me, for the whole foundation
of the poore learning I haue, and of all the furderance,
that hetherto else where I haue obtayned."—*Scho. fol.* 55.

"Before the king's majesty established his lecture at
Cambridge, I was appointed by the votes of all the
university, and was paid a handsome salary, to profess
the Greek tongue in public; and I have ever since read

a lecture in St. John's college, of which I am a fellow." (22) *To Sir W. Paget in* 1544.

1537. July 3.		[*die martis post festum Diui Petri et Pauli* (June 29) *Grant*]. Is installed M.A.
	æt. 21.	
1538. Spring.		Visits his parents in Yorkshire, whom he had not seen for seven years.
	æt. 22.	
Autumn.		Date of his earliest extant letter.
1540–1542.		Is at home in Yorkshire, for nearly two years, with quartan fever. Probably about this time he attended the archery meetings at York and Norwich. *pp.* 159. 160.
1540.	æt. 24.	'In the great snowe,' journeying 'in the hye waye betwixt Topcliffe vpon Swale; and Borrowe bridge,' he watches the nature of the wind by the snow-drifts. *p.* 157.
1541.	æt. 25.	Upon his repeated application, Edward Lee, Archbp of York, grants him a pension of 40s. (= £40 of present money) payable at the feast of Annunciation and on Michaelmas day. *see* (24). This pension ceased on the death of the Archbishop in 1544.
1541-2.		33 Hen. VIII. c. 9. 'An Acte for Mayntanance of Artyllarie and debarringe of unlaufal Games.' confirms 3 Hen. VIII. c. 3. and, *inter alia*, directs that no Bowyer shall sell a Ewe bow to any between 8 and 14 years, above the price of 12d, but shall have for such, Ewe bows from 6d to 12d: and likewise shall sell bows at reasonable prices to youth from 14 to 21 years. Ewe bows 'of the taxe called Elke' were not to be sold above 3s 4d, under penalty of 20s.—*Statutes of the Realm. iii.* 837.
1544. *Spring.	æt. 28.	Ascham writes *Toxophilus*.
After Lady Day.		Both his parents die. "How hard is my lot! I first lost my brother, such an one as not only our family, but all England could hardly match, and now to lose both my parents as if I was not already overwhelmed with sorrow!" (21) *To Cheke.*
Before July.		"I have also written and dedicated to the king's majesty a book, which is now in the press, *On the art of Shooting*, and in which I have shown how well it is fitted for Englishmen both at home and abroad, and how certain rules of art may be laid down to ensure its being learnt thoroughly by all our fellow-countrymen. This book, I hope, will be published before the king's departure, and will be no doubtful sign of my love to my country, or mean memorial of my humble learning. (22) *To Sir W. Paget.*
July—Sept. 30.		The king out of the kingdom, at the head of 30,000 men at the siege of Boulogne, in France.
1545.	æt. 29.	Ascham presents *Toxophilus* to the king, in the gallery at Greenwich. He is granted a pension of £10. *pp.* 165-166. He is ill again, and unable to reside at Cambridge.
1546.	æt. 30.	Succeeds Cheke as Public Orator of his University, in which capacity he conducts its correspondence.

1547. Jan. 28. Edward VI. comes to the throne.

Ascham's pension which ceased on the death of Henry VIII., was confirmed and augmented by Edward VI., whom he taught to write. [Ascham's pension is one of the prominent things in his life.]

1548. Feb	æt. 32.	Is Tutor to Princess Elizabeth, at Cheston. Attacked by her steward, he returns to the university.
1549. Sept.	æt. 33	
1550.	æt. 34.	While at home in the country, Ascham is appointed, at the instigation of Cheke, as Secretary to Sir Richard Morison, sent out as Ambassador to Emperor Charles V. On his way to town, has his famous interview with Lady Jane Grey at Broadgate. *Scholemaster, fol.* 12.

Secretary of Embassy.	Sept 21	The Embassy embarks at Billingsgate, and finally reaches Augsburg on Oct 28: where it appears to have remained more than a year.
	1552. Oct.	Ascham writes, probably from Spires, *A Report and Discourse written by Roger Ascham, of the affaires and state of Germany and the Emperour Charles his court, during certaine yeares while the sayd Roger was there.* Published at London, the next year, without date.

1553. July 6. Mary succeeds to the crown.

<table>
<tr><td rowspan="2" style="writing-mode: vertical-lr">Latin Secretary to Queens Mary and Elizabeth.</td><td>1553. July 7.</td><td>Writes from Brussels.
On the death of the King the Embassy is recalled.</td></tr>
<tr><td>1554. April.

May 7.

June 1. æt. 38.</td><td>Though a Protestant, Ascham escapes persecution; his pension of £10 is renewed and increased, *see p. 105.*
He is made Latin Secretary to the Queen, with a salary of 40 marks.
Resigns his Fellowship and Office of Public Orator.
Marries Margaret Howe.
He sometimes reads Greek with the Princess Elizabeth.</td></tr>
</table>

1558. Nov. 17. Elizabeth begins to reign.

		Ascham's pension and Secretaryship are continued.
	1560. Mar. 11. æt. 44.	Is made prebend of Wetwang, in York Cathedral. He had now possession of a considerable income. It would be satisfactory if he could be cleared from the suspicion of a too great love for cock-fighting.
	1563. Dec. 10. æt. 47.	The Court being at Windsor on account of the plague in London, Sir W. Cecil gave a dinner in his chamber. A conversation on Education arose on the news 'that diverse Scholers of Eaton be runne awaie from the Schole, for feare of beating.' Sir Richard Sackville, then silent, afterwards renewed the subject with Ascham; who finally writes for his grandson, Robert Sackville, *The Scholemaster,* first published by his widow in 1570.

<table>
<tr><td rowspan="3" style="writing-mode: vertical-lr">Illness and death.</td><td></td><td>His constitution had been enfeebled by frequent attacks of ague. Imprudently sitting up late to finish some Latin verses which he designed to present to the queen as a new-year's gift, and certain letters to his friends, he contracted a dangerous malady, during which he was visited and consoled by his pious friend Alexander Nowell, dean of St. Paul's, and William Gravet, a prebendary of that church and vicar of St. Sepulchre's London. Ascham died 30 Dec. 1568. His last words were "I desire to depart and to be with Christ."</td></tr>
<tr><td>1568. Dec. 30. æt. 53.</td><td></td></tr>
<tr><td>1569. Jan. 4.</td><td>He was buried at St. Sepulchre's. Nowell preached his funeral sermon, and testified that he never saw or heard of a person of greater integrity of life, or who was blessed with a more christian death. Queen Elizabeth, when informed of his decease, declared that she would rather have lost £10,000, than her tutor Ascham.</td></tr>
</table>

Buchanan did honour to his memory in the following epitaph:

Aschamum extinctum patriæ, Graiæque Camœnæ,
Et Latiæ verâ cum pietate dolent.
Principibus vixit carus, jucundis amicis,
Re modicâ, in mores dicere fama nequit.

which has been thus rendered by Archdeacon Wrangham.

O'er Ascham, withering in his narrow urn,
The muses—English, Grecian, Roman—mourn;
Though poor, to greatness dear, to friendship just:
No scandal's self can taint his hallow'd dust.

Cooper. Ath. Cantag, p. 266.

TOXOPHILUS.

INTRODUCTION.

Espite his promife, fee page 20, Afcham wrote no Englifh work on a great fubject. Writing late in life, his *Scholemafter*, he thus defends his choice in the fubjects of his books :

" But, of all kinde of paftimes, fitte for a Ientleman, I will, godwilling, in fitter place, more at large, de-clare fullie, in my booke of the Cockpitte : which I do write, to fatiffie fom, I truft, with fom reafon, that be more curious, in marking other mens doinges, than carefull in mendyng their owne faultes. And fom alfo will nedes bufie them felues in merueling, and adding thereunto vnfrendlie taulke, why I, a man of good yeares, and of no ill place, I thanke God and my Prince, do make choife to fpend foch tyme in writyng of trifles, as the fchole of fhoting, the Cockpitte, and this booke of the firft Principles of Grammer, rather, than to take fome weightie matter in hand, either of Religion, or Ciuill difcipline.

Wife men I know, will well allow of my choife herein : and as for fuch, who haue not witte of them felues, but muft learne of others, to iudge right of mens doynges, let them read that wife Poet *Horace* in his *Arte Poetica*, who willeth wifemen to beware, of hie and loftie Titles. For, great fhippes, require coft-lie tackling, and alfo afterward dangerous gouernment. Small boates, be neither verie chargeable in makyng, nor verie oft in great ieoperdie : and yet they cary many tymes, as good and coftlie ware, as greater veffels do. A meane Argument, may eafelie beare, the light burden of a fmall faute, and haue alwaife at hand, a ready excufe for ill handling : And, fome praife it is, if it fo chaunce, to be better in deede, than a man dare venture to feeme. A hye title, doth charge a man, with the heauie burden, of to great a promife, and therfore fayth *Horace* verie wittelie, that,

that Poet was a verie foole, that began hys booke, with
a goodlie verſe in deede, but ouer proude a promiſe.

 Fortunam Priami cantabo et nobile bellum,
And after, as wiſelie

 Quantò rectiùs hic, qui nil molitur ineptè. &c.
Meening *Homer,* who, within the compaſſe of a ſmal
Argument, of one harlot, and of one good wife, did
vtter ſo moch learning in all kinde of ſciences, as, by
the iudgement of *Quintilian,* he deſerueth ſo hie a
praiſe, that no man yet deſerued to ſit in the ſecond
degree beneth him. And thus moch out of my way, concerning my purpoſe in ſpending penne, and paper, and
tyme, vpon trifles, and namelie to aunſwere ſome, that
haue neither witte nor learning, to do any thyng them
ſelues, neither will nor honeſtie, to ſay well of other" *

 Certain it is, that in both *Toxophilus* and *The Schole-
maſter* (the *Cockpitte* if ever printed, is now loſt) ; not
only are the main arguments interwoven with a moſt
earneſt moral purpoſe ; but they are enlivened by
frequent and charming diſcurſions, in the which he
often lays down great principles, or illuſtrates them
from the circumſtances of his time. So that in theſe
two ways, theſe works, being not rigidly confined to the
technical ſubjects expreſſed by their titles, do 'beare,'
both in thoſe ſubjects and in the paſſing thoughts,
much of what is the higheſt truth.

 If a Yorkſhire man—who had become a ripe Engliſh
Scholer, and was alſo a fluent Engliſh writer as well as
converſant with other languages and literatures—were,
in the preſent day, to ſit down to write, for the firſt
time, in the defence and praiſe of Cricket, a book in
the Yorkſhire dialect : he would be able to appreciate
ſomewhat Aſcham's poſition when he began to write the
preſent work. For he lived in the very dawn of our
modern learning. Not to ſpeak of the heſitation and
doubt that always impedes any novelty, the abſence
of any antecedent literature left him without any model
of ſtyle. Accuſtomed as he had hitherto been to write
chiefly in Latin, he muſt have found Engliſh compoſi-
tion both irkſome and laborious. Yet his love for his

country, and his delight, even from childhood, in his native tongue overcame all difficulties. "Althoughe to haue vvritten this boke either in latin or Greeke . . . . had been more easier and fit for mi trade in study, yet neuertheleffe, I suppofinge it no point of honeftie, that mi commodite fhould ftop and hinder ani parte either of the pleafure or profite of manie, haue vvritten this Englifhe matter in the Englifhe tongue, for Englifhe men." * In fo doing, he has bequeathed to pofterity a noble fpecimen of Englifh language, expreffing genuine Englifh thought, upon a truly Englifh fubject.

Of the influence of this deliberate choice of Afcham on the literature of his time, Dr. N. Drake thus fpeaks :—

"The *Toxophilus* of this ufeful and engaging writer, was written in his native tongue, with the view of prefenting the public with a fpecimen of a purer and more correct *Englifh* ftyle than that to which they had hitherto been accuftomed; and with the hope of calling the attention of the learned, from the exclufive ftudy of the Greek and Latin, to the cultivation of their vernacular language. The refult which he contemplated was attained, and, from the period of this publication, the fhackles of Latinity were broken, and compofition in *Englifh* profe became an object of eager and fuccefsful attention. Previous to the exertions of Afcham, very few writers can be mentioned as affording any model for Englifh ftyle. If we except the Tranflation of Froiffart by Bourchier, Lord Berners, in 1523, and the Hiftory of Richard III. by Sir Thomas More, certainly compofitions of great merit, we fhall find it difficult to produce an author of much value for his vernacular profe. On the contrary, very foon after the appearance of the *Toxophilus*, we find harmony and beauty in Englifh ftyle emphatically praifed and enjoined." †

Following Plato both in the form and fubtlety of his work, Afcham writes it after the counfel of Ariftotle. "He that wyll wryte well in any tongue, mufte folowe thys councel of Ariftotle, to fpeake as the common people do, to thinke as wife men do : and fo fhoulde euery man vnderftande hym, and the iudgement of wyfe men alowe hym." ‡

Now, we muft leave the reader to liften to the pleafant talk of the two College Fellows, *Lover of Learning* and *Lover of Archery* ; as they difcourfe, befide the wheat fields in the neighbourhood of Cambridge, throughout the long fummer's afternoon, upon 'the Booke and the Bowe.'

* p. 14.   † *Shakspeare and his Times.* i. 439. Ed. 1817.   ‡ p. 18.

BIBLIOGRAPHY.

TOXOPHILUS.

* Editions not seen.

(a) Issues in the Author's life time.

I. *As a separate publication.*

1.	1545. London.	*Editio princeps.* Engraved title page, see
	1 vol. 4to.	opposite page. The Colophon is as on p. 165.

(b) Issues subsequent to the Author's death.

I. *As a separate publication.*

2.	1571. London.	TOXOPHILUS, The Schole, or partitions
	1 vol. 4to.	of shooting contayned in ij. bookes, written by Roger Ascham, 1544. And now newlye perused. Pleasaunt for all Gentlemen and Yomen of England for theyr pastime to reade, and profitable for their vse to folovve bothe in vvarre and peace. *Anno* 1571. Imprinted at London in Fleteftreate neare to Saint Dunftones Churche by Thomas Marshe.
3.	1589. London.	Same title as No. 2. AT LONDON. Printed
	1 vol. 8vo.	by ABELL IEFFES, by the consent of *H. Marsh. Anno* 1589. The Colophon is ¶ AT LONDON, Printed by Abell Ieffes, dwelling in Phillip Lane, at the Signe of the Bell. *Anno Domini* 1589.
6.	1788. Wrexham.	Same title as No. 2, of which it is a
	1 vol. 8vo.	modernized reprint. Ed. with a Dedication and Preface, by Rev. JOHN WALTERS M.A. Master of Ruthin School, and late Fellow of Jesus College, Oxford.
10.	1865. London.	1 vol. 8vo. TOXOPHILUS: &c., published
11.	1 July 1868. London. 1 vol. 8vo.	separately from Dr Giles' Edition, No. 9. *English Reprints* : see title at page 1.

II. *With other works.*

4.	1761. London.	The English Works of Roger Ascham, Pre-
	1 vol. 4to.	ceptor to Queen Elizabeth. [Life by Dr JOHNSON.] Ed. by JAMES BENNETT, Master of the Boarding School at Hoddesdon, Herts. 'Toxophilus' occupies pp 51-178.
5.	n. d. London.	1 vol. 4to. Another impression of No 4.
7.	1815. London.	Same title as No. 4 A new edition. [Ed:
	1 vol. 4to.	by J. G. COCHRANE, and limited to 250 copies. *Dr Giles.*]
8.	*n. d. London.	No. 7 'was re-issued some time afterwards,
	1 vol. 8vo.	with a new title and the addition of a half-title, but without a date.' *Dr Giles, Pref. to his Edition* No. 9.
9.	1864-5. London.	The Whole Works of Roger Ascham, now
	3 vols. [vol. 1 has 2 parts] 8vo.	first collected and revised, with a life of the author; by Rev. DR GILES, formerly Fellow of C.C.C. Oxford. 'Toxophilus' occupies ii. 1-165. [This is by far the best edition of Ascham's works.]

HAC fusa est nostris Babylonica dogmata trusa fuga.
HAC prava ad Stygias degmata trusa fuga.

HOC Scotus & Gallus fracti domitiq; iacebunt.
Subiecit Domino colla superba suo.

VE
RI
TA
S

VIN
CIT

Reioyse Englande, be gladde and merie,
TROTHE overcommeth thyne enemyes all,
The Scot, the Frenche man, the Pope, and heresie,
OVERCOMMED by Trothe, haue had a fall:
Sticke to the Trothe, and euermore   thou shall
Through Christ, King Henry, the Boke and the Bowe
All maner of enemies, quite ouerthrowe.

Gualterus Haddonus
Cantabrigien.

Mittere qui celeres summa uelit arte sagittas,
　　Ars erit ex isto summa profecta libro.
Quicquid habent arcus rigidi, neruique rotundi,
　　Sumere si libet, hoc sumere fonte licet.
Aschamus est author, magnum quem fecit Apollo
　　Arte sua, magnum Pallas & arte sua.
Docta manus dedit hunc, dedit hunc mens docta libellum :
　　Quæ uidet Ars Vsus uisa, parata facit.
Optimus hæc author quia tradidit optima scripta,
　　Conuenit hec uobis optima uelle sequi.

To the moste graciouse, and our most drad Soueraigne lord,
Kyng Henrie the. viii, by the grace of God, kyng
of Englande, Fraunce and Irelande, Defen
der of the faythe, and of the churche
of Englande and alfo of Irelande
in earth fupreme head, next vn
der Chrift, be al health
victorie, and fe-
licitie.

WHAT tyme as, mofte gracious Prince, your highnes this laft year paft, tooke that your mooft honorable and victorious iourney into Fraunce, accompanied vvith fuch a porte of the Nobilitie and yeomanrie of Englande, as neyther hath bene lyke knovven by experience, nor yet red of in Hiftorie : accompanied alfo vvith the daylie prayers, good hartes, and vvilles of all and euery one your graces fubiectes, lefte behinde you here at home in Englande : the fame tyme, I beinge at my booke in Cambrige, forie that my litle habilitie could ftretche out no better, to helpe forvvard fo noble an enterprice, yet with my good vvylle, prayer, and harte, nothinge behynde hym that vvas formofte of all, conceyued a vvonderful defire, bi the praier, vvifhing, talking, and communication that vvas in euery mans mouth, for your Graces mooft victorioufe retourne, to offer vp fumthinge, at your home cumming to your Highneffe, vvhich fhuld both be a token of mi loue and deutie tovvard your Maieftie, and alfo a figne of my good minde and zeale tovvarde mi countrie.

This occafion geuen to me at that time, caufed me

---

* This dedication is entirely omitted in second edition, 1571.

to take in hand againe, this litle purpofe of fhoting, begon of me before, yet not ended than, for other ftudies more mete for that trade of liuinge, vvhiche God and mi frendes had fet me vnto. But vvhen your Graces mofte ioifull and happie victorie preuented mi dailie and fpedie diligencie to performe this matter, I vvas compelled to vvaite an other time to prepare and offer vp this litle boke vnto your Maieftie. And vvhan it hath pleafed youre Higheneffe of your infinit goodneffe, and alfo your moft honorable Counfel to knovv and pervfe ouer the contentes, and fome parte of this boke, and fo to alovv it, that other men might rede it, throughe the furderaunce and fetting forthe of the right worfhipfull and mi Singuler good Mafter fir Vvilliam Pagette Knight, mooft vvorthie Secretarie to your highnes, and moft open and redie fuccoure to al poore honeft learned mens futes, I mooft humblie befeche your Grace to take in good vvorthe this litle treatife purpofed, begon, and ended of me onelie for this intent, that Labour, Honeft paftime and Vertu, might recoueragaine that place and right, that Idleneffe, Vnthriftie gamning and Vice hath put them fro.

And althoughe to haue vvritten this boke either in latin or Greke (vvhich thing I vvold be verie glad yet to do, if I might furelie knovv your Graces pleafure there in) had bene more eafier and fit for mi trade in ftudy, yet neuertheleffe, I fuppofinge it no point of honeftie, that mi commodite fhould ftop and hinder ani parte either of the pleafure or profite of manie, haue vvritten this Englifhe matter in the Englifhe tongue, for Englifhe men: vvhere in this I truft that your Grace (if it fhall pleafe your Higheneffe to rede it) fhal perceaue it to be a thinge Honefte for me to vvrite, pleafaunt for fome to rede, and profitable for manie to folovv, contening a paftime, honeft for the minde, holfome for the body, fit for eueri man, vile for no man, vfing the day and open place for Honeftie to rule it, not lurking in corners for miforder to abufe it.

Therefore I truft it fhal apere, to be bothe a fure token
of my zeele to fet forvvarde fhootinge, and fome figne
of my minde, tovvardes honeftie and learninge.

Thus I vvil trouble your Grace no longer, but
vvith my daylie praier, I vvill befeche God to
preferue your Grace, in al health and felicitie : to the feare and ouerthrovve
of all your ennemies : to the
pleafure, ioyfulneffe and
fuccour of al your fub-
iectes : to the vtter
deftruction
of papi-
ftrie and herefie : to the continuall fetting forth of
Goddes vvorde
and his glo
rye.

Your Graces moft
bounden Scholer,

Roger Afcham

To all gentle men and yomen of Englande.

BIas the wyfe man came to Crefus the ryche kyng, on a tyme, when he was makynge newe fhyppes, purpofyng to haue fubdued by water the out yles lying betwixt Grece and Afia minor: What newes now in Grece, faith the king to Bias? None other newes, but thefe, fayeth Bias: that the yles of Grece haue prepared a wonderful companye of horfemen, to ouerrun Lydia withall. There is nothyng vnder heauen, fayth the kynge, that I woulde fo foone wiffhe, as that they durft be fo bolde, to mete vs on the lande with horfe. And thinke you fayeth Bias, that there is anye thyng which they wolde fooner wyffhe, then that you fhulde be fo fonde, to mete them on the water with fhyppes? And fo Crefus hearyng not the true newes, but per-ceyuyng the wife mannes mynde and counfell, both gaue then ouer makyng of his fhyppes, and left alfo behynde him a wonderful example for all commune wealthes to folowe: that is euermore to regarde and fet moft by that thing wherevnto nature hath made them mooft apt, and vfe hath made them mooft fitte.

By this matter I meane the fhotyng in the long bowe, for Englifh men: which thyng with all my hert I do wyfh, and if I were of authoritie, I wolde counfel all the gentlemen and yomen of Englande, not to chaunge it with any other thyng, how good foeuer it feme to be: but that ftyll, accordyng to the oulde wont of England, youth fhoulde vfe it for the mooft honeft paftyme in peace, that men myght handle it as a moofte fure weapon in warre. Other ftronge weapons whiche bothe experience doth proue to be good, and the

wyſdom of the kinges Maieſtie and his counſel prouydes
to be had, are not ordeyned to take away ſhotyng : but
yat both, not compared togither, whether ſhuld be
better then the other, but ſo ioyned togither that the
one ſhoulde be alwayes an ayde and helpe for the other,
myght ſo ſtrengthen the Realme on all ſydes, that no
kynde of enemy in any kynde of weapon, myght paſſe
and go beyonde vs.

For this purpoſe I, partelye prouoked by the counſell
of ſome gentlemen, partly moued by the loue whiche
I haue alwayes borne towarde ſhotyng, haue wrytten
this lytle treatiſe, wherein if I haue not ſatiſfyed any
man, I truſt he wyll the rather be content with my
doyng, bycauſe I am (I ſuppoſe) the firſte, whiche hath
ſayde any thynge in this matter (and fewe begynnynges
be perfect, ſayth wyſe men) And alſo bycauſe yf I
haue ſayed a miſſe, I am content that any man amende
it, or yf I haue ſayd to lytle, any man that wyl to adde
what hym pleaſeth to it.

My minde is, in profitynge and pleaſynge euery man,
to hurte or diſpleaſe no man, intendyng none other
purpoſe, but that youthe myght be ſtyrred to labour,
honeſt paſtyme, and vertue, and as much as laye in me,
plucked from ydlenes, vnthriftie games, and vice :
whyche thing I haue laboured onlye in this booke,
ſhewynge howe fit ſhootyng is for all kyndes of men,
howe honeſt a paſtyme for the mynde, howe holſome
an exerciſe for the bodye, not vile for great men to vſe,
not coſtlye for poore men to ſuſteyne, not lurking in
holes and corners for ill men at theyr pleaſure, to miſvſe
it, but abiding in the open fight and face of the worlde,
for good men if it fault by theyr wiſdome to correct it.

And here I woulde deſire all gentlemen and yomen,
to vſe this paſtime in ſuche a mean, that the outragious-
nes of great gamyng, ſhuld not hurte the honeſtie of
ſhotyng, which of his owne nature is alwayes ioyned with
honeſtie : yet for mennes faultes oftentymes blamed
vnworthely, as all good thynges haue ben, and euermore ſhall be.

If any man woulde blame me, eyther for takynge
such a matter in hande, or els for writing it in the
Englyſhe tongue, this anſwere I may make hym, that
whan the beſte of the realme thinke it honeſt for them
to vſe, I one of the meaneſt ſorte, ought not to ſuppoſe
it vile for me to write : And though to haue written it
in an other tonge, had bene bothe more profitable for
my ſtudy, and alſo more honeſt for my name, yet I can
thinke my labour wel beſtowed, yf with a little hyn-
deraunce of my profyt and name, maye come any
fourtheraunce, to the pleaſure or commoditie, of the
gentlemen and yeomen of Englande, for whoſe ſake I
tooke this matter in hande. And as for ye Latin or
greke tonge, euery thing is ſo excellently done in
them, that none can do better : In the Englyſh tonge
contrary, euery thinge in a maner ſo meanly, bothe for
the matter and handelynge, that no man can do worſe.
For therein the leaſt learned for the moſte parte, haue
ben alwayes mooſt redye to wryte And they whiche
had leaſte hope in latin, haue bene moſte boulde in
englyſhe : when ſurelye euery man that is moſte ready
to taulke, is not mooſt able to wryte. He that wyll
wryte well in any tongue, muſte folowe thys councel of
Ariſtotle, to ſpeake as the common people do, to
thinke as wiſe men do ; and ſo ſhoulde euery man
vnderſtande hym, and the iudgement of wyſe men alowe
hym. Many Engliſh writers haue not done ſo, but
vſinge ſtraunge wordes as latin, french and Italian, do
make all thinges darke and harde. Ones I commuped
with a man whiche reaſoned the englyſne tongue to be
enryched and encreaſed therby, ſayinge : Who wyll
not prayſe that feaſte, where a man ſhall drinke at a
diner, bothe wyne, aie and beere ? Truely quod I,
they be all good, euery one taken by hym ſelfe alone,
but if you putte Maluefye and ſacke, read wyne and
white, ale and beere, and al in one pot, you ſhall make
a drynke, neyther eaſie to be knowen, nor yet holſom
for the bodye. Cicero in folowyng Iſocrates, Plato
and Demoſthenes, increaſed the latine tounge after an

other forte. This waye, bycaufe dyuers men yat write, do not know, they can neyther folowe it, bycaufe of theyr ignorauncie, nor yet will prayfe it, for verye arrogauncie, ii faultes, feldome the one out of the others companye.

Englyfh writers by diuerfitie of tyme, haue taken diuerfe matters in hande. In our fathers tyme nothing was red, but bookes of fayned cheualrie, wherein a man by redinge, fhuld be led to none other ende, but onely to manflaughter and baudrye. Yf any man fuppofe they were good ynough to paffe the time with al, he is deceyued. For furelye vayne woordes doo woorke no fmal thinge in vayne, ignoraunt, and younge mindes, fpecially yf they be gyuen any thynge thervnto of theyr owne nature. Thefe bokes (as I haue heard fay) were made the mofte parte in Abbayes, and Monafteries, a very lickely and fit fruite of fuche an ydle and blynde kinde of lyuynge.

In our tyme nowe, whan euery manne is gyuen to knowe muche rather than to liue wel, very many do write, but after fuche a fafhion, as very many do fhoote. Some fhooters take in hande ftronger bowes, than they be able to mayntayne. This thyng maketh them fummtyme, to outfhoote the marke, fummtyme to fhote far wyde, and perchaunce hurte fumme that looke on. Other that neuer learned to fhote, nor yet knoweth good fhafte nor bowe, wyll be as bufie as the beft, but fuche one commonly pluccketh doune a fyde, and crafty archers which be agaynft him, will be bothe glad of hym, and alfo euer ready to laye and bet with him: it were better for fuche one to fit doune than fhote. Other there be, whiche haue verye good bowe and fhaftes, and good knowledge in fhootinge, but they haue bene brought vp in fuche euyl fauoured fhootynge, that they can neyther fhoote fayre, nor yet nere. Yf any man wyll applye thefe thynges togyther, fhal not fe the one farre differ from the other.

And I alfo amonges all other, in writinge this lytle treatife, haue folowed fumme yonge fhooters, whiche bothe wyll begyn to fhoote, for a lytle moneye, and alfo wyll vfe to fhote ones or twife about the marke for nought, afore they beginne a good. And therfore did I take this little matter in hande, to affaye my felfe, and hereafter by the grace of God, if the iudgement of wyfe men, that looke on, thinke that I can do any good, I maye perchaunce cafte my fhafte amonge other, for better game.

Yet in writing this booke, fome man wyll maruayle perchaunce, why that I beyng an vnperfyte fhoter, fhoulde take in hande to write of makyng a perfyte archer: the fame man peraduenture wyll maruayle, howe a whetteftone whiche is blunte, can make the edge of a knife fharpe: I woulde ye fame man fhulde confider alfo, that in goyng about anye matter, there be. iiii. thinges to be confidered, doyng, faying, thinking and perfectneffe: Firfte there is no man that doth fo wel, but he can faye better, or elles fumme men, whiche be now ftarke nought, fhuld be to good. Agayne no man can vtter wyth his tong, fo wel as he is able to imagin with his minde, and yet perfectneffe it felfe is farre aboue all thinking. Than feeing that faying is one fteppe nerer perfecteneffe than doyng, let euery man leue maruey lyng why my woorde fhall rather expreffe, than my dede fhall perfourme perfecte fhootinge.

I trufte no man will be offended with this litle booke excepte it be fumme fletchers and bowiers, thinking hereby that manye that loue fhootynge fhall be taughte to refufe fuche noughtie wares as they woulde vtter. Honeft fletchers and bowiers do not fo, and they that be vnhoneft, oughte rather to amende them felues for doinge ill, than be angrie with me for fayinge wel. A fletcher hath euen as good a quarell to be angry with an archer that refufeth an ill fhaft, as a bladefmith hath to a fletcher yat forfaketh to bye of him a noughtie knyfe. For as an archer muft be content that a fletcher know a good fhafte in euery poynte for the perfecter makynge of it, So an honefte fletcher will alfo be content that a fhooter knowe a good fhafte in euery poynte for the perfiter vſing of it : bicauſe the one knoweth like a fletcher how to make it, the other knoweth lyke an archer howe to vſe it. And ſeyng the knowlege is one in them bothe, yet the ende diuerſe, ſurely that fletcher is an enemye to archers and artillery, whiche can not be content that an archer knowe a ſhafte as well for his vſe in ſhotynge, as he hym ſelfe ſhoulde knowe a ſhafte, for hys aduauntage in ſellynge. And the rather bycauſe ſhaftes be not made ſo muche to be ſolde, but chefely to be vſed. And ſeynge that vſe and occupiyng is the ende why a ſhafte is made, the making as it were a meane for occupying, ſurely the knowelege in euery poynte of a good ſhafte, is more to be required in a ſhooter than a fletcher.

Yet as I ſayde before no honeſt fletcher will be angry with me, ſeinge I do not teache howe to make a ſhafte whiche belongeth onelye to a good fletcher, but to knowe and handle a ſhafte, which belongeth to an archer. And this lytle booke I truſte, ſhall pleaſe and profite both partes : For good bowes and ſhaftes ſhall be better knowen to the commoditie of al ſhoters, and good ſhotyng may perchaunce be the more occupied to the profite of all bowyers and fletchers. And thus I praye God that all fletchers getting theyr lyuynge truly, and al archers vſynge ſhootynge honeſtly, and all maner of men that fauour artillery, may lyue continuallye in healthe and merineſſe, obeying theyr prince as they ſhulde, and louing God as they ought, to whom for al thinges be al honour and glorye for euer. Amen

TOXOPHILVS,

The schole of shootinge conteyned in tvvo bookes.

To all Gentlemen and yomen of Englande,
pleasaunte for theyr pastyme to rede,
and profitable for theyr use
to folow, both in war
and peace.

The contentes of the first booke.

A Table conteyning the second booke.

TOXOPHILVS,

A,

The first boke of the schole of shoting.

Philologus.   Toxophilus.

Philologus You studie to sore Toxophile.
    Tox. I wil not hurt my self ouer-
moche I warraunt you.
    Phi. Take hede you do not, for we
Physicions saye, that it is nether good for
the eyes in so cleare a Sunne, nor yet holsome for ye
bodie, so soone after meate, to looke vpon a mans boke.

Tox. In eatinge and studyinge I will neuer folowe
anye Physike, for yf I dyd, I am sure I shoulde haue small
pleasure in the one, and lesse courage in the other.
But what newes draue you hyther I praye you?

Phi. Small newes trulie, but that as I came on
walkynge, I fortuned to come with thre or foure that
went to shote at the pryckes: And when I sawe not
you amonges them, but at the last espyed you lokynge
on your booke here so sadlye, I thought to come and
holde you with some communication, lest your boke
shoulde runne awaye with you. For me thought by
your waueryng pace and earnest lokying, your boke
led you, not you it.

Tox. In dede as it chaunced, my mynde went faſter then my feete, for I happened here to reade in *Phedro Platonis*, a place that entretes wonderfullie of the nature of ſoules, which place (whether it were for the paſſynge eloquence of Plato, and the Greke tongue, or for the hyghe and godlie deſcription of the matter, kept my mynde ſo occupied, that it had no leiſure to loke to my feete.   For I was reding howe ſome ſoules being well fethered, flewe alwayes about heauen and heauenlie matters, other ſome hauinge their fethers mowted awaye, and droupinge, ſanke downe into earthlie thinges.

In Phedro.

Phi. I remember the place verie wel, and it is wonderfullie ſayd of Plato, and now I ſe it was no maruell though your fete fayled you, ſeing your minde flewe ſo faſt.

Tox. I am gladde now that you letted me, for my head akes with loking on it, and bycauſe you tell me ſo, I am verye ſorie yat I was not with thoſe good feloes you ſpake vpon, for it is a verie faire day for a man to ſhote in.

Phi. And me thinke you were a great dele better occupied and in better companie, for it is a very faire daye for a man to go to his boke in.

Tox. Al dayes and wethers wil ſerue for that purpoſe, and ſurelie this occaſion was ill loſt.

Phi. Yea but clere wether maketh clere mindes, and it is beſt as I ſuppoſe, to ſpend ye beſt time vpon the beſt thinges : And me thought you ſhot verie wel, and at that marke, at which euery good ſcoler ſhoulde moſte buſilie ſhote at.   And I ſuppoſe it be a great dele more pleaſure alſo, to ſe a ſoule flye in Plato, then a ſhafte flye at the prickes.   I graunte you, ſhoting is not the worſt thing in the world, yet if we ſhote, and time ſhote, we ar[e] not like to be great winners at the length. And you know alſo we ſcholers haue more erneſt and weightie matters in hand, nor we be not borne to paſtime and pley, as you know wel ynough who ſayth.

Tox. Yet the ſame man in the ſame place *Philologe*,

by your leue, doth admitte holfome, honeft
and manerlie paftimes to be as neceffarie   M. Cic. in off.
to be mingled with fad matters of the minde, as eating
and fleping is for the health of the body, and yet we
be borne for neither of bothe.   And Arif-   Arift. de mo-
totle him felfe fayth, yat although it were   ribus, 10. 0.
a fonde and a chyldifh thing to be to erneft in paftime
and play, yet doth he affirme by the authoritie of the
oulde Poet Epicharmus, that a man may vfe play for
erneft matter fake.   And in an other place,   Arift. Pol.
yat as reft is for labour, and medicines for   8. 3.
helth, fo is paftime at tymes for fad and weightie
ftudie.

   Phi. How moche in this matter is to be giuen to
ye auctoritie either of Ariftotle or Tullie, I can not
tel, feing fad men may wel ynough fpeke merily for a
merie matter, this I am fure, whiche thing this faire
wheat (god faue it) maketh me remembre, yat thofe
hufbandmen which rife erlieft, and come lateft home,
and are content to haue their diner and other drinck-
inges, broughte into the fielde to them, for feare of
lofing of time, haue fatter barnes in harueft, than
they whiche will either flepe at none time of the daye,
or els make merie with their neighbours at the ale.
And fo a fcholer yat purpofeth to be a good hufband,
and defireth to repe and enioy much fruite, of learninge, mufte tylle and fowe thereafter.   Our befte feede
tyme, which be fcholers, as it is verie tymelye, and
whan we be yonge : fo it endureth not ouerlonge, and
therefore it maye not be let flippe one houre, oure
grounde is verye harde, and full of wedes, our horfe
wherwith we be drawen very wylde as Plato fayth.
And infinite other mo lettes whiche wil   In Phedro.
make a thriftie fcholer take hede how he
fpendeth his tyme in fporte and pleye.

   Tox. That Ariftotle and Tullie fpake erneftlie, and
as they thought, the erneft matter which they entreate
vpon, doth plainlye proue.   And as for your hufbandrie, it was more probablie tolde with apt woides

propre to ye thing, then throughly proued with
reafons belongynge to our matter. Far contrariwife I
herd my felfe a good hufbande at his boke ones faye,
that to omit ftudie fomtime of the daye, and fometime of the yere, made afmoche for the encreafe of
learning, as to let the land lye fometime falloe, maketh
for the better encreafe of corne. This we fe, yf the
lande be plowed euerye yere, the corne commeth
thinne vp, the eare is fhort, the grayne is fmall, and
when it is brought into the barne and threfhed, gyueth
very euill faul. So thofe which neuer leaue poring on
their bokes, haue oftentimes as thinne inuention, as
other poore men haue, and as fmal wit and weight in
it as in other mens. And thus youre hufbandrie me
thinke, is more like the life of a couetoufe fnudge that
oft very euill preues, then the labour of a good hufband
that knoweth wel what he doth. And furelie the beft
wittes to lerning muft nedes haue moche recreation
and ceafing from their boke, or els they marre them
felues, when bafe and dompyffhe wittes can neuer be
hurte with continuall ftudie, as ye fe in luting, that a
treble minikin ftring muft alwayes be let down, but at
fuche time as when a man muft nedes playe : when
ye bafe and dull ftryng nedeth neuer to be moued
out of his place. The fame reafon I finde true in two
bowes that I haue, wherof the one is quicke of caft,
tricke, and trimme both for pleafure and profyte : the
other is a lugge flowe of caft, folowing the ftring,
more fure for to laft, then pleafaunt for to vfe. Now
fir it chaunced this other night, one in my chambre
wolde nedes bende them to proue their ftrength, but
I can not tel how, they were both left bente tyll the
nexte daye at after dyner : and when I came to them,
purpofing to haue gone on fhoting, I found my good
bowe clene caft on the one fide, and as weake as
water, that furelie (if I were a riche man) I had rather
haue fpent a crowne ; and as for my lugge, it was not
one whyt the worfe : but fhotte by and by as wel and
as farre as euer it dyd. And euen fo I am fure that

good wittes, except they be let downe like a treble
ftring, and vnbent like a good cafting bowe, they wil
neuer laft and be able to continue in ftudie. And I
know where I fpeake this *Philologe*, for I wolde not
faye thus moche afore yong men, for they wil take
foone occafion to ftudie litle ynough. But I faye it
therfore bicaufe I knowe, as litle ftudie getteth litle
learninge or none at all, fo the mooft ftudie getteth
not ye mooft learning of all. For a mans witte fore
occupied in erneft ftudie, muft be as wel recreated
with fome honeft paftime, as the body fore laboured,
muft be refrefhed with flepe and quietneffe, or els it
can not endure very longe, as the noble poete fayeth.

What thing wants quiet and meri reft endures but a fmal while.

Ouid.

And I promife you fhoting by my iudgement, is
ye mooft honeft paftime of al, and fuche one I am
fure, of all other, that hindreth learning litle or nothing at
all, whatfoeuer you and fome other faye, whiche are a
gret dele f\u0131rer againft it alwaies than you nede to be.

Phi. Hindereth learninge litle or nothinge at all?
that were a meruayle to me truelie, and I am fure feing
you fay fo, you haue fome reafon wherewith you can
defende fhooting withall, and as for wyl (for the loue
that you beare towarde fhotinge) I thinke there fhall
lacke none in you. Therfore feinge we haue fo good
leyfure bothe, and no bodie by to trouble vs : and you
fo willinge and able to defende it, and I fo redy and
glad to heare what may be fayde of it I fuppofe we
canne not paffe the tyme better ouer, neyther you for
ye honeftie of your fhoting, nor I for myne owne
mindfake, than to fe what can be fayed with it, or
agaynfte it, and fpeciallie in thefe dayes, whan fo many
doeth vfe it, and euerie man in a maner doeth common of it.

Tox. To fpeake of fhootinge Philologe, trulye I
woulde I were fo able, either as I my felfe am willing
or yet as the matter deferueth, but feing with wiffhing
we car not haue one nowe worthie, whiche fo worthie

a thinge can worthilie praife, and although I had
rather haue anie other to do it than my felfe, yet my
felfe rather then no other. I wil not fail to faye in it
what I can wherin if I faye litle, laye that of my litle
habilitie, not of the matter it felfe which deferueth no
lyttle thinge to be fayde of it.

Phi. If it deferue no little thinge to be fayde of it
Toxophile, I maruell howe it chaunceth than, that no
man hitherto, hath written any thinge of it : wherin
you muſt graunte me, that eyther the matter is noughte,
vnworthye, and barren to be written vppon, or els fome
men are to blame, whiche both loue it and vfe it, and
yet could neuer finde in theyr heart, to faye one good
woorde of it, feinge that very triflinge matters hath not
lacked great learned men to fette them out, as gnattes
and nuttes, and many other mo like thinges, wherfore eyther you may honeſtlie laye verie great faut
vpon men bycaufe they neuer yet prayfed it, or els
I may iuſtlie take awaye no litle thinge from fhooting,
bycaufe it neuer yet deferued it.

Tox. Trulye herein Philologe, you take not fo muche
from it, as you giue to it. For great and commodious
thynges are neuer greatlie prayfed, not bycaufe they
be not worthie, but bicaufe their excellencie nedeth
no man hys prayfe, hauing all theyr commendation of
them felfe not borowed of other men his lippes, which
rather prayfe them felfe, in fpekynge much of a litle
thynge than that matter whiche they entreat vpon.
Great and good thinges be not prayfed. For who
euer prayfed Hercules (fayeth the Greke prouerbe).
And that no man hitherto hath written any booke of
fhoting the fault is not to be layed in the thyng
whiche was worthie to be written vpon, but of men
which were negligent in doyng it, and this was the
caufe therof as I fuppofe. Menne that vfed fhootyng
moſte and knewe it beſt, were not learned : men that
were lerned, vfed litle fhooting, and were ignorant in
the nature of the thynge, and fo fewe menne hath bene
that hitherto were able to wryte vpon it. Yet howe

longe fhotying hath continued, what common wealthes
hath mofte vfed it, howe honefte a thynge it is for all
men, what kynde of liuing fo euer they folow, what
pleafure and profit commeth of it, both in peace and
warre, all maner of tongues and writers, Hebrue,
Greke and Latine, hath fo plentifullie fpoken of it, as
of fewe other thinges like.　So what fhooting is howe
many kindes there is of it, what goodneffe is ioyned
with it, is tolde : onelye howe it is to be learned and
brought to a perfectneffe amonges men, is not toulde.

Phi. Than *Toxophile*, if it be fo as you do faye, let
vs go forwarde and examin howe plentifullie this is
done that you fpeke, and firfte of the inuention of it,
than what honeftie and profit is in the vfe of it, bothe
for warre and peace, more than in other paftimes, lafte
of all howe it ought to be learned amonges men for
the encreafe of it, which thinge if you do, not onelye
I nowe for youre communication but many other mo,
when they fhall knowe of it, for your labour, and fhotying
it felfe alfo (if it coulde fpeke) for your kyndneffe, wyll
can you very moche thanke.

Toxoph. What good thynges men fpeake of fhoting
and what good thinges fhooting bringes to men as my
wit and knowlege will ferue me, gladly fhall I fay my
mind.　But how the thing is to be learned I will furely
leue to fome other which bothe for greater experience in
it, and alfo for their lerninge, can fet it out better than I.

Phi. Well as for that I knowe both what you can do
in fhooting by experience, and yat you can alfo fpeke
well ynough of fhooting, for youre learning, but go on
with the firft part.　And I do not doubt, but what my
defyre, what your loue toward it, the honeftie of
fhoting, the profite that may come thereby to many
other, fhall get the feconde parte out of you at the laft.

Toxoph. Of the firft finders out of fhoting, diuers ⲵ
men diuerflye doo wryte.　Claudiane the　　Claudianus
poete fayth that nature gaue example of　　in histri.
fhotyng firft, by the Porpentine, which doth fhote his
prickes, and will hitte any thinge that fightes with it :

whereby men learned afterwarde to immitate the fame
in findyng out both bowe and fhaftes.
Plinie referreth it to Schythes the fonne   Plin. 7. 56
of Iupiter.   Better and more noble wryters bringe
fhoting from a more noble inuentour: as Plato,
Calimachus, and Galene from Apollo.   In sympo.
Yet longe afore thofe dayes do we reade   In hym.
in the bible of fhotinge expreflye. And   Gen. 21.
alfo if we fhall beleue Nicholas de Lyra,   Nic. de lyra.
Lamech killed Cain with a fhafte. So this
great continuaunce of fhoting doth not a lytle praife
fhotinge : nor that neither doth not a litle fet it oute,
that it is referred to th[e] inuention of Apollo, for the
which poynt fhoting is highlye praifed of   Galen in ex-
Galene : where he fayth, yat mean craftes   hor. ad bo-
be firft found out by men or beaftes, as   nas artes.
weauing by a fpider, and fuche other : but high and
commendable fciences by goddes, as fhotinge and
muficke by Apollo. And thus fhotynge for the neceffitie of it vfed in Adams dayes, for the nobleneffe of
it referred to Apollo, hath not ben onelie commended
in all tunges and writers, but alfo had in greate price,
both in the beft commune wealthes in warre tyme for
the defence of their countrie, and of all degrees of men
in peace tyme, bothe for the honeftie that is ioyned
with it, and the profyte that foloweth of it.

Philol. Well, as concerning the fyndinge oute of it,
litle prayfe is gotten to fhotinge therby, feinge good
wittes maye moofte eafelye of all fynde oute a trife-
lynge matter. But where as you faye that moofte commune wealthes haue vfed it in warre tyme, and all degrees of men maye verye honeftlye vfe it in peace
tyme : I thynke you can neither fhewe by authoritie,
nor yet proue by reafon.

Toxophi. The vfe of it in warre tyme, I wyll declare
hereafter. And firfte howe all kindes and fortes of men
(what degree foeuer they be) hath at all tymes afore,
and nowe maye honeftlye vfe it : the example of moofte
noble men verye well doeth proue.

Cyaxares the kynge of the Medees, and
great graundefather to Cyrus, kepte a forte
of Sythians with him onely for this purpofe, to teache
his fonne Aftyages to fhote. Cyrus being a
childe was brought vp in fhoting, which
thinge Xenophon wolde neuer haue made mention on,
except it had ben fitte for all princes to haue vfed : feing
that Xenophon wrote Cyrus lyfe (as Tullie
fayth) not to fhewe what Cyrus did, but
what all maner of princes both in paftimes and erneft
matters ought to do.

Herod. in clio.

*Xen. in infti
Cyri. 1.*

*Ad Quint.
Fra. 1. 1.*

Darius the firft of that name, and king of Perfie
fhewed plainly howe fit it is for a kinge to loue and
vfe fhotynge, whiche commaunded this fentence to be
grauen in his tombe, for a Princelie memorie and
prayfe.

> *Darius the King lieth buried here*   Strabo. 15.
> *That in fhoting and riding had neuer pere.*

Agayne, Domitian the Emperour was fo cunning in
fhoting that he coulde fhote betwixte a mans
fingers ftanding afarre of, and neuer hurt
him.   Comodus alfo was fo excellent, and had fo fure
a hande in it, that there was nothing within his retche
and fhote, but he wolde hit it in what
place he wolde : as beaftes runninge,
either in the heed, or in the herte, and neuer myffe, as
Herodiane fayeth he fawe him felfe, or els he coulde
neuer haue beleued it.

Tranq. Suet.

Herodia. 1.

Phi. In dede you praife fhoting very wel, in yat
you fhewe that Domitian and Commodus loue
fhotinge, fuche an vngracious couple I am fure as a
man fhall not fynde agayne, if he raked all hell for
them.

Toxoph. Wel euen as I wyll not commende their
ilneffe, fo ought not you to difpraife their goodneffe,
and in dede, the iudgement of Herodian vpon Commodus is true of them bothe, and that was this : that

beſide ſtrength of bodie and good ſhotinge, they hadde no princelie thing in them, which ſaying me thinke commendes ſhoting wonderfullie, callinge it a princelie thinge.

Furthermore howe commendable ſhotinge is for princes : Themiſtius the noble philoſopher   Themiſt. ſheweth in a certayne oration made to   in ora, 6. Theodoſius th[e] emperoure, wherin he doeth com- mende him for. iii. thinges, that he vſed of a childe. For ſhotinge, for rydinge of an horſe well, and for feates of armes.

Moreouer, not onelye kinges and emperours haue ben brought vp in ſhoting, but alſo the beſt commune wealthes that euer were, haue made goodlie actes and lawes for it, as the Perſians which vnder Cyrus con- quered in a maner all the worlde, had a   Herod. in clio. lawe that their children ſhulde learne thre thinges, onelie from v. yeare oulde vnto. xx. to ryde an horſe well, to ſhote well, to ſpeake truthe   Leo de stra- alwayes and neuer lye. The Romaines   tag. 20. (as Leo the[e]mperour in his boke of ſleightes of warre[2] telleth) had a lawe that euery man ſhoulde vſe ſhoting in peace tyme, while he was. xl. yere olde and that euerye houſe ſhoulde haue a bowe, and. xl. ſhaftes ready for all nedes, the omittinge of whiche lawe (ſayth Leo) amonges the youthe, hath ben the onely occaſion why the Romaynes loſt a great dele of their empire. But more of this I wil ſpeake when I come to the profite of ſhoting in warre. If I ſhuld rehearſe the ſtatutes made of noble princes of Englande in parliamentes for the ſettyng forwarde of ſhoting, through this realme, and ſpecially that acte made for ſhoting the thyrde yere of the reygne of our mooſt drad ſoueraygne lorde king Henry the. viii. I could be very long. But theſe fewe examples ſpecially of ſo great men and noble common wealthes, ſhall ſtand in ſtede of many.

Phi. That ſuche princes and ſuche commune welthes haue moche regarded ſhoting, you haue well declared. But why shotinge ought so of it selfe to be regarded, you haue scarcelye yet proued.

Tox. Examples I graunt out of histories do shew a thing to be so, not proue a thing why it shuld be so. Yet this I suppose, yat neither great mens qualities being commendable be without great authoritie, for other men honestly to folow them : nor yet those great learned men that wrote suche thinges, lacke good reason iustly at al tymes for any other to approue them. Princes beinge children oughte to be brought vp in shoting : both bycause it is an exercise moost holsom, and also a pastyme moost honest : wherin labour prepareth the body to hardnesse, the minde to couragiousnesse, sufferyng neither the one to be marde with tendernesse, nor yet the other to be hurte with ydlenesse : as we reade how Sardanapalus and suche other were, bycause they were not brought vp with outwarde honest payneful pastymes to be men : but cockerde vp with inwarde noughtie ydle wantonnnesse to be women. For how fit labour is for al youth, Iupiter or els Minos amonges them of Grece, and Lycurgus amonges the Lacedemonians, do shewe by their lawes, which neuer or- *Cic. 2. Tus. Qu.* deyned any thing for ye bringyng vp of youth that was not ioyned with labour. And the labour which is in shoting of al other is best, both bycause it encreaseth strength, and preserueth health moost, beinge not vehement, but moderate, not ouerlaying any one part with wery-somnesse, but softly exercisynge euery parte with equalnesse, as the armes and breastes with drawinge, the other parties with going, being not so paynfull for the labour as pleasaunt for the pastyme, which exercise by the iudgement of the best physicions, is most alowable. By shoting also is the mynde honestly exercised where a man alwaies desireth to *Gal. 2. de* be best (which is a worde of honestie) and *san. tuend.* that by the same waye, that vertue it selfe doeth, couetinge to come nighest a moost perfite ende or meane standing betwixte. ii. extremes, escheweing

ſhorte, **or** gone, or eitherſyde wide, **for** the which
cauſes Ariſtotle him ſelfe ſayth that ſhoting *Arist. 1. de*
and vertue is very like. Moreouer that *morib.*
ſhoting of all other is the mooſt honeſt paſtyme, and
hath leeſt occaſion to noughtineſſe ioyned with it. ii.
thinges very playnelye do proue, which be as a man
wolde ſaye, the tutours and ouerſeers to ſhotinge:
Daye light and open place where euerye man doeth
come, the maynteyners and kepers of ſhoting, from all
vnhoneſt doing. If ſhotinge faulte at any tyme, it
hydes it not, it lurkes not in corners and hudder-
mother: but openly accuſeth and bewrayeth it ſelfe,
which is the nexte waye to amendement, as wyſe
men do ſaye. And theſe thinges I ſuppoſe be ſignes,
not of noughtineſſe, for any man to diſalowe it: but
rather verye playne tokens of honeſtie, for euerye man
to prayſe it.

The vſe of ſhotinge alſo in greate mennes chyldren
ſhall greatlye encreaſe the loue and vſe of ſhotinge in
all the reſidue of youth. For meane mennes myndes
loue to be lyke greate menne, as Plato *Iso. in nic.*
and Iſocrates do ſaye. And that euerye
bodye ſhoulde learne to ſhote when they be yonge,
defence of the commune wealth, doth require when
they be olde, which thing can not be done mightelye
when they be men, excepte they learne it perſitelye
when they be boyes. And therfore ſhotinge of all
paſtymes is mooſt fitte to be vſed in childhode:
bycauſe it is an imitation of mooſt erneſt thinges to
be done in manhode.

Wherfore, ſhoting is fitte for great mens children,
both bycauſe it ſtrengthneth the body with holſome
labour, and pleaſeth the mynde with honeſt paſtime
and alſo encourageth all other youth erneſtlye to folowe
the ſame. And theſe reaſons (as I ſuppoſe) ſtirred vp
both great men to bring vp their chyldren in ſhotinge,
and alſo noble commune wealthes ſo ſtraytelye to commaunde ſhoting. Therfore ſeinge Princes moued by
honeſt occaſions, hath in al commune wealthes vſed

ſhotynge, I ſuppoſe there is none other degree of men, neither lowe nor hye, learned nor leude, yonge nor oulde.

Phil. You ſhal nede wade no further in this matter *Toxophile*, but if you can proue me thatſcholers and men gyuen to learning maye honeſt-lie vſe ſhoting, I wyll ſoone graunt you that all otherſortes of men maye not onelye lefullie, but ought of dutie to vſe it. But I thinke you can not proue but that all theſe examples of ſhotinge brought from ſo longe a tyme, vſed of ſo noble princes, confirmed by ſo wyſe mennes lawes and iudgementes, are ſette afore temporall men, onelye to followe them : whereby they may the better and ſtronglyer defende the commune wealth withall. And nothing belongeth to ſcholers and learned men, which haue an other parte of the commune wealth, quiete and peaceable put to their cure and charge, whoſe ende as it is diuerſe from the other, ſo there is no one waye that leadeth to them both.

Toxo. I graunte *Philologe*, that ſcholers and lay men haue diuerſe offices and charges in the commune wealth, whiche requires diuerſe bringing vp in their youth, if they ſhal do them as they ought to do in their age. Yet as temporall men of neceſſitie are compelled to take ſomewhat of learning to do their office the better withall : So ſcholers maye the boldlyer borowe ſomewhat of laye mennes paſtimes, to mayn-teyne their health in ſtudie withall. And ſurelie of al other thinges ſhoting is neceſſary for both ſortes to learne. Whiche thing, when it hath ben euermore vſed in Englande how moche good it hath done, both oulde men and Chronicles doo tell : and alſo our enemies can beare vs recorde. For if it be true (as I haue hearde ſaye) when the kynge of Englande hath ben in Fraunce, the preeſtes at home bicauſe they were archers, haue ben able to ouerthrowe all Scotlande. Agayne ther is an other thing which aboue all other doeth moue me, not onely to loue ſhotinge, to prayſe ſhoting, to exhorte all other to ſhotinge, but alſo to vſe ſhoting my ſelfe: and that is our kyng his mooſt royall purpoſe and wyll, whiche in all his ſtatutes generallye doth commaunde men, and with his owne mouthe mooſt gentlie doeth exhorte men, and by his greate gyftes and rewardes, greatly doth encourage men, and with his mooſt princelie example very oft doth prouoke all other men to the ſame. But here you wyll come in with temporal man and ſcholer: I tell you plainlye, ſcholer or vnſcholer, yea if I were. xx. ſcholers, I wolde thinke it were my dutie, bothe with exhortinge men to ſhote, and alſo with ſhoting my ſelfe to helpe to ſet forwarde that thing which the kinge his wiſdome, and his counſell, ſo greatlye laboureth to go forwarde: whiche thing ſurelye they do, bycauſe they knowe it to be in warre, the defence and wal of our countrie, in peace, an exerciſe mooſt holſome for the body, a paſtime mooſt honeſt for the mynde, and as I am able to proue my ſelfe, of al other moſte fit and agreable with learninge and learned men.

Phi. If you can proue this thing ſo playnly, as you ſpeake it erneſtly, then wil I, not only thinke as you do, but become a ſhooter and do as you do. But yet beware I ſaye, leſt you for the great loue you bear towarde ſhotinge, blindlie iudge of ſhootinge. For loue and al other to erneſt affections be not for nought paynted blinde. Take hede (I ſaye) leaſt you prefer ſhootinge afore other paſtimes, as one Balbinus through blinde affection, preferred his louer before all other wemen, although ſhe were deformed with a polypus in her noſe. And although ſhooting maye be mete ſometyme for ſome ſcholers, and ſo forthe: yet the fitteſt alwayes is to be preferred. Therefore if you will nedes graunt ſcholers paſtime and recreation of their mindes, let them vſe (as many of them doth) Muſyke, and playing on inſtrumentes, thinges moſte ſemely for all ſcholers, and moſte regarded alwayes of Apollo and the Muſes.

Tox. Euen as I can not deny, but ſome muſike is

fit for lerning so I trust you can not chose but graunt, that shoting is fit also, as Calimachus doth signifie in this verse.

Both merie songes and good shoting deliteth Apollo. Cal. hym. 2.

Butas concerning whether of them is **Œ** moste fit for learning, and scholers to vse, you may saye what you will for your pleasure, this I am sure that Plato and Aristotle bothe, in their bokes en- treatinge of the common welthe, where they shew howe youthe shoulde be brought vp in. iiii. thinges, in redinge, in writing, in exercise of bodye, and singing, do make mention of Musicke and all kindes of it, wherein they both agre, that Musicke vsed amonges the Lydians is verie ill for yong men, which be stu- dentes for vertue and learning, for a certaine nice, softe, and smoth swetnesse of it, whiche woulde rather entice them to noughtines, than stirre them to honestie.

An other kinde of Musicke inuented by the Dorians, they both wonderfully prayse, alowing it to be verie syt for the studie of vertue and learning, becausse of a manlye, rough and stoute sounde in it, whyche shulde encourage yong stomakes, to attempte manlye matters. Nowe whether these balades and roundes, these gali- ardes, pauanes and daunces, so nicelye fingered, so swetely tuned, be lyker the Musike of the Lydians or the Dorians, you that be learned iudge. And what so euer ye iudge, this I am sure, yat lutes, harpes, all maner of pypes, barbitons, sambukes, with other instrumentes euery one, whyche standeth by fine and quicke fingeringe, be condemned of Aris-   Aristot. pol. totle, as not to be brought in and vsed   8. 6. amonge them, whiche studie for learning and vertue.

Pallas when she had inuented a pipe, cast it away, not so muche sayeth Aristotle, becausse it deformed her face, but muche rather bycausse suche an Instrumente belonged nothing to learnynge. Howe suche Instru- mentes agree with learning, the goodlye agrement betwixt Apollo god of learninge, and Marsyas the

Satyr, defender of pipinge, doth well declare, where
Marfyas had his fkıne quite pulled ouer his head for
his labour.

Muche mufike marreth mennes maners, fayth Galen,
although fome man wil faye that it doth not fo, but
rather recreateth and maketh quycke a mannes mynde,
yet me thinke by reafon it doth as hony doth to a
mannes ftomacke, whiche at the firft receyueth it
well, but afterwarde it maketh it vnfit, to abyde any
good ftronge norifhynge meate, or els anye holfome
fharpe and quicke drinke. And euen fo in a maner
thefe Inftrumentes make a mannes wit fo fofte and
fmoothe fo tender and quaifie, that they be leffe able
to brooke, ftrong and tough ftudie. Wittes be not
fharpened, but rather dulled, and made blunte, wyth
fuche fweete fofteneffe, euen as good edges be blonter,
whiche menne whette vpon fofte chalke ftones.

And thefe thinges to be true, not onely Plato Ariftotle
and Galen, proue by authoritie of reafon,   Herodotus
but alfo Herodotus and other writers,   in Clio.
fhewe by playne and euident example, as that of
Cyrus, whiche after he had ouercome the Lydians,
and taken their kinge Crefus prifoner, yet after by
the meane of one Pactyas a verye headie manne
amonges the Lydians, they rebelled agaynfte Cyrus
agayne, then Cyrus had by an by, broughte them to
vtter deftruction, yf Crefus being in good fauour with
Cyrus had not hertelie defyred him, not to reuenge
Pactyas faulte, in fhedynge theyr blood. But if he
would folowe his counfell, he myght brynge to paffe,
that they fhoulde neuer more rebel agaynft hym, And
yat was this, to make them weare long kyrtils, to ye
foot lyke woomen, and that euerye one of them fhoulde
haue a harpe or a lute, and learne to playe and fing
whyche thinge if you do fayth Crefus (as he dyd in dede)
you fhall fe them quickelye of men, made women.
And thus lutinge and finginge take awaye a manlye
ftomake, whiche fhulde enter and pearce depe and
harde ftudye.

Euen fuche an other ftorie doeth Nympho-   Nymphod.
dorus an olde greke Hiftoriographer write,
of one Sefoftris kinge of Egypte, whiche ftorie becaufe
it is fomewhat longe, and very lyke in al poyntes to the
other and alfo you do well ynoughe remembre it, feynge
you read it fo late in Sophoclis commen-   Comment.
taries, I wyll nowe paffe ouer. Therefore   in Antig.
eyther Ariftotle and Plato knowe not what was good
and euyll for learninge and vertue, and the example
of wyfe hiftories be vainlie fet afore vs or els the min-
ftrelfie of lutes, pipes, harpes, and all other that ftandeth
by fuche nice, fine, minikin fingering (fuche as the
moofte parte of fcholers whom I knowe vfe, if they vfe
any) is farre more fitte for the womannifhneffe of it to
dwell in the courte among ladies, than for any great
thing in it, whiche fhoulde helpe good and fad ftudie,
to abide in the vniuerfitie amonges fcholers. But perhaps you knowe fome great goodneffe of fuche muficke
and fuche inftrumentes, whervnto Plato and Ariftotle
his brayne coulde neuer attayne, and therfore I will
faye no more agaynft it.

ℙ𝖍𝖎. Well Toxophile is it not ynoughe for you to
rayle vpon Mufike, excepte you mocke me to? but to
fay the truth I neuer thought my felfe thefe kindes of
muficke fit for learninge, but that whyche I fayde was
rather to proue you, than to defende the matter. But
yet as I woulde haue this forte of muficke decaye
amonge fcholers, euen fo do I wyffhe from the
bottome of my heart, that the laudable cuftome of
Englande to teache chyldren their plainefong and
prikfong, were not fo decayed throughout all the
realme as it is. Whiche thing howe profitable it was
for all fortes of men, thofe knewe not fo wel than whiche
had it moft, as they do nowe whiche lacke it mofte.
And therfore it is true that Teucer fayeth in Sophocles.

Seldome at all good things be knowen how good to be   Sophocles
Before a man fuche things dc miffe out of his handes.   in Aiace.

That milke is no fitter nor more naturall for the

bringing vp of children than mufike is, both Gallen proueth by authoritie, and dayly vfe teacheth by experience. For euen the little babes lacking the vfe of reafon, are fcarfe fo well ftilled in fuckyng theyr mothers pap, as in hearynge theyr mother fyng.

Agayne how fit youth is made, by learning to fing, for grammar and other fciences, bothe we dayly do fee, and Plutarch learnedly doth proue, and Plato wifelie did alowe, which receyued no fcholer in to his fchole, that had not learned his fonge before.

The godlie vfe of prayfing God, by finginge in the churche, nedeth not my prayfe, feing it is fo prayfed through al the fcripture, therfore nowe I wil fpeke nothing of it, rather than I fhuld fpeke to litle of it.

Befyde al thefe commodities, truly. ii. degrees of menne, which haue the higheft offices vnder the king in all this realme, fhal greatly lacke the vfe of Singinge, preachers and lawiers, bycaufe they fhal not without this, be able to rule their breftes, for euery purpofe. For where is no diftinction in telling glad thinges and fearfull thinges, gentilnes and cruelnes, foftenes and vehementnes, and fuche lyke matters, there can be no great perfwafion.

For the hearers, as Tullie fayeth, be muche affectioned, as he is that fpeaketh. At his wordes be they drawen, yf he ftande ftill in one facion, their mindes ftande ftill with hym : If he thundre, they quake : If he chyde, they feare : If he complayne, they fory with hym : and finally, where a matter is fpoken, with an apte voyce, for euerye affection, the hearers for the mofte parte, are moued as the fpeaker woulde. But when a man is alwaye in one tune, lyke an Humble bee, or els nowe vp in the top of the churche, nowe downe that no manne knoweth where to haue hym : or piping lyke a reede, or roring lyke a bull, as fome lawyers do, whiche thinke they do beft, when they crye lowdeft, thefe fhall neuer greatly mooue, as I haue knowen many wel learned, haue done, bicaufe theyr voyce was not flayed afore, with learnyng to fynge.

For all voyces, great and small, base and shril, weke or softe, may be holpen and brought to a good poynt, by learnyng to synge.

Whether this be true or not, they that stand moofte in nede, can tell best, whereof some I haue knowen, whiche, becaufe they learned not to fing, whan they were boyes, were fayne to take peyne in it, whan they were men. If any man shulde heare me Toxophile, that woulde thinke I did but fondly, to suppose that a voice were so neceffarie to be loked vpon, I would afke him if he thought not nature a foole, for making such goodly inftrumentes in a man, for wel vttring his woordes, or els if the. ii. noble orators Demofthenes and Cicero were not fooles, wherof the one dyd not onelie learne to fing of a man: But alfo was not afhamed to learne howe he shoulde vtter his foundes aptly of a dogge, the other fetteth oute no poynte of rhetorike, fo fullie in all his bookes, as howe a man shoulde order his voyce for all kynde of matters.

Therfore feinge men by fpeaking, differ and be better than beaftes, by fpeakyng wel, better than other men, and that finging is an helpe towarde the fame as dayly experience doth teache, example of wyfe men doth alowe, authoritie of learned men doth approue wherwith the foundacion of youth in all good common wealthes alwayes hath bene tempered; furelye if I were one of the parliament houfe, I woulde not fayle, to put vp a bill for the amendment of this thynge, but becaufe I am lyke to be none this yeare, I wil fpeake no more of it, at this time.

Tox. It were pitie truly *Philologe*, that the thinge shoulde be neglected, but I truft it is not as you fay.

Phi. The thing is to true, for of them that come daylye to ye vniuerfitie, where one hath learned to finge, vi. hath not. But nowe to oure shotinge Toxophile agayne, wherin I suppose you can not fay fo muche for shotyng to be fitte for learninge, as you haue spoken agaynfte Muficke for the fame.

Therfore as concerning Mufike, I can be content to

graunt you your mynde: But as for fhooting, furely I
fuppofe that you can not perfwade me, by no meanes,
that a man can be earneft in it, and earneft at his
booke to: but rather I thynke that a man with a bowe
on his backe, and fhaftes vnder hys girdell, is more fit
to wayte vpon Robin Hoode, than vpon Apollo or the
Mufes.

Tox. Ouer erneft fhooting furely I will not ouer
erneftlye defende, for I euer thought fhooting fhoulde
be a wayter vpon lerning not a maftres ouer learning.
Yet this I maruell not a litle at, that ye thinke a man
with a bowe on hys backe is more like Robin Hoode
feruaunt, than Apollofe, feing that Apollo him felfe in
Alceftis of Euripides, whiche tragidie you red openly
not long ago, in a maner glorieth faying this verfe.

It is my wont alwaies my bowe with me to beare.   Euripid. in
                                                       Alceft.

Therfore a learned man ought not to much to be
afhamed to beare that fome tyme, whiche Apollo god
of lerning him felfe was not afhamed always to beare.
And bycaufe ye woulde haue a man wayt vpon the
Mufes, and not at all medle with fhotyng I maruell
that you do not remembre howe that the ix. mufes
their felfe as fone as they were borne, wer put to norfe
to a lady called Euphemis whiche had a fon named
Erotus with whome the nine Mufes for his excellent
fhootinge, kepte euer more companie withall, and vfed
dayly to fhoote togither in ye mount Pernafus; and at
laft it chaunced this Erotus to dye, whofe death the
Mufes lamented greatly, and fell all vpon theyr knees
afore Iupiter theyr father, and at theyr requeft,
Erotus for fhooting with the Mufes in earth was made
a figne, and called Sagittarius in heauen. Therfore
you fe, that if Apollo and the Mufes either were
examples in dede, or onelye fayned of wife men to be
examples of learninge, honeft fhoting maye well
ynough be companion with honeft ftudie.

Phi. Well Toxophile, if you haue no ftronger
defence of fhoting then Poëtes, I feare yf your com-

panions which loue shotinge, hearde you, they wolde thinke you made it but a triflyng and fabling matter, rather then any other man that loueth not shotinge coulde be perfuaded by this reafon to loue it.

Toxo. Euen as I am not fo fonde but I knowe that thefe be fables, fo I am fure you be not fo ignoraunt, but you knowe what fuche noble wittes as the Poetes had, ment by such matters: which oftentymes vnder the couering of a fable, do hyde and wrappe in goodlie preceptes of philofophie, with the true iudgement of thinges. Whiche to be true fpeciallye in Homer and Euripides, Plato, Ariftotle, and Galene playnelye do fhewe: when through all their workes (in a maner) they determine all controuerfies, by thefe. ii. Poetes and fuche lyke authorities. Therfore if in this matter I feme to fable, and nothynge proue, I am content you iudge fo on me: feinge the fame iudgement fhall condemne with me Plato, Ariftotle, and Galene, whom in that errour I am wel content to folowe. If thefe oulde examples proue nothing for fhoting, what faye you to this? that the beft learned and fageft men in this Realme, which be nowe alyue, both loue fhoting and vfe fhoting, as the beft learned biffhoppes that be: amonges whome *Philologe*, you your felfe knowe. iiii. or. v. which as in all good learning, vertue and fage-neffe they gyue other men example what thing they fhoulde do, euen fo by their fhoting, they playnely fhewe what honeft paftime, other men giuen to learning, may honeftly vfe. That erneft ftudie muft be recreated with honeft paftime fufficientlye I haue proued afore, both by reafon and authoritie of the beft learned men that euer wrote. Then feing paftymes be lefull, the mooft fitteft for learning, is to be fought for. A paftyme, faith Ariftotle, muft be lyke a medicine. Medicines ftande by contra- *Arift. po. 7.* ries, therfore the nature of ftudying confidered, the fitteft paftyme fhal foone appeare. In ftudie euery parte of the body is ydle, which thing caufeth groffe and colde humours, to gather togyther and vexe

ſcholers verye moche, the mynde is altogyther bent
and ſet on worke. A paſtyme then muſt be had where
euery parte of the bodye muſt be laboured to ſeparate
and leſſen ſuche humours withal: the mind muſt be
vnbent, to gather and fetche againe his quickneſſe
withall. Thus paſtymes for the mynde onelye, be
nothing fit for ſtudentes, bycauſe the body which is
mooſt hurte by ſtudie, ſhulde take away no profyte
thereat. This knewe Eraſmus verye well, when he was
here in Cambrige: which when he had ben ſore at
his boke (as Garret our bookebynder hath verye ofte
tolde me) for lacke of better exerciſe, wolde take his
horſe, and ryde about the markette hill, and come
agayne. If a ſcholer ſhoulde vſe bowles or tennies,
the laboure is to vehement and vnequall, whiche is
condempned of Galene: the example very ill for other
men, when by ſo manye actes they be made vnlawfull.

Running, leaping, and coyting be to vile for ſcholers,
and ſo not fit by Ariſtotle his iudgement: walking
alone into the felde, hath no token of   Ariſtot.
courage in it, a paſtyme lyke a ſimple man   pol. 7. 17.
which is neither fleſh nor fiſſhe. Therfore if a man
woulde haue a paſtyme holeſome and equall for euerye
parte of the bodye, pleaſaunt and full of courage
for the mynde, not vile and vnhoneſte to gyue ill example
to laye men, not kepte in gardynes and corners, not
lurkynge on the nyght and in holes, but euermore in
the face of men, either to rebuke it when it doeth ill,
or els to teſtifye on it when it doth well: let him ſeke
chefely of all other for ſhotynge.

Philol. Suche commune paſtymes as men com-
menlye do vſe, I wyll not greatlye allowe to be fit for
ſcholers: ſeinge they maye vſe ſuche exer-   Gal. de. ſan
ciſes verye well (I ſuppoſe) as Galene him   tuend. 2.
ſelfe doth allowe.

Toxoph. Thoſe exerciſes I remember verye well, for
I read them within theſe two dayes, of the whiche,
ſome be theſe: to runne vp and downe an hyll, to
clyme vp a longe powle, or a rope, and there hange a

while, to holde a man by his armes and waue with his heeles, moche lyke the paftyme that boyes vfe in the churche when their mafter is awaye, to fwinge and totter in a belrope : to make a fifte, and ftretche out bothe his armes, and fo ftande lyke a roode. To go on a man his tiptoes, ftretching out th[e] one of his armes forwarde, the other backewarde, which if he blered out his tunge alfo, myght be thought to daunce Anticke verye properlye. To tumble ouer and ouer, to toppe ouer tayle : To fet backe to backe, and fe who can heaue an other his heles higheft, with other moche like : whiche exercifes furelye mufte nedes be naturall, bycaufe they be fo childiffhe, and they may be alfo holefome for the body : but furely as for pleafure to the minde or honeftie in the doinge of them, they be as lyke fhotinge as Yorke is foule Sutton. Therfore to loke on al paftymes and exercifes holfome for the bodye, pleafaunt for the mynde, comlye for euery man to do, honeft for all other to loke on, profitable to be fette by of euerye man, worthie to be rebuked of no man, fit for al ages perfons and places, onely fhoting fhal appeare, wherin all thefe commodities maye be founde.

Phil. To graunt Toxophile, that ftudentes may at tymes conuenient vfe fhoting as mooft holfome and honeft paftyme : yet to do as fome do, to fhote hourly daylie, wekelye, and in a maner the hole yere, neither I can prayfe, nor any wyfe man wyl alowe, nor you your felfe can honeftlye defende.

Toxoph. Surely Philologe, I am very glad to fe you come to that poynte that mooft lieth in your ftomake, and greueth you and other fo moche. But I trufte after I haue fayd my mynde in this matter, you fhal confeffe your felfe that you do rebuke this thing more than ye nede, rather then you fhal fynde that any man may fpende by anye poffibilitie, more tyme in fhotinge then he ought. For firft and formooft the hole tyme is deuyded into. ii. partes, the daye and the night : whereof the night maye be both occupyed in many honeft bufineffes, and alfo fpent in moche vnthriftineſſe, but in no wiſe it can be applyed to ſhot-ing. And here you ſe that halfe oure tyme, graunted to all other thinges in a maner both good and ill, is at one ſwappe quite taken awaye from ſhoting. Now let vs go forward, and ſe how moche of halfe this tyme of ours is ſpent in ſhoting. The hole yere is deuided into. iiii. partes, Spring tyme, Somer, faule of the leaſe, and winter wherof the whole winter, for the roughneſſe of it, is cleane taken away from ſhoting : except it be one day amonges. xx. or one yeare amonges. xl. In Somer, for the feruent heate, a man maye ſaye likewyſe : except it be ſomtyme agaynſt night. Now then ſpring tyme and faule of the leafe be thoſe which we abuſe in ſhoting. But if we con-ſider how mutable and chaungeable the wether is in thoſe ſeaſons, and howe that Ariſtotle him ſelfe ſayth, that mooſte parte of rayne ſauleth in theſe two tymes : we ſhall well perceyue, that where a man wolde ſhote one daye, he ſhall be ſayne to leaue of. iiii. Now when tyme it ſelfe graunteth vs but a litle ſpace to ſhote in, lette vs ſe if ſhoting be not hindered amonges all kyndes of men as moche otherwayes. Firſt, yong children vſe not, yong men for feare of them whom they be vnder to moche dare not : ſage men for other greater buſineſſes, wyll not : aged men for lacke of ſtrengthe, can not : Ryche men for couetouſneſſe ſake, care not : poore men for coſt and charge, may not : maſters for their houſholde keping, hede not : ſeruauntes kept in by their maiſters very oft, ſhall not : craftes men for getting of their lyuing, verye moche leyſure haue not : and many there be that oft beginnes, but for vnaptneſſe proues not : and mooſt of all, whiche when they be ſhoters gyue it ouer and lyſte not, ſo that generallye men euerye where for one or other conſideration moche ſhoting vſe not. Ther-fore theſe two thinges, ſtrayteneſſe of tyme, and euery man his trade of liuing, are the cauſes that ſo fewe men ſhotes : as you maye ſe in this greate towne, where as there be a thouſande good mens bodies, yet ſcarſe. x.

yat vfeth any great fhoting. And thofe whome you fe fhote the mooft, with how many thinges are the[y] drawen (or rather driuen) from fhoting. For firft, as it is many a yere or they begyn to be great fhoters, euen fo the great heate of fhotinge is gone within a yere or two : as you knowe diuerfe Philologe your felfe, which were fometyme the beft fhoters, and now they be the beft ftudentes.

If a man faule fycke, farewell fhoting, maye fortune as long as he lyueth. If he haue a wrentche, or haue taken colde in his arme, he may hang vp his bowe (I warraunt you) for one feafon. A litle blayne, a fmall cutte, yea a filie poore worme in his finger, may kepe him from fhoting wel ynough. Breaking and ill luck in bowes I wyll paffe ouer, with an hundred mo fere thinges, whiche chaunceth euerye daye to them that fhote mooft, wherof the leeft of them may compell a man to leaue fhoting. And thefe thinges be fo trewe and euident, that it is impoffible either for me craftelye to fayne them, or els for you iuftly to deny them. Than feing how many hundred thinges are required altogyther to giue a man leaue to fhote, and any one of them denied, a man can not fhote : and feing euery one of them maye chaunce, and doth chaunce euery day, I meruayle any wyfe man wyll thynke it poffible, that any greate tyme can be fpent in fhoting at all.

Phi. If this be true that you faye Toxo-phile, and in very dede I can denye no-thinge of it, I meruayle greatly how it chaunceth, that thofe, whiche vfe fhoting be fo moche marked of men, and ofttymes blamed for it, and yat in a maner as moche as thofe which pleye at cardes and dife. And I fhal tell you what I hearde fpoken of the fame matter. A man no fhoter, (not longe agoo) **Cardes** **and dyfe.** wolde defende playing at cardes and dife, if it were honeftly vfed, to be as honeft a paftime as youre fhot-inge : For he layed for him, that a man might pleye for a litle at cardes and dyfe, and alfo a man might fhote away all that euer he had. He fayd a payre of cardes

D

coſt not paſt. ii.d. and that they neded not ſo moche
reparation as bowe and ſhaftes, they wolde neuer hurte
a man his hande, nor neuer weare his gere. A man
ſhulde neuer ſlee a man with ſhoting wyde at the cardes. In wete and drye, hote and coulde, they woulde
neuer forſake a man, he ſhewed what great varietie
there is in them for euerye mans capacitie: if one game
were harde, he myght eaſelye learne an other: if a
man haue a good game, there is greate pleaſure in it:
if he haue an ill game, the payne is ſhorte, for he
maye ſoone gyue it ouer, and hope for a better: with
many other mo reaſons. But at the laſt he concluded,
that betwixt playinge and ſhoting, well vſed or ill vſed,
there was no difference: but that there was leſſe coſte
and trouble, and a greate deale more pleaſure in
playing, then in ſhotynge.

Tox. I can not deny, but ſhoting (as all other good
thinges) may be abuſed. And good thinges ungoodlye
vſed, are not good, ſayeth an honorable biſhoppe in
an erneſter matter then this is: yet we muſte beware
that we laye not mennes faultes vpon the thing which
is not worthie, for ſo nothing ſhulde be good. And
as for ſhoting, it is blamed and marked of men for that
thing (as I ſayde before) which ſhoulde be rather a
token of honeſtie to prayſe it, then any ſigne of
noughtineſſe to diſalowe it, and that is bycauſe it is in
euerye man his ſight, it ſeketh no corners, it hydeth it
not: if there be neuer ſo litle fault in it, euerye man
ſeeth it, it accuſeth it ſelfe. For one houre ſpente in
ſhoting is more ſene and further talked of, then. xx.
nightes ſpent in dyſing, euen as a litle white ſtone is ſene
amonges. iii. hundred blacke. Of thoſe that blame
ſhotinge and ſhoters, I wyll ſaye no more at this tyme
but this, that beſide that they ſtoppe and hinder ſhoting,
which the kinges grace wolde haue forwarde, they be
not moche vnlyke in this poynt to Wyll Somer the
king his foole, which ſmiteth him that ſtandeth alwayes
before his face, be he neuer ſo worſhipfull a man, and
neuer greatly lokes for him whiche lurkes behinde an
other man his backe, that hurte him in dede.

But to him that compared gamning with ſhoting ſomewhat wyll I anſwere, and bycauſe he went afore me in a compariſon : and compariſons ſayth learned men, make playne matters : I wyl ſurely folowe him in the ſame. Honeſt thynges (ſayeth Plato) be knowen from vnhoneſt thinges, by this In phedro. difference, vnhoneſtie hath euer preſent pleaſure in it, hauing neyther good pretence going before, nor yet any profit folowing after ; which ſaying deſcrybeth generallye, bothe the nature of ſhooting and gamning whiche is good, and which is euyl, verie well.

Gamninge hath ioyned with it, a vayne preſente pleaſure, but there foloweth, loſſe of name, loſſe of goodes, and winning of an hundred gowtie, dropſy diſeaſes, as euery man can tell. Shoting is a peynfull paſtime, wherof foloweth health of body quiknes of witte, habilitie to defende oure countrye, as our enemies can beare recorde.

Loth I am to compare theſe thinges togyther, and yet I do it not bicauſe there is any compariſon at al betwixte them, but therby a man ſhal ſe how good the one is, howe euil the other. For I thinke ther is ſcarſe ſo muche contrariouſnes, betwixte hotte and colde, vertue and vice, as is betwixte theſe. ii. thinges : For what ſo euer is in the one, the clean contrarye is in the other, as ſhall playnlye appere, if we conſider, bothe their beginnynges, theyr encreaſynges, theyr fructes, and theyr endes, whiche I wyl ſoone rydde ouer.

❡ The fyrſte brynger in to the worlde of ſhootynge, was Apollo, whiche for his Pla. in. ſymp. wiſdome, and great commodities, brought amonges men by him, was eſtemed worthie, to be counted as a God in heauen. Diſyng ſurely is a baſtarde borne, becauſe it is ſaid to haue. ii. fathers, and yet bothe noughte : The one was an vngracious God, called *Theuth*, which for his noughtines Plato came neuer in other goddes companyes, in Phedro. and therfore Homer doth deſpiſe onſe to name him,

in all his workes. The other father was   Herodot. n
a Lydian borne, whiche people for fuche   Clio.
gamnes, and other vnthriftines, as boowlyng and
hauntyng of tauernes, haue bene euer had in moft
vile reputation, in all ftoryes and writers.

The Fofterer vp of fhoting is Labour, ye companion
of vertue, the maynteyner of honeftie, the encreafer of
health and welthineffe, whiche admytteth nothinge in a
maner in to his companye, that ftandeth not, with
vertue and honeftie, and therefore fayeth the oulde
poete Epicharmus very pretelye in Xenophon, that
God felleth vertue, and all other good   Xen de dict.
things to men for labour. The Nource   et fact. Soc.
of dife and cardes, is werifom Ydleneffe, enemy of
vertue, ye drowner of youthe, that tarieth in it, and
as Chaufer doth faye verie well in the Parfons tale,
the greene path waye to hel, hauinge this thing appro-
priat vnto it, that where as other vices haue fome
cloke of honeftie, onely ydlenes can neyther do wel,
nor yet thinke wel. Agayne, fhooting hath two
Tutours to looke vpon it, out of whofe companie,
fhooting neuer ftirreth, the one called Daye light, ye
other Open place, whyche. ii. keepe fhooting from euyl
companye, and fuffers it not to haue to much fwinge, but
euermore keepes it vnder awe, that it darre do nothyng
in the open face of the worlde, but that which is good
and honeft. Lykewyfe, dyfinge and cardynge, haue.
ii. Tutours, the one named Solitarioufenes, whyche
lurketh in holes and corners, the other called Night
an vngratioufe couer of noughtyneffe, whyche two
thynges be very Inkepers and receyuers of all noughtyneffe and noughtye thinges, and thereto they be in a
maner, ordeyned by Nature. For on the nighte tyme
and in corners, Spirites and theues, rattes and mife,
toodes and oules, nyghtecrowes and poulcattes, foxes
and foumerdes, with all other vermine, and noyfome
beaftes, vfe moofte ftyrringe, when in the daye lyght,
and in open places whiche be ordeyned of God for
honefte thynges, they darre not ones come, whiche
thinge Euripides noted verye well, fayenge.

Il thinges the night, good thinges the daye doth haunt and vse.

Iphi. in. Tau.

Companions of fhoting, be prouidens, good heed giuing, true meatinge, honeft comparifon, whyche thinges agree with vertue very well. Cardinge and dyfinge, haue a forte of good felowes alfo, goynge commonly in theyr companye, as blynde Fortune, ftumbling chaunce, fpittle lucke, falfe dealyng, crafty conueyaunce, braynleffe brawlynge, falfe forfwerynge, whiche good feloes wyll fone take a man by the fleue, and caufe him take his Inne, fome wyth beggerye, fome wyth goute and dropfie, fome with thefte and robbery, and feldome they wyl leaue a man before he comme eyther to hangyng or els fomme other extreme mifery. To make an ende, howe fhoting by al mennes lawes hath bene alowed, cardyng and dyfing by al mennes iudgementes condemned, I nede not fhewe the matter is fo playne.

Therfore, whan the Lydians fhall inuent better thinges than Apollo, when flothe and ydlenes fhall encreafe vertue more than labour, whan the nyghte and lurking corners, giueth leffe occafion to vnthriftineffe, than lyght daye and opennes, than fhal fhotynge and fuche gamninge, be in fumme comparifon lyke. Yet euen as I do not fhewe all the goodnes, whiche is in fhotynge, whan I proue it ftandeth by the fame thinges that vertue it felfe ftandeth by, as brought in by God, or Godlyelyke men, foftered by labour, committed to the fauegarde of lyght and opennes, accompanied with prouifion and diligens, loued and allowed by euery good mannes fentence. Euen lykewyfe do I not open halfe the noughtines whiche is in cardyng and difing, whan I fhewe howe they are borne of a defperate mother, norifhed in ydlenes, encrefed by licence of nyght and corners, accompanied wyth Fortune, chaunce, deceyte, and craftines: condemned and banifhed, by all lawes and iudgementes.

For if I woulde enter, to defcrybe the monftruoufenes of it, I fhoulde rather wander in it, it is fo brode,

than haue any readye paffage to the ende of the matter:
whofe horriblenes is fo large, that it paffed the eloquence of oure Englyfhe Homer, to compaffe it: yet
becaufe I euer thought hys fayinges to haue as muche
authoritie, as eyther Sophocles or Euripides in Greke,
therfore gladly do I remembre thefe verfes of hys.

> *Hafardry is very mother of lefinges,*
> *And of deceyte, and curfed fweringes,*
> *Blafphemie of Chrift, manflaughter, and wafte alfo,*
> *Of catel of tyme, of other thynges mo.*

¶ *Mother of lefinges*) trulye it maye well be called fo,
if a man confydre howe manye wayes, and how many
thinges, he lofeth thereby, for firfte he lofeth his
goodes, he lofeth his tyme, he lofeth quycknes of wyt,
and all good luft to other thinges, he lofeth honeft
companye, he lofeth his good name and eftimation,
and at lafte, yf he leaue it not, lofeth God, and
heauen and all: and in ftede of thefe thinges winneth
at length, eyther hangyng or hell.

¶ *And of deceyte*) I trowe if I fhoulde not lye, there
is not halfe fo muche crafte vfed in no one thinge in
the worlde, as in this curfed thynge. What falfe dife
vfe they? as dife ftopped with quickfiluer and heares,
dife of a vauntage, flattes, gourdes to chop and
chaunge whan they lyfte, to lette the trew dife fall
vnder the table, and fo take vp the falfe, and if they
be true dife, what fhyfte wil they make to fet ye one of
them with flyding, with cogging, with foyfting, with
coytinge as they call it. Howe wyll they vfe thefe
fhiftes, whan they get a playne man that can no fkyll
of them? Howe will they go about, yf they perceyue
an honeft man haue money, which lift not playe, to
prouoke him to playe? They wyl feke his company,
they wil let hym paye nought, yea and as I hearde a
man ones faye that he dyd, they wil fend for hym to
fome houfe, and fpend perchaunce, a crown on him,
and at laft wyll one begin to faye: what my mafters,
what fhall we do? fhall euerye man playe his xii. d.
whyles an apple rofte in the fyre, and than we wyll

drinke and departe : Naye wyl an other faye, as falfe
as he, you can not leaue whan you begyn, and therfore I wyll not playe : but yet yf you wyll gage, that
euery man as he hath loft his. xii. d. fhall fit downe, I
am content, for furely I woulde winne no mannes
money here, but euen as much as wolde paye for mye
fupper. Than fpeketh the thyrde, to the honeft man
that thought not to playe, what wylle you playe your.
xii. pence if he excufe hym, tufh man wyll the other
faye, fticke not in honeft company for. xii. d. I wyll
beare your halfe, and here is my money.

Nowe al this is to make him to beginne, for they
knowe if he be ones in, and be a loofer, yat he wyl
not flicke at his. xii. d. but hopeth euer to gette it
agayne, whiles perhaps, he loofe all. Than euery one
of them fetteth his fhiftes abroche, fome with falfe
dife, fome with fettynge of dyfe, fome with hauinge
outelandifhe fyluer coynes guylded, to put away at a
tyme for good gold. Than if ther come a thing in
controuerfie, mufte you be iudged by the table, and
than farewell the honeft man hys parte, for he is borne
downe on euerye fyde.

Nowe fir, befyde all thefe thinges they haue certayne
termes, as a man woulde faye, appropriate to theyr
playing : wherby they wyl drawe a mannes money,
but paye none, whiche they cal barres, that furely he
that knoweth them not, maye foone be debarred of
all that euer he hath, afore he lerne them. Yf a
playne man lofe, as he fhall do euer, or els it is a
wonder, than the game is fo deuilyfh, that he can
neuer leaue : For vayn hope (which hope fayth Euripides, deftroyeth many a man and Citie)
dryueth hym on fo farre, that he can neuer   In fuppli.
retourne backe, vntyl he be fo lyght, that he nede feare
no theues by the waye. Nowe if a fimple man happen
onfe in his lyfe, to win of fuche players, than will they
eyther entreate him to kepe them company whyles he
hath loft all agayne, or els chey will vfe the mofte
dyuelifhe fafhion of all, For one of the players that

ſtandeth nexte him, ſhall haue a payre of falſe diſe,
and caſt them out vpon the bourde, the honeſt man
ſhall take them and caſt them, as he did the other, the
thirde ſhall eſpye them to be falſe diſe, and ſhall crye
oute, harde, with all the othes vnder God, that he hath
falſelye wonne theyr moneye, and than there is
nothynge but houlde thy throte from my dagger, than
euery man layeth hande on the ſimple man, and
taketh all theyr moneye from him, and his owne also,
thinking himſelfe wel, that he ſcapeth with his lyfe.

Curſed ſwerying, blaſphemie of Chriſte.) Theſe halfe
verſes Chaucer in an other place, more at large doth
well ſet out, and verye liuely expreſſe, ſayinge.

> *Ey by goddes precious hert and his nayles*
> *And by the blood of Chriſte, that is in Hales,*
> *Seuen is my chaunce, and thine is ſinke and treye,*
> *Ey goddes armes, if thou falſly playe,*
> *This dagger ſhall thorough thine herte go*
> *This frute commeth of the beched boones twco*
> *Forſweringe, Ire, falſnes and Homicide. &c.*

Thoughe theſe verſes be very erneſtlie wrytten, yet
they do not halfe ſo griſely ſette out the horyblenes of
blaſphemy, which ſuche gamners vſe, as it is in dede,
and as I haue hearde my ſelfe. For no man can wryte
a thing ſo earneſtlye, as whan it is ſpoken wyth ieſture,
as learned men you knowe do ſaye. Howe will you
thinke that ſuche furiouſenes wyth woode countenaun-
ces, and brenning eyes, with ſtaringe and bragging,
with heart redie to leape out of the belly for ſwelling,
can be expreſſed ye tenth part, to the vttermoſt.
Two men I herd my ſelfe, whoſe ſayinges be far more
griſely, than Chaucers verſes. One, whan he had loſt
his moneye, ſware me God, from top to toe with, one
breath, that he had loſt al his money for lacke of
ſweringe : The other, loſyng his money, and heaping
othes vpon othes, one in a nothers necke, mooſt
horrible and not ſpekeable, was rebuked of an honeſt
man whiche ſtode, by for ſo doynge, he by and by
ſtarynge him in the face, and clappyng his fiſte with all

his moneye he had, vpon the boorde, fware me by the
flefhe of God, that yf fweryng woulde helpe him but
one ace, he woulde not leue one pece of god vnfworne,
neyther wythin nor without. The remembraunce of
this blafphemy Philologe, doth make me quake at the
heart, and therefore I wyll fpeake no more of it.

And fo to conclude wyth fuche gamnying, I thynke
there is no vngracioufenes in all thys worlde, that
carieth fo far from god, as thys faulte doth. And yf
there were anye fo defperate a perfone, that woulde
begynne his hell here in earth, I trowe he fhoulde not
fynde hell more lyke hell it felfe, then the lyfe of thofe
men is which dayly haunt and vfe fuche vngracious games.

𝕻𝖍𝖎𝖑. You handle this gere in dede: And I fuppofe
if ye had ben a prentice at fuche games, you coulde
not haue fayd more of them then you haue done, and
by lyke you haue had fomwhat to do with them.

𝕿𝖔𝖝. In dede, you may honeftlye gather that I hate
them greatly, in that I fpeake agaynft them: not that
I haue vfed them greatlye, in that I fpeake of them.
For thynges be knowen dyuerfe wayes, as Socrates (you
knowe) doeth proue in Alcibiades. And if euery man
fhulde be that, that he fpeaketh or wryteth vpon, then
fhulde Homer haue bene the beft capitayne, mooft
cowarde, hardye, hafty, wyfe and woode, fage and
fimple: And Terence an oulde man and a yong, an
honeft man and a bawde: with fuche lyke. Surelye
euerye man ought to praye to God dayly, to kepe them
from fuche unthriftyneffe, and fpeciallye all the youth
of Englande: for what youth doth begynne, a man
wyll folowe commonlye, euen to his dyinge daye:
whiche thinge Adraftus in Euripides pretelye doth expreffe, fayinge.

What thing a man in tender age hath moft in vre
That fame to death alwayes to kepe he fhal be fure   Euripides
Therfore in age who greatly longes good frute to mowe   in suppli.
In youth he muft him felfe aplye good feede to fowe.

For the foundation of youth well fette (as Plato doth

faye) the whole bodye of the commune wealth fhal
floryfhe therafter. If the yonge tree growe croked, when
it is oulde, a man fhal rather breake it than ftreyght it.
And I thinke there is no one thinge yat crokes youth
more then fuche vnlefull games. Nor let no man
fay, if they be honeftly vfed they do no harme. For
how can that paftyme whiche neither exercifeth the
bodye with any honeft labour, nor yet the minde with
any honeft thinking, haue any honeftie ioyned with it.
Nor let no man affure hym felfe that he can vfe it
honeftlye: for if he ftande therein, he may fortune
haue a faule, the thing is more flipperye then he
knoweth of. A man maye (I graunt) fyt on a brante
hyll fyde, but if he gyue neuer fo lytle forwarde, he
can not ftoppe though he woulde neuer fo fayne, but
he muft nedes runne heedling, he knoweth not how
farre. What honeft pretences, vayne pleafure layeth
dayly (as it were entifements or baytes, to pull men
forwarde withall) Homer doeth well fhewe, by the
Sirenes, and Circes. And amonges all in that fhyp
there was but one Vlyffes, and yet he hadde done to
as the other dyd, yf a goddeffe had not taught hym:
And fo lykewyfe I thinke, they be eafye to numbre,
whiche paffe by playing honeftlye, excepte the grace
of God faue and kepe them. Therfore they that
wyll not go to farre in playing, let them folowe this
counfell of the Poete.

Stoppe the begynninges.

Philolo. Well, or you go any further, I pray you
tell me this one thing: Doo ye fpeake agaynfte meane
mennes playinge onlye, or agaynfte greate mennes
playinge to, or put you anye difference betwixte them?

Toxophi. If I fhulde excufe my felfe herein, and
faye that I fpake of the one, and not of the other, I
feare leafte I fhoulde as fondlye excufe my felfe, as a
certayne preacher dyd, whome I hearde vpon a tyme
fpeake agaynfte manye abufes, (as he fayde) and at
laft he fpake agaynft candelles, and then he fearynge,

leaſt ſome men woulde haue bene angrye and
offended with him, naye ſayeth he, you muſt take me
as I meane : I ſpeake not agaynſt greate candelles, but
agaynſt lytle candels, for they be not all one (quoth he) I
promyſe you : And ſo euerye man laughed him to ſcorne.

In dede as for greate men, and greate mennes matters, I lyſt not greatlye to meddle. Yet this I woulde
wyſſhe that all great men in Englande had red ouer diligentlye the Pardoners tale in Chaucer, and there they
ſhoulde perceyue and ſe, howe moche ſuche games
ſtand with theyr worſhyppe, howe great ſoeuer they be.
What great men do, be it good or yll, meane men communelye loue to followe, as many learned men in many
places do ſaye, and daylye experience doth playnelye
ſhewe, in coſtlye apparrell and other lyke matters.

Therefore, ſeing that Lordes be lanternes to leade
the lyfe of meane men, by their example, eyther to
goodneſſe or badneſſe, to whether ſoeuer they liſte : and
ſeinge alſo they haue libertie to lyſte what they will, I
pray God they haue will to liſt that which is good, and
as for their playing, I wyll make an ende with this ſaying
of Chaucer.

Lordes might finde them other maner of pleye
Honest ynough to driue the daye awaye.

But to be ſhorte, the beſt medicine for all ſortes of
men both high and lowe, yonge and oulde, to put
awaye ſuche vnlawfull games is by the contrarye, lykewyſe as all phyſicions do alowe in phyſike. So let
youthe in ſteade of ſuche vnlefull games, whiche ſtande
by ydleneſſe, by ſolitarineſſe, and corners, by night
and darkeneſſe, by fortune and chaunce, by crafte and
ſubtiltie, vſe ſuche paſtimes as ſtand by labour : vpon
the daye light, in open ſyght of men, hauynge ſuche an
ende as is come to by conning, rather then by crafte :
and ſo ſhulde vertue encreaſe, and vice decaye. For
contrarye paſtimes, muſt nedes worke contrary mindes
in men, as all other contrary thinges doo.

And thus we ſe Philologe, that ſhoting is not onely

the mooſt holeſome exerciſe for the bodye, the mooſt
honeſt paſtime for the mynde, and that for all ſortes
of men : But alſo it is a mooſt redy medicine, to
purge the hole realme of ſuche peſtilent gamning, wherwith many tymes : it is ſore troubled and ill at eaſe.

Phi. The more honeſtie you haue proued by ſhoting *Toxophile*, and the more you haue perſwaded me
to loue it, ſo moche trulye the ſorer haue you made
me with this laſt ſentence of yours, wherby you plainly
proue that a man maye not greatly vſe it.　For if
ſhoting be a medicine (as you ſaye that it is) it maye
not be vſed very oft, left a man ſhuld hurt him ſelfe
ith all, as medicines moche occupyed doo.　For Aristotle him ſelfe ſayeth, that medicines be no meate to
lyue withall : and thus ſhoting by the ſame reaſon,
maye not be moche occupyed.

Tox. You playe your oulde wontes Philologe, in
dalying with other mens wittes, not ſo moche to
proue youre owne matter, as to proue what other men
can ſay.　But where you thinke that I take awaye
moche vſe of ſhoting, in lykening it to a medicine : bycauſe men vſe not medicines euery daye, for ſo ſhoulde
their bodyes be hurt : I rather proue daylye vſe of
ſhoting therby.　For although Ariſtotle ſayeth that
ſome medicines be no meate to lyue withall, whiche is
true :　Yet Hippocrates ſayth that our　　Hippo. de
daylye meates be medicines, to withſtande　　med. purg.
euyll withall, whiche is as true.　For he maketh two
kyndes of medicines, one our meate that we vſe dailye,
whiche purgeth ſoftlye and ſlowlye, and in this ſim-
ilitude maye ſhoting be called a medicine, wherewith
dayly a man maye purge and take away al vnlefull
deſyres to other vnlefull paſtymes, as I proued before.
The other is a quicke purging medicine, and ſeldomer
to be occupyed, excepte the matter be greater, and I
coulde deſcribe the nature of a quicke medicine,
which ſhoulde within a whyle purge and plucke oute
all the vnthriftie games in the Realme, through which
the commune wealth oftentymes is ſycke.　For not

onelv good quicke wittes to learnyng be thereby
brought out of frame, and quite marred : But alſo
many wittes, either to attempt matters of high courage
in warre tyme, or els to atcheue matters of weyght
and wiſdome in peace tyme, be made therby very
quaſie and faynt.　For loke throughoute all hiſtories
written in Greke, Latyne, or other language, and you
ſhal neuer finde that realme proſper in the whiche
ſuche ydle paſtymes are vſed.　As concerning the
medicyne, although ſome wolde be miſcontent, if they
hearde me meddle anye thynge with it : Yet betwixte
you and me here alone, I maye the boldlyer ſaye my
fantaſie, and the rather bycauſe I wyll onelye wyſh for
it, whiche ſtandeth with honeſtie, not determyne of it
which belongeth to authoritie.　The medicine is this,
that wolde to God and the kynge, all theſe vnthriftie
ydle paſtymes, whiche be very bugges, that the Pſalme
meaneth on, walking on the nyght and in
corners, were made felonye, and ſome of　Psalm. 90.
that punyſhment ordeyned for them, which is appoynted for the forgers and falſifyers of the kynges
coyne.　Which puniſhment is not by me　Demost. con-
now inuented, but longe agoo, by the　tra Leptinem.
mooſte noble oratour Demoſthenes : which meru-
ayleth greatly that deathe is appoynted for falſifyers and forgers of the coyne, and not as greate
punyſhmente ordeyned for them, whiche by theyr
meanes forges and falſifyes the commune wealthe.
And I ſuppoſe that there is no one thyng that
chaungeth ſooner the golden and ſyluer wyttes of men
into copperye and braſſye wayes then diſing and ſuche
vnlefull paſtymes.

And this quicke medicine I beleue wolde ſo throwlye
pourge them, that the daylye medicines, as ſhoting and
other paſtymes ioyned with honeſt labour ſhoulde
eaſeiyer withſtande them.

Phil. The excellent commodityes of ſhotynge in
peace tyme, Toxophile, you haue very wel and ſuffi-
ciently declared.　Wherby you haue ſo perſuaded me,

that God wyllyng hereafter I wyll both loue it the better,
and alfo vfe it the ofter.   For as moche as I can gather
of all this communication of ours, the tunge, the nofe,
the handes and the feete be no fytter membres, or
inftrumentes for the body of a man, then is fhotinge
for the hole bodye of the realme.   God hath made
the partes of men which be beft and mooft necceffarye,
to ferue, not for one purpofe onelye, but for manye :
as the tunge for fpeaking and tafting, the nofe for
fmelling, and alfo for auoyding of all excrementes,
which faule oute of the heed, the handes for receyuynge
of good thinges, and for puttyng of all harmefull
thinges, from the bodye.   So fhotinge is an exercyfe of
healthe, a paftyme of honeft pleafure, and fuche one
alfo that ftoppeth or auoydeth all noyfome games
gathered and encreafed by ill rule, as noughtye humours
be, whiche hurte and corrupte fore that parte of the
realme, wherin they do remayne.

But now if you can fhewe but halfe fo moche profyte in warre of fhotynge, as you haue proued pleafure
in peace, then wyll I furelye iudge that there be fewe
thinges that haue fo manifolde commodities, and vfes
ioyned vnto them as it hath.

Tox. The vpperhande in warre, nexte the   **G**
goodneffe of God (of whome al victorie
commeth, as fcripture fayth) ftandeth   Mach 1. 3.
chefely in thre thinges : in the wyfedome of the Prince,
in the fleyghtes and pollicies of the capitaynes, and in
the ftrength and cherefull forwardneffe of the fouldyers.
A Prince in his herte muft be full of mercy and peace,
a vertue mooft pleafaunt to Chrift, mooft agreable to
mans nature, mooft profytable for ryche and poore.

For than the riche man enioyeth with great pleafure
that which he hath : the poore may obtayne with his
labour, that which he lacketh.   And although there
is nothing worfe then war, wherof it taketh his
name, through the which great men be in daunger,
meane men without fuccoure, ryche men in feare,
bycaufe they haue fomwhat : poore men in care,

bvcause they haue nothing: And so euery man in
thougnt and miserie: Yet it is a ciuill medicine, wherewith a prince maye from the bodye of his commune
wealtn, put of that daunger whiche maye faule: or
elles recouer agayne, whatsoeuer it hath lost. And
therfore as Isocrates doth saye, a prince
must be a warriour in two thinges, in con-   Ad Nico.
ninge and knowledge of all sleyghtes and feates of
warre, and in hauing al necessarye habilimentes belongyng to the same. Whiche matter to entreate at
large, were ouerlonge at this tyme to declare, and ouer-
moche for my learning to perfourme.

After the wisdome of the prince, are valiant capitaynes moost necessary in warre, whose office and
dutye is to knowe all fleightes and pollicies for all
kyndes of warre, which they maye learne. ii. wayes,
either in daylye folowing and haunting the warres or
els bicause wisdome bought with strypes, is many
tymes ouercostlye: they maye bestowe sometyme in
Vegetius, which entreateth suche matters in Latin
metelye well, or rather in Polyenus, and Leo the
Emperour, which setteth out al pollicies and duties
of capitaynes in the Greke tunge very excellentlye.
But chefelye I wolde wisshe (and if I were of authoritie) I wolde counsel al the yong gentlemen of this
realme, neuer to lay out of theyr handes. ii. authors
Xenophon in Greke, and Cæsar in Latyn, where in
they shulde folowe noble Scipio Africanus,
as Tullie doeth saye: In whiche. ii. authours   De. Sen.
besydes eloquence a thinge moste necessary of all other,
for a captayne, they shulde learne the hole course
of warre, whiche those. ii. noble menne dyd not more
wyselye wryte for other men to learne, than they dyd
manfully exercise in the fyelde, for other men to followe.

The strengthe of war lyeth in the souldier, whose
chyefe praysc and vertue, is obedience towarde his
captayne, sayth Plato. And Xenophon   Obedience.
being a gentyle authour, moste christianlye   Plat. leg. 12.
doeth saye, euen by these woordes, that   Xen. Agef.

that fouldyer which firfte ferueth god, and than obeyeth
hys captayne, may boldelie with all courage, hope to
ouerthrowe his enemy. Agayne, without obedience,
neither valiant man, ftout horfe, nor goodly
harnes doth any good at al. which obedience of ye fouldier toward his captane, brought the
whole empyre of ye worlde, into the Romanes handes.
and whan it was brought, kepte it lenger, than euer it
was kept in any common welth before or after.

And this to be true, Scipio Africanus, the mofte
noble captayne that euer was amonge the
Romaynes, fhewed very playnly, what tyme
as he went into Afryke, to deftroye Cartage. For he
reftinge hys hoofte by the waye in Sicilie, a daye or twoo,
and at a tyme ftanding with a great man of Sicilie, and
looking on his fouldiers how they exercifed themfelues
in kepyng of araye, and other feates, the gentleman
of Sicilie afked Scipio, wherin lay hys chyefe hope to
ouercome Cartage : He anfwered, in yonder feloes of
myne whom you fe play : And why fayth the other,
bycaufe fayeth Scipio, that if I commaunded them to
runne in to the toppe of this high caftel, and caft
them felues doune backeward vpon thefe rockes, I am
fure they woulde do it.

Salluft alfo doth write, yat there were mo Romanes
put to death of theyr captaynes for
fetting on theyr enemyes before they had
licence, than were for running away out of the fyelde,
before they had foughten. Thefe two examples do
proue, that amonges the Romaynes, the obedience of
the fouldyer was wonderfull great, and the feueritie of
the Captaynes, to fe the fame kepte wonderfull ftrayte.
For they wel perceyued that an hofte full of obe-
dyence, falleth as feldome into the handes of theyr
enemies as that bodye fawleth into Jeoperdye, the
whiche is ruled by reafon. Reafon and Rulers beynge
lyke in offyce, (for the one ruleth the body of man, the
other ruleth the bodye of the common wealthe) ought
to be lyke of condicions, and oughte to be obeyed in

Xen. Hippar.

Plutarchus.

Sal. in. Cat.

all maner of matters. Obedience is nouryſſhed by feare and loue, Feare is kept in by true iuſtice and equitie, Loue is gotten by wiſdome, ioyned with liberalitie: For where a ſouldyer ſeeth ryghteouſeneſſe ſo rule, that a man can neyther do wronge nor yet take wronge, and that his capitayne for his wyſedome, can mayntayne hym, and for his liberalitie will maintayne him, he muſt nedes both loue him and feare him, of the whiche procedeth true and vnſayned obedience. After this inwarde vertue, the nexte good poynt in a ſouldier, is to haue and to handle his weapon wel, whereof the one muſt be at the appoyntment of the captayne, the other lyeth in the courage and exerciſe of the ſouldier: yet of al weapons the beſt is, as Euripides doth ſay, wherwith with leeſt daunger of our ſelf we maye hurt our enemye mooſt. And that is (as I ſuppoſe) artillarie. Artillarie now a dayes is taken for. ii. thinges: Gunnes and Bowes, which how moch they do in war, both dayly experience doeth teache, and alſo Peter Nannius a learned man of Louayn, in a certayne dialoge[3] doth very well ſet out, wherein this is moſt notable, that when he hath ſhewed excedyng commodities of both, and ſome diſcommodities of gunnes, as infinite coſt and charge, comberſome carriage: and yf they be greate, the vncertayne leuelyng, the peryll of them that ſtand by them, the eſyer auoydyng by them that ſtande far of: and yf they be lytle, the leſſe both feare and ieoperdy is in them, beſyde all contrary wether and wynde, whiche hyndereth them not a lytle: yet of all ſhotyng he cannot reherſe one diſcommoditie.

ℙℏⅈ. That I meruayle greatly at, ſeing Nannius is ſo well learned, and ſo exerciſed in the authours of both the tunges: for I my ſelfe do remember that ſhotying in war is but ſmally prayſed, and that of diuers captaynes in dyuers authors. For firſt in Euripides (whom you ſo highly praiſe) and very well, for Tullie thynketh euerye verſe in him to be an authoritie, what I praye you, doth Lycus that ouercame Thebes, ſay as con-

In Herc. fu.

cernyng ſhoting? whoſe words as farre as I remembre, be theſe, or not muche vnlyke.

> *What prayſe hath he at al, whiche neuer durſt abide,*
> *The dint of a ſpeares poynt thruſt againſt his ſide*
> *Nor neuer bouldlie buckeler bare yet in his leſte hande*
> *Face to face his enemies bront ſtiſſelie to wythſtande,*
> *But alwaye truſteth to a bowe and to a fethered ſticke*
> *Harnes euer moſt fit for him which to flie is quicke,*   Eurip. in
> *Bowe and ſhaſte is Armoure meteſt for a cowarde*   Herc. furent.
> *Which dare not ones abide the bronte of battel ſharpe and harde.*
> *But he a man of manhode moſt is by mine aſſent*
> *Which with harte and corage boulde, fullie hath him bent,*
> *His enemies looke in euery ſloure ſloutelie to a bide,*
> *Face to face, and fote to fote, tide what may be tide.*

Agayne Teucer the beſt Archer amonges all the
Grecians, in Sophocles is called of Menelaus, a boweman, and a ſhooter as in   Soph in
villaynie and reproche, to be a thing of no   Sia. flag.
price in warre. Moreouer Pandarus the beſt ſhooter in
the worlde, whome Apollo hym ſelfe taught to ſhoote,
bothe he and his ſhotynge is quyte con-
temned in Homer, in ſo much that Homer   Iliad. 5.
(which vnder a made fable doth alwayes hyde hys
iudgement of thinges) doeth make Pandarus him ſelfe
crye out of ſhooting, and caſt his bowe awaye, and
take him to a ſpeare, makynge a vowe that if euer he
came home, he woulde breake his ſhaftes, and burne
his bowe, lamentyng greatly, that he was ſo fonde to
leaue at home his horſe and charyot wyth other
weapons, for the truſt yat he had in his bowe. Homer
ſignifieng thereby, that men ſhoulde leue ſhoting out
of warre, and take them to other wepons more fitte
and able for the ſame, and I trowe Pandarus woordes
be muche what after thys ſorte.

> *Ill chaunce ill lucke me hyther broughte*
> *Ill fortune me that daye befell,*
> *Whan firſt my bowe fro the pynne I roughte*
> *For Hectors ſake, the Grekes to quell.*

But yf that God fo for me fhap
That home agayne I maye ones come,
Let me neuer inioye that hap,
Nor euer twyfe looke on the fonne,
If bowe and fhaftes I do not burne
Whyche nowe fo euel doth ferue my turne.

But to let paffe al Poetes, what can be forer faid agaynft any thing, than the iudgement of Cyrus is agaynft fhotynge, whiche doth cauſe his Perſians beyng the beſt fhooters to laye awaye theyr bowes and take them to fweardes and buckelers, fpeares and dartes, and other lyke hande weapons. The which thing Xenophon fo wyfe a philoſopher, fo experte a captayne in warre hym felfe, woulde neuer haue written, and fpecially in that booke wherein he purpofed to fhewe, as Tullie fayeth in dede, not the true hiftorie, but the example of a perfite wife prince and common welthe, excepte that iudgement of chaungyng Artillerie, in to other wepons, he had alwayes thought beft to be folowed, in all warre. Whofe counfell the Parthians dyd folowe, whan they chafed Antonie ouer the mountaines of Media, whiche being the beft fhoters of the worlde, lefte theyr bowes, and toke them to fpeares and morifpikes.

Xen. Cyri. Inft. 6.

Epift. 1. ad Q. Fra.

Plutarch M. Ant.

And thefe fewe examples I trowe, of the beft fhooters, do well proue that the beft fhotinge is not the beft thinge as you call it in warre.

𝕿𝖔𝖝. As concernynge your firft example, taken oute of Euripides, I maruayle you wyl bring it for ye difprayfe of fhotyng, feyng Euripides doth make thofe verfes, not bicaufe he thinketh them true, but bicaufe he thinketh them fit for the perfon that fpake them. For in dede his true iudgement of fhoting, he doth expreffe by and by after in the oration of the noble captaine Amphytrio agaynfte Lycus, wherein a man maye doubte, whether he hath more eloquentlye confuted Lycus fayenge, or more worthelye fette oute the prayfe of fhootynge.

And as I am aduifed, his woordes be muche hereafter as I fhall faye.

Againft the wittie gifte of fhotinge in a bowe Eurip. in.
Fonde and leud woordes thou leudlie doeft out throwe, Herc. fur
Whiche, if thou wilte heare of me a woorde or twayne
Quicklie thou mayft læerne howe fondlie thou doeft blame,

Firfte he that with his harneis him felfe doth wal about,
That fcarce is lefte one hole through which he may pepe out,
Such bondmen to their harneis to fight are nothinge mete
But fonoft of al other are troden vnder fete.

Yf he be ftronge, his felovves faynt, in whome he putteth his truft,
So loded with his harneis muft nedes lie in the duft,
Nor yet from death he cannot ftarte, if ones his weapon breke,
Howe ftoute, howe ftrong, howe great, howe longe,
        fo euer be fuche a freke.

But who fo euer can handle a bowe fturdie ftiffe and ftronge
Wherwith lyke hayle manie fhaftes he fhootes into the thickeft thronge:
This profite he takes, that ftanding a far his enemie he maye fpill
Whan he and his full fafe fhall ftande out of all daunger and ill.
And this in War is wifedome mofte, which workes our enemies woo.
Whan we fhal be far from all feare and ieoperdie of our foo.

Secondarily euen as I do not greatlye regarde what Menelaus doth fay in Sophocles to Teucer, bycaufe he fpake it bothe in anger, and alfo to hym that he hated, euen fo doo I remembre very well in Homer, that when Hector and the Troians woulde haue fet fyre on the greke fhippes, Teucer with his bowe made them recule backe agayne, when Menelaus   Iliad. 8. tooke hym to his feete, and ranne awaye.

Thirdlye as concerning Pandarus, Homer doth not difprayfe the noble gyfte of fhotynge, but therby euery man is taught, that whatfoeuer, and how good foeuer a weapon a man doth vfe in war, yf he be hym   Hom. Ili. 5. felfe a couetoufe wretche, a foole wythoute counfell, a peacebreaker as Pandarus was, at laft he fhall throughe the punifhment of God fall into his enemyes handes, as Pandarus dydde, whome Diomedes throughe the helpe of Minerua miferablye flue.

And bycaufe you make mencion of Homer, and

Troye matters, what can be more prayfe for anye thynge, I praye you, than that is for fhootyng, that Troye coulde neuer be deftroyed without the helpe of Hercules fhaftes, whiche thinge doeth fignifie, that although al the worlde were gathered in an army togyther, yet without fhotinge they can neuer come to theyr purpofe, as Vlyffes in Sophocles very plainlye doth faye vnto Pyrrhus, as concernyng Hercules fhaftes to be caried vnto Troye.

Nor you without them, nor without you they do ought.   Soph. phil.

Fourthlye where as Cyrus dyd chaunge   Xen. Cyri.
parte of his bowemen, wherof he had plen-   Instit. 6.
tie, into other menne of warre, wherof he lacked, I will not greatlye difpute whether Cyrus did well in that poynt in thofe dayes or no, bycaufe it is not playne in Xenophon howe ftrong fhooters the Perfians were, what bowes they had, what fhaftes and heades they occupyed, what kynde of warre theyr enemies vfed.

But trulye as for the Parthians, it is playne, in Plutarche, that in chaungyng theyr bowes   Plu. in. M.
in to fpeares, they brought theyr felfe   Anton.
into vtter deftruction. For when they had chafed the Romaynes many a myle, through reafon of theyr bowes, at the laft the Romaynes afhamed of their fleing, and remembrynge theyr owlde noblenessse and courage, ymagined thys waye, that they woulde kneele downe on theyr knees, and fo couer all theyr body wyth theyr fhyldes and targattes, that the Parthians fhaftes might flyde ouer them, and do them no harme, which thing when the Parthians perceyued, thinking that ye Romaynes wer forweryed with laboure, watche, and hungre: they layed downe their bowes, and toke fperes in their handes, and fo ranne vpon them: but the Romaynes perceyuinge them without their bowes, rofe vp manfully, and flewe them euery mother fon, faue a fewe that faued them felues with runnyng awaye. And herein our archers of Englande far paffe the Parthians, which for fuche a purpofe, when they

ſhall come to hande ſtrokes, hath euer redy, eyther at
his backe hangyng, or els in his next felowes hande a
leaden maule, or ſuche lyke weapon, to beate downe
his enemyes withall.

Phi. Well *Toxophile*, ſeing that thoſe examples whiche
I had thought to haue ben cleane agaynſt ſhoting, you
haue thus turned to the hygh prayſe of ſhotinge : and
all this prayſe that you haue now ſayd on it, is rather
come in by me than ſought for of you : let me heare
I praye you nowe, thoſe examples whiche you haue
marked of ſhotyng your ſelfe : whereby you are, and
thinke to perſuade other, yat ſhoting is ſo good in warre.

Tox. Examples ſurely I haue marked very many :
from the begynning of tyme had in memorie of wrytyng, throughout all commune wealthes, and Empires
of the worlde : wherof the mooſte part I wyll paſſe
ouer, left I ſhoulde be tedioufe : yet ſome I wyll
touche, bycauſe they be notable, bothe for me to tell
and you to heare.

And bycauſe the ſtorye of the Iewes is for the tyme
mooſt auncient, for the truthe mooſte credible, it ſhalbe
mooſt fitte to begynne with them. And although I
knowe that God is the onely gyuer of victorie, and not
the weapons, for all ſtrength and victorie (ſayth Iudas
Machabeus) cometh from heauen : Yet
ſurely ſtrong weapons be the inſtrumentes   Mach. 1. 3.
wherwith god doth ouercome yat parte,
which he wil haue ouerthrown. For God   Ⱨ
is well pleaſed wyth wyſe and wittie feates of warre :
As in metinge of enemies, for truſe takyng, to haue
priuilye in a buſhment harneſt men layd
for feare of treaſon, as Iudas Machabeus   Mach. 2. 14.
dyd wyth Nicanor Demetrius capitayne : And to haue
engines of warre to beate downe cities with all : and
to haue ſcout watche amonges our enemyes to knowe
their counſayles, as the noble captaine
Ionathas brother to Iudas Machabeus did   Mach. 1. 12.
in the countrie of Amathie againſt the mighty hoſte of
Demetrius. And beſyde al this, god is pleaſed to haue

goodly tombes for them which do noble feates in warre,
and to haue their ymages made, and alſo their cote
Armours to be ſet aboue theyr tombes, to   Mach. 1. 13.
their perpetual laude and memorie : as the
valiaunt capitayne Symon, dyd cauſe to be made for
his brethren Iudas Machabeus and Ionathas, when
they were ſlayne of the Gentiles.   And thus of what
authoritie feates of warre, and ſtrong weapons be,
ſhortly and playnelye we maye learne: But amonges
the Iewes as I began to tell, I am ſure there was
nothing ſo occupyed, or dydde ſo moche good as bowes
dyd : inſomoche that when the Iewes had any great
vpperhande ouer the Gentiles, the fyrſte thinge alwayes
that the captayne dyd, was to exhort the people to
gyue all the thankes to God for the victorye, and not to
theyr bowes, wherwith they had ſlayne their   Joſue. 23.
enemyes : as it is playne that the noble
Ioſue dyd after ſo many kynges thruſt downe by hym.

God, when he promyſeth helpe to the Jewes, he vſeth
no kynde of ſpeakyng ſo moche as this, that he wyll
bende his bowe, and die his ſhaftes in the   Deutero. 32
Gentiles blood : whereby it is manifeſt, that
eyther God wyll make the Iewes ſhoote ſtronge ſhotes
to ouerthrowe their enemies : or at leeſte that ſhotinge
is a wonderful mightie thing in warre, whervnto ye
hygh power of God is lykened.   Dauid in the Pſalmes
calleth bowes the veſſels of death, a bytter   Pſal. 7. 63.
thinge, and in an other place a myghty   75.
power, and other wayes mo, which I wyll let paſſe,
bycauſe euerye man readeth them daylye : But yet
one place of ſcripture I muſt nedes remembre,
which is more notable for ye prayſe of ſhoting, then
any yat euer I red in any other ſtorie, and that is,
when Saul was ſlayne of ye Philiſtians   Regum 1. 31.
being mightie bowmen, and Ionathas his
ſonne with him, that was ſo good a ſhoter, as ye
ſcripture ſayth, that he neuer ſhot ſhafte in vayne,
and yat the kyngdome after Saules deathe came vnto
Dauid : the firſt ſtatute and lawe that euer Dauid

made after he was king, was this, that al
ye children of Ifrael fhulde learne to fhote,   Regum. 2. 1.
according to a lawe made many a daye before yat tyme
for the fetting out of fhoting as it is written (fayeth
Scripture) *in libro Iuftorum*, whiche booke we haue not
nowe : And thus we fe plainelye what greate vfe of
fhoting, and what prouifion euen from the begynnynge
of the worlde for fhotyng, was amonge the Iewes.

The Ethiopians which inhabite the furtheft part
South in the worlde, were wonderfull bowmen : in
fomoche that when Cambyfes king of   Herodotus in
Perfie being in Egipt, fent certayne am-   Thalia.
baffadours into Ethiope to the kynge there, with many
great gyftes : the king of Ethiop perceyuinge them
to be efpyes, toke them vp fharpely, and blamed
Cambyfes greatly for fuch vniuft enterprifes : but
after that he had princely entertayned them, he fent
for a bowe, and bente it and drewe it, and then vnbent
it agayne, and fayde vnto the ambaffadours, you fhall
commende me to Cambyfes, and gyue him this bowe
fro me, and byd him when any Perfian can fhote in
this bowe, let him fet vpon the Ethiopians : In the
meane whyle let hym gyue thankes vnto God, whiche
doth not put in the Ethiopians mynde to conquere
any other mans lande.   This bowe, when it came
amonge the Perfians, neuer one man in fuche an infinite hoft (as Herodotus doth faye) could ftyrre the
ftryng, faue onely Smerdis the brother of Cambyfes,
whiche ftyrred it two fingers, and no further : for the
which act Cambyfes had fuche enuy at him, that he
afterward flewe him : as doth appeare in the ftorye.

Sefoftris the mooft mightie king that euer was in
Egipt, ouercame a great parte of the worlde, and that
by archers : he fubdued the Arabians, the Iues, the
Affyrians : he went farther into Scythia then any man
els : he ouercame Thracia, euen to the borders of
Germanie.   And in token how he ouercame al men
he fet vp in many places great ymages to his owne
lykeneffe, hauynge in the one hande a bowe, in the

other a sharpe heeded shafte: that men
myght knowe, what weapon is hooste
vsed, in conqueryng so manye people.

Herod. in.
Euterpe.
Diod. Sic. 2.

Cyrus, counted as a god amonges the Gentyles, for
his noblenesse and felicitie in warre : yet at
the last when he set vpon the Massagetanes
(which people neuer went without their bowe nor their
quiuer, nether in warre nor peace) he and all his were
slayne, and that by shotyng, as appeareth in the storye.

Herod. in clio.

Polycrates the prince of Samos (a very little yle)
was lorde ouer all the Greke sees, and with-
stode the power of the Persians, onely by
the helpe of a thousande archers.

Herod. in thalia.

The people of Scythia, of all other men loued, and
vsed moost shotyng, the hole rychesse and househoulde
stuffe of a man in Scythia, was a yocke of oxen, a
plough, his nagge and his dogge, his bowe and his
quiuer : which quiuer was couered with the skynne of
a man, whiche he toke or slewe fyrste in battayle.
The Scythians to be inuincible by reason of their
shotyng, the greate voyages of so manye noble con-
querours spent in that countrie in vayne, doeth well
proue : But specially that of Darius the myghtie kyng
of Persie, which when he had taryed there a great
space, and done no good, but had forweryed his
hoste with trauayle and hunger : At last the men
of Scythia sent an ambassadour with. iiii.
gyftes : a byrde, a frogge, a mouse, and.

Herod. in.
Melpomen.

v. shaftes. Darius meruaylyng at the straungenesse
of the gyftes, asked the messenger what they signyfyed :
the messenger answered, that he had no further com-
maundement, but onely to delyuer his gyftes, and
retourne agayne with all spede : but I am sure (sayeth
he) you Persians for your great wysdome, can soone
boult out what they meane. When the messenger was
gone, euery man began to say his verdite. Darius
Iudgment was this, that ye Scythians gaue ouer into
the Persians handes, their lyues, their hole power,
both by lande and see, signifyinge by the mouse the

earthe, by the frogge the water, in which they both
liue, by ye birde their lyues which lyue in the ayer, by
the fhaft their hole power and Empire, that was maynteyned alwayes by fhotinge. Gobryas a noble and
wyfe captayne amonges the Perfians, was of a cleane
contrary minde, faying, nay not fo, but the Sythians
meane thus by their gyftes, that except we get vs
wynges, and flye into the ayer lyke birdes, or run into
ye holes of the earthe lyke myfe, or els lye lurkyng in
fennes and mariffes lyke frogges, we fhall neuer returne
home agayne, before we be vtterly vndone with their
fhaftes : which fentence fanke fo fore into their hertes,
yat Darius with all fpede poffible, brake vp his campe,
and gat hym felfe homewarde. Yet howe moche the
Perfians them felues fet by fhotinge, wherby they
encreafed their empire fo moche, doth appeare by.
iii. manifeft reafons: firfte that they brought   Herod. in clio.
vppe theyr youth in the fchole of fhoting,   Xenoph. in
vnto. xx. yere of age, as dyuerfe noble   cyrop.
Greke authours do faye.   Strab. ii.

Agayne, bycaufe the noble kyng Darius thought hym
felfe to be prayfed by nothyng fo moch, as to be counted
a good fhoter, as doth appeare by his fepulchre,
wherin he caufed to be written this fentence.

Darius the King lieth buried here   Strab. 15.
That in fhoting and riding had neuer pere.

Thirdlye the coyne of the Perfians, both golde and
filuer had the Armes of Perfie vpon it, as is   Plutarch. in
cuftomably vfed in other realmes, and that   Agefila.
was bow and arowes : by the which feate they declared,
how moch they fet by them.

The Grecians alfo, but fpecially the noble Athe-
nienfes, had all their ftrength lyinge in   Suidas.
Artillarie : and for yat purpofe the citie of
Athens had a thoufand. men which were onely archers,
in dayly wages, to watche and kepe the citie from al
ieoperdie and fodein daunger : which archers alfo fhuld
cary to prifon and warde any mifdoer at ye commaunde-

ment of the hygh officers, as playnlye doth appeare in
Plato. And furely the bowmen of Athens   Plato in pro-
did wonderful feates in many battels, but   tagora.
fpecially when Demofthenes the valiaunt captayne flue
and toke prifoners all the Lacedemonians befyde ye
citie of Pylos, where Neftor fomtyme was lord: the
fhaftes went fo thicke that day (fayth
Thucydides) that no man could fe theyr   Thucydid. 4.
enemies. A Lacedemonian taken prifoner, was afked
of one at Athens, whether they were ftoute fellowes that
were flayne or no, of the Lacedemonians: he anfwered
nothing els but this: make moche of thofe fhaftes of
youres, for they knowe neyther ftoute nor vnftoute:
meanynge thereby, that no man (though he were neuer
fo ftout) came in their walke, that efcaped without
death.

Herodotus defcrybing the mighty hooft   Herod. in
of Xerxes efpecially doth marke out, what   Polym.
bowes and fhaftes they vfed, fignifying yat therin lay
their chefe ftrength. And at the fame tyme Attoffa,
mother of Xerxes, wyfe to Darius, and doughter of
Cyrus, doeth enquire (as Aefchylus fheweth
in a Tragedie) of a certayne meffenger   Efch. in Perf.
that came from Xerxes hofte, what ftronge and fearfull bowes the Grecians vfed: wherby it is playne, that
Artillarie was the thing, wherin both Europe and Afia
at thofe dayes trufted mooft vppon.

The beft parte of Alexanders hofte were arch.ers as
playnelye doth appeare in Arianus, and other yat
wrote his life: and thofe fo ftronge archers, that they
onely, fundrye tymes ouercame their enemies, afore
any other neded to fyght: as was fene in
the battayl which Nearchus one of Alex-   Arianus. 8.
anders capitaynes had befyde the ryuer of Thomeron.
And therfore as concerning all thefe kyngdomes and
commune wealthes, I maye conclude with this fentence of Plinie, whofe wordes be, as I fup-   Plin. lib. 16.
pofe thus: If any man woulde remembre   Cap. 36.
the Ethiopians, Egyptians, Arabians, the men of Inde,

of Scythia, fo many people in ye eaſt of the Sarmatianes, and all the kyngdomes of the Parthians, he ſhall well perceyue halfe the parte of the worlde, to lyue in ſubiection, ouercome by the myght and power of ſhotinge.

In the commune wealth of Rome, which exceded all other in vertue, nobleneſſe, and dominion litle mention is made of ſhoting, not bycauſe it was litle vſed amonges them, but rather bycauſe it was bothe ſo neceſſarye and commune, that it was thought a thing not neceſſarye or requyred of anye man to be ſpoken vpon, as if a man ſhoulde deſcribe a greate feaſte, he woulde not ones name bread, although it be mooſte common and neceſſary for all : but ſurely yf a feaſte beynge neuer ſo great, lacked bread, or had fewſty and noughty bread, all the other daynties ſhulde be vnſauery, and litle regarded, and than woulde men talke of the commodity of bread, whan they lacke it, that would not ones name it afore, whan they had it : And euen ſo dyd the Romaynes as con-cernynge ſhootyng. Seldome is ſhootinge named, and yea it dyd the moſte good in warre, as didde appere, verye playnlye in that battell, whiche Scipio Aphricanus had with the Numantines in Spayne, whome he coulde neuer ouercome, before he ſette bowemen amonges his horſe men, by whoſe myght they were clean vanquiſhed.

Agayne, Tiberius fyghtynge with Armenius and Ing-uiomerus princis of Germanie, had one wing of archers on horſeback, an other of   Cor, Tac. 2 archers on foot, by whoſe might the Germanes were ſlayne downe ryghte, and ſo ſcattered and beate oute of the feelde, that the chaſe laſted. x. myles, the Ger-manes clame vp in to trees for feare, but the Romanes dyd fetche them downe with theyr ſhaftes as they had ben birdes, in whyche battell the Romaynes loſt ſewe or none, as doth appeare in the hiſtorie.

But as I began to ſaye, the Romaynes dyd not ſo muche prayſe the goodneſſe of ſhootinge, whan they had it, as they dyd lament the lacke of it, whan they

wanted it, as Leo the. v. the noble Emperour doth
playnly teſtifie in ſundrie places in thoſe bokes whiche he
wrote in Greke, of the fleyghtes and pollicies of warre.[2]

Phil. Surelie of that booke I haue not heard before,
and howe came you to the ſyghte of it.

Tox. The booke is rare trulie, but this laſte yeare
when maſter Cheke tranſlated the ſayd booke out of
greke in to Latin, to ye kinges maieſtie, he of his
gentleneſſe, wolde haue me very ofte in hys chamber,
and for the familiaritie that I had wyth hym, more
than manye other, woulde ſuffer me to reade of it,
whan I woulde, the whiche thing to do, ſurelye I was
very deſirous and glad, becauſe of the excellent
handelynge of all thynges, that euer he taketh in
hande. And verily *Philologe*, as ofte as I remembre the
departynge of that man from the vniuerſitie, (whiche
thinge I do not ſeldome) ſo ofte do I well perceyue
our moſte helpe and ſutheraunce to learnynge, to haue
gon awaye with him. For by ye great commoditie
yat we toke in hearyng hym reade priuatly in his
chambre, all Homer, Sophocles, and Euripides,
Herodotus, Thucydides, Xenophon, Iſocrates and
Plato, we feele the great diſcommoditie in not hearynge
of hym, Ariſtotle and Demoſthenes, whiche. ii. authours
with all diligence laſt of all he thought to haue redde
vnto us. And when I conſider howe manye men he
ſuccoured with his helpe, and hys ayde to abyde here
for learninge, and howe all men were prouoked and
ſtyrred vp, by his councell and daylye example, howe
they ſhulde come to learning, ſurely I perceyue that
ſentence of Plato to be true, which ſayeth that there is
nothyng better in any common wealthe, than that there
ſhoulde be alwayes one or other, excellent paſſyng
mar, whoſe lyfe and vertue, ſhoulde plucke forwarde
the will, diligence, laboure and hope of all other, that
folowyng his footeſteppes, they myght comme to the
ſame ende, whereunto labour, lerning and vertue, had
conueied him before. The great hinderance of learning,
in iackinge thys man greatly I ſhulde lament, if this diſ-

commoditie of oures, were not ioyned with the commoditie and health, of ye hole realme, for which purpofe,
our noble king full of wyfedome hath called vp this
excellent man full of learnynge, to teache noble prince
Edwarde, an office ful of hope, comforte and folace to al
true hertes of England: For whome al England dayly
doth praye, yat he paffing his Tutour in
learnyng and knowledge folowynge his   Cor. Tac. 2.
father in wifedome and felicitie, accordyng to yat example which is fet afore his eyes, may fo fet out and
mayntayne goddes worde to the abolifhment of al papif-
try, the confufion of al herefie, that thereby he feared of
his ennemies, loued of al his fubiectes, maye bring to
his own glory, immortal fame and memorie, to this
realme, welthe, honour, and felicitie, to true and vn-
fayned religion perpetuall peace, concorde, and vnitie.

But to retourne to fhootynge agayne, what Leo
fayeth of fhootynge amonges the Romaynes, hys
woordes, be fo muche for the prayfe of fhootynge,
and the booke alfo fo rare to be gotten, that I learned
the places by harte, whyche be as I fuppofe, euen
thus. Fyrfte in his fixte booke, as concerning what
harneys is beft: Lette all the youth of Rome be
compelled to vfe fhootyng, eyther more or leffe, and
alwayes to bear theyr bowe and theyr quiuer aboute
with them, untyll they be. xl. yeares oulde.

For fithens fhootynge was necglected and decayed
among the Romaynes, many a battayle and fyelde
hath been lofte. Agayne in the II. booke
and. 50. chapiter, (I call that by bookes and   Leo. II. 50.
chapiters, whyche the greke booke deuideth by chapiters and paragraphes) Let your fouldyers haue theyr
weapons wel appoynted and trimmed, but aboue all
other thynges regarde mofte fhootinge, and therfore
lette men when there is no warre, vfe fhootynge at
home: For the leauynge of, onely of fhotynge, hath
broughte in ruyne and decaye, the hole Empire
of Rome. Afterwarde he commaundeth agayne, hys
capitayne by thefe wordes: Arme your hofte as I

haue appoynted you, but fpecially with
bowe and arrowes plentie. For fhootynge
is a thinge of muche myghte and power in warre,
and chyefely agaynſt the Sarracenes and Turkes, whiche
people hath all their hope of victorie in theyr bowe
and fhaftes : Befydes all this, in an other place, he
wryteth thus to his Captayne : Artillerie is eafie to be
prepared, and in time of great nede, a thinge moſte
profitable, therfore we ſtraytlye commaunde you to
make proclamation to al men vnder our dominion.
which be eyther in war or peace, to all
cities, borowes and townes, and fynally to
all maner of men, that euerye feare perſone haue bowe
and fhaftes of his owne, and euerye houſe befyde this,
to haue a ſtanding bearyng bowe, and. xl. fhaftes
for all nedes, and that they exercife them felues in
holtes, hilles, and dales, playnes and wodes, for all
maner of chaunces in warre.

Howe muche fhooting was vſed among the olde
Romanes and what meanes noble captaynes and Emperours made, to haue it encreafe amonge them, and
what hurte came by the decaye of it, thefe wordes, of
Leo the emperour, which in a maner I haue reherfed
woorde for woorde, playnly doth declare. And yet
fhotynge, although they fet neuer fo muche by it, was
neuer fo good than, as it is nowe in Englande, whiche
thing to be true, is very probable, in that Leo doth
faye, that he woulde haue his fouldiers take of theyr
arrowe heads, and one fhote at an other, for theyr
exercife, whiche playe yf Englyſhe archers vſed, I
thinke they fhoulde fynde fmal play and
leſſe pleaſure in it at all.

The great vpperhande maynteyned alwayes in warre
by artillery, doeth appeare verye playnlye by this reafon
alfo, that whan the ſpanyardes, franchmen, and ger-
manes, grekes, macedonians, and egyptians, eche contry
vfing one finguler weapon, for whyche they were greatelye
feared in warre, as the Spanyarde *Lancea*, the Franche-
man *Gefa*, the German *Framea*, the Grecian *Machera*,

Leo. 18. 21.

Leo. 20. 79.

Leo. 7. 18.

the Macedonian *Sariſſa*, yet coulde they not eſcape, but be ſubiectes to the Empire of Rome, whan the Pertians hauyng all theyr hope in artillerie, gaue no place to them, but ouercame the Romanes, ofter than the Romaynes them, and kepte battel with them, many an hundred yeare, and flue the ryche Craſſus and hys ſon wyth many a ſtoute Romayne more, with their bowes. They draue Marcus Antonius ouer the hylles of Media in Armenia, to his great ſhame and reproch. They flue Iulianus Apoſtata, and Antonius Caracalla, they helde in perpetual pryſon, ye moſt noble emperour Valerian in deſpite of all the Romaynes and many other princes, whiche wrote for his delyueraunce, as Bel ſolis called kynge of kynges, Valerius kynge of Caduſia, Arthabeſdes kyng of Armenia, and many other princes more, whom ye Parthians by reaſon of theyr artillerie, regarded neuer one whitte, and thus with the Romaynes, I maye conclude, that the borders of theyr empyre were not at the funne ryſinge and funne ſettynge, as Tullye ſayeth : but ſo farre they went, as artillarie woulde gyue them leaue. For I thinke all the grounde that they had, eyther northewarde, farther than the borders of Scythia, or Eaſtewarde, farther than the borders of Parthia, a man myght haue boughte with a ſmall deale of money, of whiche thynge ſurely ſhotyng was the cauſe.

M Craſs.
Plutarch.
M Anto.
Iuliano.

From the ſame contrie of Scythia the Gothians Hunnes, and Wandalians came wyth the ſame wepons of artillarie, as Paulus Diaconus doth ſaye, and ſo berafte Rome of her empyre wyth fyre, ſpoyle, and waſte, ſo yat in ſuche a learned citie was lefte ſcarce one man behynde, that had learnynge or leyſoure to leue in writinge to them whiche ſhoulde come after howe ſo noble an Empyre, in ſo ſhorte a whyle, by a rable of banyſhed bondemen, wythoute all order and pollicie, ſaue onelye theyr naturalle and daylye exerciſe in artillarye, was broughte to ſuche thraldome and ruine.

Paul Diac.

After them the Turkes hauing an other name, but yet

the fame people, borne in Scythia, brought vp onely in artillarie, by the fame weapon
P Mela. 1.
haue fubdued and beraft from the Chriften men all Afia and Aphrike (to fpeake vpon,) and the mooft noble countries of Europe, to the greate diminifhing of Chrifte his religion, to the great reproche of cowardyfe of al chriftianitie, a manifeft token of gods high wrath and difpleafure ouer the fynne of the worlde, but fpeciallye amonges Chriften men, which be on flepe made drunke with the frutes of the flefh, as infidelitie, difobedience to Goddes worde, and herefie, grudge, illwyll, ftryfe, open battayle, and priuie enuye, coueytoufneffe, oppreffion, vnmercifulneffe, with innumerable fortes of vnfpeakeable daylye bawdrye: which thinges furely, yf God holde not his holy hand ouer vs, and plucke vs from them, wyl bryng vs to a more Turkifhneffe and more beaftlye blynde barbaroufneffe: as callyng ill thinges good, and good thynges ill, contemnyng of knowledge and learnynge, fettynge at nought, and hauyng for a fable, God and his high prouidence, wyll bring vs (I fay) to a more vngracious Turkifhneffe (if more Turkifhneffe can be then this) than if the Turkes had fworne, to bring al Turkye agaynft vs. For thefe frutes furelye muft neades fprynge of fuch feede, and fuch effect nedes folowe of fuche a caufe: if reafon, truthe, and God, be not altered, but as they are wont to be. For furely no Turkyfhe power can ouerthrowe vs, if Turkyffhe lyfe do not caft vs downe before.

If god were wyth vs, it buted not the turke to be agaynft vs, but our vnfaythful finfull lyuyng, which is the Turkes moder, and hath brought hym vp hitherto, mufte nedes turne god from vs, becaufe fyn and he hath no felowfhyp togither. If we banifhed ill liuyng out of chriftendome, I am fure the Turke fhulde not onelye, not ouercome vs, but fcarce haue an hole to runne in to, in his own countrye.

But Chriftendome nowe I may tell you Philologe is muche lyke a man that hath an ytche on him, and lyeth

F

dronke alſo in his bed, and though a theſe come to the
dore, and heaueth at it, to come in, and ſleye hym, yet
he lyeth in his bed, hauing more pleaſure to lye in a
ſlumber and ſcratche him ſelfe wher it ytcheth euen to
the harde bone, than he hath redynes to ryſe up luſtelye,
and dryue him awaye that woulde robbe hym and ſleye
hym. But I truſte Chriſte wyl ſo lyghten and lyſte vp
Chriſten mennes eyes, that they ſhall not ſlepe to death,
nor that the turke Chriſtes open enemy, ſhall euer boſte
that he hath quyte ouerthrowen vs. But as I began to
tell you, ſhootynge is the cheſe thinge, wherewith God
ſuffereth the turke to punyſh our noughtie liuinge wyth
all: The youthe there is brought vp in　　Caſp. de re-
ſhotyng, his priuie garde for his own perſon,　　bus Turc.
is bowmen, the might of theyr ſhootynge is wel knowen
of the Spanyardes, whiche at the towne called Newecaſtell
in Illirica, were quyte ſlayne vp, of the turkes arrowes:
whan the Spanyardes had no vſe of theyr gunnes, by
reaſon of the rayne. And nowe laſt of all, the emperour his maieſtie him ſelfe, at the Citie of Argier in
Aphricke had his hooſte ſore handeled wyth the Turkes
arrowes, when his gonnes were quite diſpatched and
ſtode him in no ſeruice, bycauſe of the raine that fell,
where as in ſuche a chaunce of raine, yf he had had
bowmen, ſurelye there ſhoote myghte peraduenture
haue bene a litle hindred, but quite diſpatched and
marde, it coulde neuer haue bene.

But as for the Turkes I am werie to talke of them
partlye becauſe I hate them, and partlye bycauſe I am
now affectioned euen as it were a man that had bene
longe wanderyng in ſtraunge contries and would fayne
be at home to ſe howe well his owne frendes proſper
and leade theyr lyfe, and ſurelye me thincke I am verie
merye at my harte to remember how I ſhal finde at
home in Englande amonges Englyſh men, partlye by
hyſtories, of them that haue gone afore vs, agayne by
experience of them whych we knowe, and lyue with
vs as greate noble feates of warre doone by Artillarye,
as euer was done at any tyme in any other common

welthe. And here I muſt nedes remember a certaine
Frenchman called Textor, that writeth a
boke whiche he nameth Officina,[4] wherin he
weueth vp many brokenended matters and ſettes out
much riſraffe, pelfery, trumpery, baggage and beggerie
ware clamparde vp of one that would ſeme to be fitter
for a ſhop in dede than to write any boke. And
amonges all other yll packed vp matters, he thruſtes
vp in a hepe togyther all the good ſhoters that euer
hathe bene in the worlde as he ſaythe hymſelfe, and
yet I trow Philologe that of all the examples whiche I
now by chaunce haue reherſed out of the beſt Authors
both in greke and latin, Textor hath but. ii. of them,
which. ii. ſurely yf they were to reken agayne, I wold
not ones name them, partly bycauſe they were noughtie
perſons, and ſhoting ſomoche the worſe, bycauſe they
loued it, as Domitian and Commodus the emperours :
partelye bycauſe Textor hath them in his boke, on
whom I loked on bychaunce in the bookebynders
ſhope, thynkynge of no ſuche matter. And one thing
I wyl ſay to you *Philologe,* that if I were diſpoſed to do
it, and you hadde leyſure to heare it, I coulde ſoone do as
Textor doth, and reken vp ſuche a rable of ſhoters that
be named here and there in poetes, as wolde holde vs
talkyng whyles tomorowe : but my purpoſe was not to
make mention of thoſe which were feyned of Poetes
for theyr pleaſure, but of ſuche as were proued in hiſtories for a truthe : but why I bringe in Textor was
this : At laſte when he hath rekened all ſhoters that
he can, he ſayeth thus, Petrus Crinitus [5]
wryteth, that the Scottes whiche dwell beyonde Englande be verye excellent ſhoters, and the
beſt bowmen in warre. This ſentence whether Crinitus wrote it more leudly of ignoraunce, or Textor
confirmeth it more piuyſhlye of enuye, may be called
in queſtion and doubte : but this ſurelye do I knowe
very well that Textor hath both red in Gaguinus the
Frenche hyſtorie,[6] and alſo hath hearde his father or
graundfather taulke (except perchaunce he was borne

Textor.

P. Crin. 3 10.

and bred in a Cloyfter) after that fort of the fhotynge of Englifshe men, that Textor neded not to haue gone fo piuifhlye beyonde Englande for fhoting, but myght very foone, euen in the firft towne of Kent, haue founde fuche plentie of fhotinge, as is not in al the realme of Scotland agayne. The Scottes furely be good men of warre in theyr owne feate as can be : but as for fhotinge, they neyther can vfe it for any profyte, nor yet wil chalenge it for any prayfe, although mafter Textor of his gentleneffe wold gyue it them. Textor neaded not to haue fylled vppe his booke with fuche lyes, if he hadde read the ftorye of Scotlande, whiche Ioannes Maior doeth wryte: wherein he myghte haue learned, that when Iames Stewart fyrft   Ioan Ma. 6 kyng of that name, at the Parliament holden at Saynt Iohnnes towne or Perthie, commaunded vnder payne of a greate forfyte, that euerye Scotte fhoulde learne to fhote : yet neyther the loue of theyr countrie, the feare of their enemies, the auoydying of punifhment, nor the receyuinge of anye profyte that myght come by it, coulde make them to be good Archers : whiche be vnapte and vnfytte therunto by Gods prouidence and nature.

Therfore the Scottes them felues proue Textor a lyer, bothe with authoritie and alfo daily experience, and by a certayne Prouerbe that they haue amonges them in theyr communication, wherby they gyue the whole prayfe of fhotynge honeftlye to Englyffhe men, faying thus : that euery Englyffhe Archer beareth vnder hys gyrdle. xxiiii. Scottes.

But to lette Textor and the Scottes go : yet one thynge woulde I wyffhe for the Scottes, and that is this, that feinge one God, one faythe, one compaffe of the fee, one lande and countrie, one tungue in fpeakynge, one maner and trade in lyuynge, lyke courage and ftomake in war, lyke quickneffe of witte to learning, hath made Englande and Scotlande bothe one, they wolde fuffre them no longer to be two : but cleane gyue ouer the Pope, which feketh none other thinge (as many a noble and wyfe Scottifh man doth knowe) but to fede vp diffention and parties betwixt them and vs, procuryng that thynge to be two, which God, nature, and reafon, wold haue one.

Howe profytable fuche an attonement were for Scotlande, both Iohannes Maior,[7] and Ector Boetius[8] whiche wrote the Scottes Chronicles do tell, and alfo all the gentlemen of Scotlande with the poore communaltie, do wel knowe : So that there is nothing that ftoppeth this matter, faue onelye a fewe freers, and fuche lyke, whiche with the dregges of our Englyfh Papiftrie lurkyng now amonges them, ftudy nothing els but to brewe battell and ftryfe betwixte both the people : Wherby onely they hope to maynetayne theyr Papifticall kyngdome, to the deftruction of the noble blood of Scotlande. that then they maye with authoritie do that, whiche neither noble man nor poore man in Scotlande yet doeth knowe. And as for Scottifhe men and Englifhe men be not enemyes by nature, but by cuftome : not by our good wyll, but by theyr owne follye : whiche fhoulde take more honour in being coupled to Englande, then we fhulde take profite in being ioyned to Scotlande.

Iohn Maior. 6. hift. Scot.

Wales being headye, and rebelling many yeares agaynft vs, laye wylde, vntylled, vnhabited, without lawe, iuftice, ciuilitie and ordre : and then was amonges them more ftealing than true dealing, more furetie for them that ftudyed to be noughte, then quyetneffe for them that laboured to be good : when nowe thanked be God, and noble Englande, there is no countrie better inhabited, more ciuile, more diligent in honeft craftes, to get bothe true and pientifull lyuynge withall. And this felicitie (my mynde gyueth me) within thefe few dayes fhal chaunce alfo to Scotlande, by the godly wyfedome of oure moofte noble Prince kynge Henrye the. viii. by whome God hath wrought more wonderfull thynges then euer by any prince before : as banifhing the byfhop of Rome and herifie, bringyng to light god his worde and veritie, eftablifhing fuche iuftice and equitie, through euery parte of this his realme, as neuer was sene afore.

To suche a Prince of suche a wysdome, God hath reserued this mooste noble attonement : wherby neither we shalbe any more troubled, nor the Scottes with their best countries any more destroyed, nor ye see, whiche God ordeyneth profytable for both, shall from eyther be any more stopped : to the great quietnesse, wealth, and felicitie of all the people dwellynge in this Ile, to the high renoume and prayse of our mooste noble kyng, to the feare of all maner of nacions that owe ill wyll to either countrie, to the hygh pleasure of God, which as he is one, and hateth al diuision, so is he best of all pleased, to se thinges which be wyde and amysse, brought to peace and attonement. But Textor (I beshrowe him) hath almooste broughte vs from our communication of shoting. Now sir by my iudgement, the Artillarie of England farre excedeth all other realmes : but yet one thing I doubt and longe haue surely in that point doubted, when, or by whom, shotyng was first brought in to Englande, and for the same purpose as I was ones in companye wyth syr Thomas Eliot knight, which surelie for his lerning in all kynde of knowlege bringeth much worshyp to all the nobilitie of Englande, I was so bould to aske hym, yf he at any tyme, had marked any thing, as concernynge the bryngynge in of shootynge in to Englande : he aunswered me gentlye agayne, that he had a worcke in hand which he nameth, *De rebus memorabilibus Angliæ*, which I trust we shal se in print shortlye,[7] and for the accomplyshmente of that boke, he had read and perused ouer many olde monumentes of Englande, and in seking for that purpose, he marked this of shootynge in an excedyng olde cronicle, the which had no name, that what tyme as the Saxons came first into this realme in kyng Vortigers dayes, when they had bene here a whyle and at last began to faull out with the Brittons, they troubled and subdewed the Brittons wyth nothynge so much, as with theyr bowe and fhaftes, whiche wepon beynge ftraunge and not fene here before, was wonderfull terrible vnto them, and this beginninge I can thynke verie well to be true. But now as concerning many examples for the prayfe of Englifh archers in warre, furely I wil not be long in a matter yat no man doubteth in, and thofe few yat I wil name, fhal either be proued by ye hiftories of our enemies, or els done by men that nowe liue.

Kynge Edward the thirde at the battel of Creffie ageinft Philip ye Frenche king as Gaguinus the french Hiftoriographer plainlye doeth tell, flewe that daye all the nobilite of Fraunce onlye wyth hys archers.

Such lyke battel alfo fought ye noble black prince Edwarde befide Poeters, where Iohn ye french king with hys fonne and in a maner al ye peres of Fraunce were taken befide. xxx. thoufand. which that daye were flayne, and verie few Englyfhe men, by reafon of theyr bowes.

Kynge Henrie the fifte a prince pereles and mofte vyctorioufe conqueroure of all that euer dyed yet in this parte of the world, at the battel of Agin court with. vii. thoufand. fyghtynge men, and yet many of them fycke, beynge fuche Archers as the Cronycle fayeth that moofte parte of them drewe a yarde, flewe all the Cheualrie of Fraunce to the nomber of .XL. thou-fand. and moo, and loft not pafte. xxvi. Englyffhe men.

The bloudye Ciuil warre of England betwixt the houfe of Yorke and Lancafter, where fhaftes flewe of both fydes to the deftruction of mannye a yoman of Englande, whom foreine battell coulde neuer haue fubdewed bothe I wyll paffe ouer for the pyttyefulneffe of it, and yet may we hyghelye prayfe GOD in the remembraunce of it, feynge he of hys prouydence hath fo knytte to gether thofe. ii. noble houfes, with fo noble and pleafunte a flowre.

The excellent prince Thomas Hawarde nowe Duke of Northfolk, for whofe good profperite with al his noble familie al Englifh hertes dayly doth pray with bowmen of England flew kyng Iamie with many a noble Scot euen brant agenft Flodon hil, in which battel ye ftoute archers of Chefhire and Lanchaffhire for one day beftowed to ye death for their prince and country fake, hath gotten immortall name and prayfe for euer.

The feare onely of Englyfh Archers hathe done more wonderfull thinges than euer I redde in anye hiftorye greke or latin, and mooft wonderfull of all now of late befide Carlile betwixt Efke and Leuen at Sandy fikes, where the hoole nobilite of Scotlande for fere of the Archers of Englonde (next the ftroke of God) as both Englyfh men and Scotyfhe men that were prefent hath toulde me were drowened and taken prifoners.

Nor that noble acte alfo, whyche althoughe it be almoft loft by tyme, commeth not behynd in worthineffe, whiche my fynguler good frende and Mafter Sir William Walgraue and Sir George Somerfet dyd with with a few Archers to ye number as it is fayd of. xvi. at the Turne pike befyde Hammes where they turned with fo fewe Archers, fo many Frenchemen to flight, and turned fo many oute of theyr Iackes, whych turne turned all fraunce to fhame and reproche and thofe. ii. noble knightes to perpetuall prayfe and fame.

And thus you fe Philologe, in al countries Afia, Aphrike and Europe, in Inde, Aethiop, Aegypt and Iurie, Parthia, Perfia, Greece, and Italie, Schythia, Turky, and Englande, from the begynninge of the world euen to thys daye, that fhotynge hath had the cheife ftroke in warre.

Phi. Thefe examples furelye apte for the   **I** prayfe of fhotynge, nor feyned by poetes, but proued by trewe hiftories, diftinct by tyme and order, hath delyted me excedyng muche, but yet me thynke that all thys prayfe belongeth to ftronge fhootynge and drawynge of myghtye bowes not to prickyng and nere fhotinge, for which caufe you and many other bothe loue and vfe fhootyng.

Tox. Euer more Philologe you wyl haue some ouertwhart reafon to drawe forthe more communica-

tion withall, but neuerthelesse you shall perceaue if
you wyl, that vse of prickyng, and desyre of nere
shootynge at home, are the onelye causes of stronge
shootyng in warre, and why? for you se, that the
strongest men, do not drawe alwayes the strongest
shoote, whiche thyng proueth that drawinge stronge,
liethe not so muche in the strength of man, as in the
vse of shotyng, And experience teacheth the same in
other thynges, for you shal se a weake smithe, whiche
wyl wyth a lipe and turnyng of his arme, take vp a
barre of yron, yat another man thrise as stronge, can
not stirre. And a stronge man not vsed to shote, hath
his armes breste and shoulders, and other partes wherewith he shuld drawe stronglye, one hindering and stop-
pinge an other, euen as a dosen stronge horses not
vsed to the carte, lettes and troubles one another.
And so the more stronge man not vsed to shote, shootes
moost vnhansumlye, but yet if a strong man with vse
of shooting coulde applye all the partes of hys bodye
togyther to theyr moost strengthe, than should he both
drawe stronger than other, and also shoote better than
other. But nowe a stronge man not vsed to shoote, at
a girde, can heue vp and plucke in sunder many a
good bowe, as wild horses at a brunte doth race and
pluck in peces many a stronge carte. And thus
stronge men, without vse, can do nothynge in shoting
to any purpose, neither in warre nor peace, but if they
happen to shoote, yet they haue done within a shoote
or two when a weake man that is vsed to shoote, shal
serue for all tymes and purposes, and shall shoote. x.
shaftes, agaynst the others. iiii. and drawe them vp to
the poynte, euerye tyme, and shoote them to the mooste
aduauntage, drawyng and withdrawing his shafte when
he list, markynge at one man, yet let driuyng at an
other man : whyche thynges in a set battayle, although
a man, shal not alwayes vse, yet in bickerynges, and at
ouerthwarte meatinges, when fewe archers be togyther,
they do mooste good of all.

Agayne he that is not vsed to shoote, shall euermore

with vntowardneſſe of houldynge his bowe, and
nockynge his ſhafte, not lookyng to his ſtryng be-
tyme, put his bowe alwayes in ieoperdy of breakynge,
and than he were better to be at home, moreouer he
ſhal ſhoote very fewe ſhaftes, and thoſe full vnhand-
ſumlye, ſome not halfe drawen, ſome to hygh and ſome
to lowe, nor he can not driue a ſhoote at a tyme, nor
ſtoppe a ſhoote at a neede, but oute muſte it, and
verye ofte to euel profe.

Phi. And that is beſt I trow in war, to let it go, and
not to ſtoppe it.

Tox. No not ſo, but ſomtyme to houlde a ſhafte at
the heade, whyche if they be but few archers, doth
more good with the feare of it, than it ſhoulde do if it
were ſhot, with the ſtroke of it.

Phi. That is a wonder to me, yat the feare of a diſpleaſure, ſhoulde do more harme than the diſpleaſure it ſelfe.

Tox. Yes, ye knowe that a man whiche fereth to be
banyſhed, out of hys cuntrye, can neyther be mery,
eate, drynke nor ſleape for feare, yet when he is ban-
iſhed in dede, he ſlepeth and eateth, as well as any
other.　And many menne doubtyng and fearyng
whether they ſhoulde dye or no, euen for verye feare
of deathe, preuenteth them ſelfe with a more bytter
deathe then the other death ſhoulde haue bene in
deade.　And thus feare is euer worſe than the thynge
feared, as is partelye proued, by the communication
of Cyrus and Tigranes, the kynges ſunne　　Ciri. ped. 3.
of Armenie, in Xenophon.

Phi. I graunte Toxophile, that vſe of ſhotyng
maketh a man drawe ſtrong, to ſhoote at moſt aduauntage, to kepe his gere, whiche is no ſmall thinge in war,
but yet me thinke, that the cuſtomable ſhoting at
home, ſpeciallye at buttes and prickes, make nothynge
at all for ſtronge ſhooting which doth moſte good in
war.　Therfore I ſuppoſe yf men ſhulde vſe to goo
into the fyeldes, and learne to ſhote myghty ſtronge
ſhootes, and neuer care for any marke at al, they
ſhulde do muche better.

Tox. The trouthe is, that fashion muche vsed, woulde do muche good, but this is to be feared, leaſt that waye coulde not prouoke men to vſe muche ſhotyng, bycauſe ther ſhulde be lytle pleaſure in it. And that in ſhoting is beſte, yat prouoketh a man to vſe ſhotinge moſte: For muche vſe maketh men ſhoote, bothe ſtrong and well, whiche two thinges in ſhootinge, euery man doeth deſyre. And the chyefe mayntayner of vſe, in any thyng, is comparyſon, and honeſte contention. For whan a manne ſtryueth to be better than an other, he wyll gladly vſe that thing, though it be neuer ſo paynful wherein he woulde excell, whiche thynge Ariſtotle verye pretelye doth note, ſayenge.

Where is compariſon, there is victorie: where is victorie, there is pleaſure: And where is pleaſure, no man careth what labour or payne he taketh, bycauſe of the prayſe, and pleaſure, thathe ſhall haue, in doynge better than other men. Ariſto. rheto. ad Theod.

Agayne, you knowe, Heſiodus wryteth to hys brother Perſes, yat al craftes men, by contending one honeſtly with an other, do encreaſe theyr cunnyng with theyr ſubſtance. And therfore in London, and other great Cities, men of one crafte, moſte commonly, dwelle togyther, bycauſe in honeſt ſtryuyng togyther, who ſhall do beſt, euery one maye waxe bothe cunninger and rycher, ſo lykewyſe in ſhootynge, to make matches to aſſemble archers togyther, to contende who ſhall ſhoote beſt, and winne the game, encreaſeth ye vſe of ſhotynge wonderfully amonges men. Heſio. in ope et die.

Phi. Of Vſe you ſpeake very much Toxophile but I am ſure in al other matters, Vſe can do nothing, wythoute two other thinges be ioyned wyth it, one is a natural Aptneſſe to a thinge, the other is a true waye or knowledge, howe to do the thing, to which. ii. yf Vſe be ioyned, as thirde felowe, of them thre, procedeth perfectneſſe and excellencie: If a manne lacke the firſt two, Aptneſſe and Cunnyng, Vſe can

do lytle good, at all. For he yat woulde be an oratour
and is nothinge naturallye fitte for it, that is to faye
lacketh a good wytte and memorie, lacketh a good
voyce, countenaunce and body, and other fuche like,
ye[t] yf he had all thefe thinges, and knewe not what,
howe, where, when nor to whome he fhulde fpeake,
furelye the vfe of fpekynge, woulde brynge out
none other frute but playne follye and bablyng,
fo yat Vfe is the lafte and the leaft necceffarye, of all
thre, yet no thing can be done excellently without
them al thre. And therfore Toxophile I my felfe
bicaufe I neuer knewe, whether I was apte for fhooting
or no, nor neuer knewe waye, howe I fhulde learne to
fhoote I haue not vfed to fhoote : and fo I thinke fiue
hundred more in Englande do befyde me. And
furelye yf I knewe that I were apte, and yat you woulde
teach me howe to fhoote, I woulde become an archer,
and the rather, bycaufe of the good communication,
the whiche I haue had with you this daye, of
fhotyng.

    Tox. Aptneffe, Knowlege, and Vfe, euen as you
faye, make all thinges perfecte. Aptneffe is the fyrft
and chyefeft thinge, without whiche the other two do
no good at all. Knowledge doeth encreafe al maner
of Aptneffe, bothe leffe and more. Vfe fayth Cicero,
is farre aboue all teachinge. And thus they all three
mufte be had, to do any thinge very well, and yf anye
one be awaye, what fo euer is done, is done verye
meanly. Aptneffe is ye gyfte of nature, Knowlege,
is gotten by ye helpe of other : Vfe lyeth in our owne
diligence and labour. So that Aptneffe and vfe be
ours and within vs, through nature and labour: Knowledge not ours, but commynge by other: and therfore mooft dilligently, of all men to be fought for.
Howe thefe three thinges ftande with the artillery of
Englande, a woorde or twoo I will faye.

    All Englifhe men generally, be apte for fhotyng,
and howe? Lyke as that grounde is plentifull and
frutefull, whiche withoute any tyllynge, bryngeth out

corne, as for example, yf a man shoulde go to the
myll or market with corne, and happen to spyl some in
the waye, yet it wolde take roote and growe, bycause
ye soyle is so good : so England may be thought very
frutefull and apt to brynge oute shooters, where
children euen from the cradell, loue it : and yong
men without any teachyng so diligentlye vse it.
Agayne, lykewyse as a good grounde, well tylled, and
well husbanded, bringeth out great plentie of byg
eared corne, and good to the faule : so if the youthe
of Englande being apte of it selfe to shote, were taught
and learned how to shote, the Archers of England
shuld not be only a great deale ranker, and mo then
they be : but also a good deale bygger and stronger
Archers then they be.   This commoditie shoulde
folowe also yf the youth of Englande were taught to
shote, that euen as plowing of a good grounde for
wheate, doth not onely make it mete for the seede,
but also riueth and plucketh vp by the rootes, all
thistles, brambles and weedes, whiche growe of theyr
owne accorde, to the destruction of bothe corne and
grounde : Euen so shulde the teaching of youth to
shote, not only make them shote well, but also
plucke awaye by the rootes all other desyre to
noughtye pastymes, as disynge, cardyng, and boouling, which without any teaching are vsed euery
where, to the great harme of all youth of this realme.
And lykewise as burnyng of thistles and diligent
weding them oute of the corne, doth not halfe
so moche ryd them, as when ye ground is falloed and
tilled for good grayne, as I haue hearde many a good
husbandman say : euen so, neither hote punishment,
nor yet diligent searching oute of suche vnthriftinesse
by the officers, shal so throwly wede these vngracious
games out of the realme, as occupying and bringyng
vp youth in shotynge, and other honest pastyme.
Thirdly, as a grounde which is apt for corne and also
wel tilled for corne : yet if a man let it lye stil and do
not occupye it. iii. or. iiii. yeare : but then wyll sow it,

if it be wheate (fayth *Columella*) it wil turne into rye:
fo if a man be neuer fo apte to fhote, nor neuer fo wel
taught in his youth to fhote, yet if he giue it ouer,
and not vfe to fhote, truly when he fhalbe eyther
compelled in war tyme for his country fake, or els
prouoked at home for his pleafure fake, to faule to his
bowe: he fhal become of a fayre archer, a ftark
fquyrter and dribber. Therefore in fhotynge, as in
all other thinges, there can neyther be many in number, nor excellent in dede: excepte thefe. iii. thynges,
Aptneffe, Knowledge, and Vfe goo togyther.

Phil. Very well fayde *Toxophile*, and I promyfe you,
I agree to this iudgement of yours altogyther and
therefore I can not a lytle maruayle, why Englyffhe
men brynge no more helpe to fhotynge, then nature
it felfe gyueth them. For you fe that euen children
be put to theyr owne fhiftes in fhotyng, hauing
nothynge taughte them: but that they maye chofe,
and chaunce to fhoote ill, rather then well, vn-
aptlye foner then fitlye, vntowardlye, more eafely then
welfauouredlye, whiche thynge caufeth manye neuer
begynne to fhoote: and moo to leaue it of when they
haue begone, and mooft of all to fhote both worfe and
weaker, then they might fhote, if they were taught.

But peraduenture fome men wyll faye, that wyth
vfe of fhootynge a man fhall learne to fhoote, true it
is he fhall learne, but what fhal he learne? marye to
fhoote noughtly. For all Vfe, in all thynges, yf it be
not ftayed with Cunnyng, wyll verie eafely brynge a
man to do yat thynge, what fo euer he goeth aboute
with muche illfauorednes and deformitie.

Which thinge how much harme it doth in learning both *Craffus* excellencie dothe proue in
Tullie, and I my felfe haue experiens in my
lytle fhootyng. And therfore *Toxophile*, you muft
nedes graunt me that ether Englifhe men do il, in not
ioynyng Knowlege of fhooting to Vfe, or els there is
no knowlege or cunninge, which can be gathered of
fhooting.

De Orat. 1.

Tox. Learnyng to shoote is lytle regarded in England, for this confideration, bycaufe men be fo apte
by nature they haue a greate redy forwardneffe and
wil to vfe it, al though no man teache them, al thoughe
no man byd them, and fo of theyr owne corage they
runne hedlynge on it, and fhoote they ill, fhote they
well, greate hede they take not. And in verie dede
Aptneffe with Vfe may do fumwhat without Knowlege, but not the tenthe parte, if fo be they were
ioyned with knowlege.

Whyche thre thynges be feperate as you fe, not of
theyr owne kynde, but through the negligence of men
whyche coupleth them not to gyther. And where
ye doubte whether there can be gadered any
knowlege or arte in fhootyng or no, furely I thynke
that a man being wel exercifed in it and fumwhat
honeftly learned with all, myght foone with diligent
obferuynge and markynge the hole nature of fhootynge, find out as it were an Arte of it, as Artes in
other matters haue bene founde oute afore, feynge
that fhootyng ftandeth by thofe thinges, which maye
both be thorowlye perceued, and perfitly knowen,
and fuche that neuer failes, but be euer certayne,
belongynge to one mooft perfect ende, as fhootyng
ftreight, and keping of a length bring a man to hit
the marke, ye chefe end in fhootyng : which two
thynges a man may attaine vnto, by diligent vfynge,
and well handlynge thofe inftrumentes, which belong
vnto them. Therfore I can not fee, but there lieth
hyd in the nature of Shootynge, an Arte, whiche by
notynge, and obferuynge of him, that is exercifed in
it, yf he be any thyng learned at al, maye be taught,
to the greate forderaunce of Artillarie through out al
this Realme. And trewlye I meruell gretelye, that
Englyffhe men woulde neuer yet, feke for the Arte
of fhootynge, feinge they be fo apte vnto it, fo prayfed
of there frendes, fo feared of there enne-
myes for it. Vegetius woulde haue may-   *Vegetius.*
fters appointed, whyche fhoulde teache youthe to

fhoote faire. Leo the Emperour of Rome,
fheweth the fame cuftome, to haue bene   Leo. 6. 5.
alwayes amongeft ye olde Romaynes : whych cuftome
of teachyng youth to fhoote (faythe he) after it was
omitted, and litle hede taken of, brought the hole
Empire of Rome, to grete Ruine. *Schola Perfica*,
that is the Scole of the Perfians, appoynted to brynge vp youthe, whiles   Strabo. 11.
they were. xx. yeres olde in fhooting, is as
notably knowne in Hiftories as the Impire of ye
Perfians : whych fchole, as doth apere in Cornelius
Tacitus, as fone as they gaue ouer and fell
to other idle paftimes, brought bothe them   Cor. Tac. 2.
and ye Parthians vnder ye fubiection of the Romaines.
Plato would haue common maifters and
ftipendes, for to teache youthe to fhoote,   De leg. 7.
and for the fame purpofe he would haue a brode
feylde nere euery Citie, made common for men to vfe
fhotyng in, whyche fayeng the more reafonably it is
fpoken of Plato, the more vnreafonable is theyr dede
whiche woulde ditche vp thofe feeldes priuatly for
ther owne profyt, whyche lyeth open generallye for
the common vfe : men by fuche goodes be made
rycher not honefter fayeth Tullie. Yf men can be
perfwaded to haue fhootynge taughte, this
aucthoritie whyche foloweth will perfwade   De Offi. 2.
them, or els none, and that is as I haue ones fayde
before, of Kynge Dauyd, whofe fyrfte acte and ordi-
naunce was after he was kynge that all Iudea fhould
learne to fhoote. Yf fhotyng could fpeake, fhe would
accufe England of vnkyndneffe and flouthfulneffe, of
vnkyndneffe toward her bycaufe fhe beyng left to a
lytle blynd vfe, lackes her beft maintener which is
cunnynge : of flouthfulneffe towarde theyr owne felfe,
bycaufe they are content wyth that whych aptneffe and
vfe doth graunt them in fhootynge, and wyl feke for
no knowlege as other noble common welthes haue
done : and the iuftlier fhootynge myght make thys
complaynt, feynge that of fence and weapons there is

made an Arte, a thyng in no wyfe to be compared to fhootynge.

For of fence all moofte in euerye towne, there is not onely Mafters to teache it, wyth his Pro-uoftes Vfhers Scholers and other names of arte and Schole, but there hath not fayld alfo, whyche hathe diligently and well fauouredly written it and is fet out in Printe that euery man maye rede it.

What difcommoditie doeth comme by the lacke of knowlege, in fhootynge, it were ouer longe to rehearce. For manye that haue bene apte, and loued fhootynge, bycaufe they knewe not whyche way to houlde to comme to fhootynge, haue cleane tourned them felues from fhootynge.

And I maye telle you Philologe, the lacke of teach-ynge to fhoote in Englande, caufeth very manye men, to playe with the kynges Actes, as a man dyd ones eyther with the Mayre of London or Yorke I can not tel whether, whiche dyd commaund by proclamation, euerye man in the Citie, to hange a lanterne wyth a candell, afore his dore : whiche thynge the man dyd, but he dyd not lyght it : And fo many bye bowes bicaufe of the acte, but yet they fhote not : not of euyll wyll, but bycaufe they knowe not howe to fhoote. But to conclude of this matter, in fhoting as in all other thynges, Apteneffe is the fyrfte, and chyefe thynge, whiche if it be awaye, neyther Cunnynge or Vfe, doeth anye good at all, as the Scottes and Fraunce men, wyth know-ledge and Vfe of fhootynge, fhall become good Archers, whan a cunnynge fhypwright fhall make a ftronge fhyppe, of a Salowe tree : or whan a hufband-man fhall becom ryche, wyth fowyng wheat on New-market heath.   Cunnynge mufte be had, bothe to fet out, and amende Nature, and alfo to ouerfee, and correcte vfe : which vfe yf it be not led, and gouerned wyth cunnyng, fhall fooner go amiffe, than ftrayght.

Vfe maketh perfitneffe, in doinge that thynge,

Aptnesse.

Cunnynge.

G

whervnto nature maketh a man apte, and knowlege maketh a man cunninge before. So yat it is not ſo doubtful, which of them three hath mooſt ſtroke in ſhoting as it is playne and euident, that all thre muſt be had, in excellent ſhootynge.

Phi. For this communicacion Toxophile I am very glad, and yat for myn owne ſake bicauſe I truſt now, to become a ſhoter, And in dede I thought a fore, Engliſh men moſt apte for ſhoting, and I ſawe them dayelye vſe ſhotyng, but yet I neuer founde none, that woulde talke of anye knowlege whereby a man might come to ſhotynge. Therfore I truſt that you, by the vſe you haue had in ſhoting, haue ſo thorowly marked and noted the nature of it, that you can teache me as it were by a trade or waye how to come to it.

Tox. I graunte, I haue vſed ſhootinge meetly well, that I myght haue marked it wel ynoughe, yf I had bene diligent. But my much ſhootynge, hath cauſed me ſtudie litle, ſo that thereby I lacke learnynge, whych ſhulde ſet out the Arte or waye in any thynge. And you knowe that I was neuer ſo well ſene, in the Poſteriorums of Ariſtotle as to inuent and ſearche out general Demonſtrations for the ſetting forth of any newe Science. Yet by my trothe yf you wyll, I wyll goe with you into the fealdes at any tyme and tel you as much as I can, or els you maye ſtande ſome tyme at the prickes and looke on them which ſhoote beſt and ſo learne.

Phi. Howe lytle you haue looked of Ariſtotle, and how muche learnynge, you haue loſt by ſhotynge I can not tell, but this I woulde ſaye and yf I loued you neuer ſo ill, that you haue bene occupyed **in** ſumwhat els beſyde ſhotynge. But to our purpoſe, as I wyll not requyre a trade in ſhotinge to be taught me after the futteltye of Ariſtotle, euen ſo do I not agre wyth you in this poynt, that you wold haue me learne to ſhoote with lokyng on them which ſhoote beſt, for to I knowe I ſhould neuer come to ſhote meanelye. For in ſhotyng as in all other thynges which be gotten by teachynge, there muſt be ſhewed a waye and a path which fhal leade a man to ye beft and cheiffeft poiɴt whiche is in fhootynge, whiche you do marke youre felfe well ynough, and vttered it alfo in your communication, when you fayde there laye hyd in ye nature of fhootyng a certayne waye whych wel perceyued and thorowlye knowen, woulde bring a man wythout any wanderyng to ye befte ende in fhotyng whych you called hitting of the pricke. Therfore I would refer all my fhootinge to that ende which is beft, and fo fhuld I come the foner to fome meane. That whiche is beft hath no faulte, nor can not be amended. So fhew to me beft fhootynge, not the befte fhoter, which yf he be neuer fo good, yet hath he many a faulte eafelye of any man to be efpyed. And therfore meruell not yf I requyre to folowe that example whych is without faulte, rather than that which hath fo manye faultes. And thys waye euery wyfe man doth folow in teachynge any maner of thynge. As Ariftotle when he teacheth a man to be good he fettes not before hym Socrates lyfe whyche was ye beft man, but chiefe goodneffe it felfe accordynge to whych he would haue a man direɕte his lyfe.

Tox. This waye which you requyre of me *Philologe*, is to hard for me, and to hye for a fhooter to taulke on, and taken as I fuppofe out of the middes of Philofophie, to ferche out the perfite ende of any thyng, ye which perfite ende to fynde out, fayth Tullie, is the hardeft thynge in the worlde, the onely occafyon and caufe, why fo many feɕtes of Ora. ad. Bru. Philofophers hathe bene alwayfe in learnynge. And althoughe as Cicero faith a man maye ymagine and dreame in his mynde of a perfite ende in any thynge, yet there is no experience nor vfe of it, nor was neuer fene yet amonges men, as alwayes to heale the fycke, euer more to leade a fhyppe without daunger, at al times to hit the prick : fhall no Phyficion, no fhypmafter, no fhoter euer do. And Ariftotle faith that in all deades there are two pointes to be marked, poffibilitie and excellencie, but Arift. pol. 8. 6.

chefely a wife man muft folowe and laye hand on poffibilitie for feare he leafe bothe. Therfore feyng that
which is mooft perfect and beft in fhootyng as alwayes
to hit ye pricke, was neuer fene nor hard tel on yet
amonges men, but onelye ymagined and thought vpon
in a man his mynde, me thinck this is the wifeft counfel and beft for vs to folow rather that which a man
maye come to, than yat whyche is vnpoffible to be
attained to, lefte iuftely that fayeng of ye wyfe mayde
Ifmene in Sophocles maye be verifyed on vs.

A foole he is that takes in hande he can not ende. Soph. Ant.

Phi. Well yf the perfite ende of other matters, had
bene as perfitlye knowne, as the perfite ende of
fhotynge is, there had neuer bene fo manye fectes of
Philofophers as there be, for in fhoting both man and
boye is in one opinion, that alwayes to hit the pryck is
moofte perfecte end that can be imagyned, fo that we
fhall not nede gretly contend in this matter. But
now fir, whereas you thynke yat a man in learning to
fhoote or any thyng els, fhuld rather wyfelye folow
poffibilitie, than vainly feke for perfite excellencie,
furelye I wyl proue yat euery wyfe man, yat wifely
wold learne any thyng, fhal chiefly go aboute yat
wherevnto he knoweth wel he fhal neuer come. And
you youre felfe I fuppofe fhal confeffe ye fame to be
ye beft way in teachyng, yf you wyl anfwere me to
thofe thinges whych I wyl afke of you.

Tox. And yat I wyl gladlye, both bycaufe I thynke
it is vnpoffible for you to proue it, and alfo bycaufe I
defire to here what you can faye in it.

Phi. The ftudie of a good Phyficion Toxophile, I trow
be to know al difeafes and al medicines fit for them.

Tox. It is fo in dede.

Phi. Bicaufe I fuppofe he would gladly at al tymes
heale al difeafes of al men.

Tox. Ye truely.

Phi. A good purpofe furely, but was ther euer
phyficion yet among fo many whyche had laboured

in thys ftudy, that at al times coulde heale all difeafes?

Tox. No trewly; nor I thyncke neuer fhalbe.

Phi. Than Phyficions by lyke, ftudie for yat, whiche none of them commeth vnto. But in learning of fence I pray you what is yat which men mooft labor for?

Tox. That they may hit a nother I trow and neuer take blow theyr felfe.

Phi. You fay trothe, and I am fure euery one of them would faine do fo when fo euer he playethe. But was there euer any of them fo conning yet, which at one tyme or other hath not be[n] touched?

Tox. The beft of them all is glad fomtyme to efcape with a blowe.

Phil. Than in fence alfo, men are taught to go aboute that thing, whiche the beft of them all knowethe he fhall neuer attayne vnto. Moreouer you that be fhoters, I pray you, what meane you, whan ye take fo greate heade, to kepe youre ftandynge, to fhoote compaffe, to looke on your marke fo diligently, to caft vp graffe diuerfe tymes and other thinges more, you know better than I. What would you do than I pray you?

Tox. Hit ye marke yf we could.

Phil. And doth euery man go about to hit the marke at euery fhoote?

Tox. By my trothe I trow fo, and as for my feife I am fure I do.

Phil. But al men do not hit it at al tymes.

Tox. No trewlye for that were a wonder.

Phil. Can any man hit it at all tymes?

Tox. No man verilie.

Phil. Than by likely to hit the pricke alwayes, is vnpoffible. For that is called vnpoffible whych is in no man his power to do.

Tox. Vnpoffible in dede.

Phil. But to fhoote wyde and far of the marke is a thynge poffyble.

Tox. No man wyll denie that.

Phil. But yet to hit the marke alwayſe wɛre an
excellent thyng.

Tox. Excellent ſurelie.

Phil. Than I am ſure thoſe be wiſer men, which
couete to ſhoote wyde than thoſe whiche couete to hit
the prycke.

Tox. Why ſo I pray you.

Phil. Becauſe to ſhote wyde is a thynge poſſyble,
and therfore as you ſaye youre ſelfe, of euery wyſe
man to be folowed. And as for hittinge ye prick,
bycauſe it is vnpoſſible, it were a vaine thynge to go
aboute it; but in good ſadneſſe *Toxophile* thus you ſe
that a man might go throghe all craftes and ſciences,
and proue that anye man in his ſcience coueteth that
which he ſhal neuer gette.

Tox. By my trouth (as you ſaye) I can not denye,
but they do ſo: but why and wherfore they ſhulde do
ſo, I can not learne.

Philo. I wyll tell you, euerye crafte and ſcience
ſtandeth in two thynges: in Knowing of his crafte, and
Working of his crafte: For perfyte knowlege bringeth
a man to perfyte workyng. This knowe Paynters,
karuers, Taylours, ſhomakers, and all other craftes
men, to be true. Nowe, in euery crafte, there is a
perfite excellencie, which may be better knowen in a
mannes mynde, then folowed in a mannes dede: This
perfyteneſſe, bycauſe it is generally layed as a brode
wyde example afore al men, no one particuler man
is able to compaſſe it; and as it is generall to al men,
ſo it is perpetuall for al time whiche proueth it a
thynge for man vnpoſſible: although not for the capacitie of our thinkyng whiche is heauenly, yet ſureiye
for the habilitie of our workyng whyche is worldiye.

God gyueth not full perfyteneſſe to one man (ſayth
Tullie) leſt if one man had all in any one
ſcience, ther ſhoulde be nothyng leſte for
an other. Yet God ſuffereth vs to haue the perfvt
knowledge of it, that ſuch a knowledge dilligenuly

De. Inuen ₂.

folowed, might bring forth accordyng as a man doth
labour, perfyte woorkyng. And who is he, that in
learnynge to wryte. woulde forfake an excellent example, and folowe a worfe?

Therfore feing perfytenesse it felfe is an example for
vs, let euerye man studye howe he maye come nye it,
which is a poynt of wyfdome, not reafon with God
why he may not attaine vnto it, which is vayne
curofitie.

Tox. Surely this is gaily faid Philologe, but yet this
one thinge I am afraide of, left this perfitnesse which
you fpeke on will difcourage men to take any thynge
in hande, bycaufe afore they begin, they know, they
fhal neuer come to an ende. And thus difpayre fhall
difpatche, euen at the fyrfte entrynge in, many a good
man his purpofe and intente. And I thinke both you
your felfe, and al other men to, woulde counte it mere
folie for a man to tell hym whome he teacheth, that
he fhal neuer optaine that, whyche he would fainest
learne. And therfore this fame hyghe and perfite
waye of teachyng let vs leue it to hygher matters, and
as for fhootynge it fhalbe content with a meaner
waye well ynoughe.

Phi. Where as you faye yat this hye perfitnesse will
difcorage men, bycaufe they knowe, they fhall neuer
attayne vnto it, I am fure cleane contrarie there is
nothynge in the world fhall incourage men more than
it. And whye? For where a man feith, that though
a nother man be neuer fo excellente, yet it is poffible
for hym felfe to be better, what payne or labour wyl
that man refufe to take? yf the game be onfe wonne,
no man wyl fet forth hys foote to ronne. And thus
perfitnefse beynge fo hyghe a thynge that men maye
looke at it, not come to it, and beynge fo plentifull
and indifferent to euerye bodye that the plentifulnesse
of it may prouoke all men to labor, bycaufe it hath
ynoughe for all men, the indifferencye of it shall encourage euerye one to take more paine than hys fel-
lowe, bycaufe euerye man is rewarded accordyng to his

nye commyng, and yet whych is moſte meruel of al,
ye more men take of it, the more they leue behynd for
other, as Socrates dyd in wyſdome, and Cicero in elo-
quens, whereby other hath not lacked, but hathe fared
a greate deele ye better. And thus perfitneſſe it ſelfe
bycauſe it is neuer obteyned, euen therfore only doth
it cauſe ſo many men to be ſo well ſene and perfite in
many matters, as they be. But where as you thynke
yat it were fondneſſe to teache a man to ſhoote, in
lokyng at the moſt perfitneſſe in it, but rather woulde
haue a manne go ſome other way to worke, I truſt no
wyſe man wyl diſcomend that way, except he thincke
himſelfe wyſer than Tullye, whiche doeth playnlye ſaye,
that yf he teached any maner of crafte
as he dyd Rhetorike he would labor to   De Orat. 3.
bringe a man to the knowlege of the mooſt perfitneſſe of it, whyche knowlege ſhould euer more leade
and gyde a manne to do that thynge well whiche he
went aboute. Whych waye in al maner of learnyng
to be beſt, Plato dothe alſo declare in Euthydemus,
of whome Tullie learned it as he dyd many other
thynges mo. And thus you ſe Toxophile by what
reaſons and by whoſe authoritie I do require of you
this waye in teachynge me to ſhoote, which waye I
praye you withoute any more delaye ſhew me as far
forth as you haue noted and marked.

Tox. You cal me to a thyng Philologe which I am
lothe to do. And yet yf I do it not beinge but a
ſmale matter as you thynke, you wyll lacke frendeſhypp
in me, yf I take it in hande and not bring it to paſſe
as you woulde haue it, you myghte thyncke great want
of wyſdome in me.

But aduyſe you, ſeing ye wyll nedes haue it ſo, the
blame ſhalbe yours, as well as myne : yours for
puttynge vpon me ſo inſtauntlye, myne in receyuynge
ſo fondly a greater burthen then I am able to beare.

Therfore I, more wyllvnge to fulfyll your mynde, than
hopyng to accomplyſh that which you loke for, ſhall
ſpeake of it, not as a maſter of ſhotynge, but as one not

altogyther ignoraunt in fhotynge. And one thynge I am glad of, the funne drawinge downe fo faft into the weft, fhall compell me to drawe a pace to the ende of our matter, fo that his darkneffe fhall fomethyng cloke myne ignoraunce. And bycaufe you knowe the orderynge of a matter better then I: Afke me generallye of it, and I fhall particularly anfwere to it. Phi.

Very gladly Toxophile : for fo
by ordre, thofe thynges
whiche I woulde
knowe, you fhal
tell the bet-
ter : and
thofe
thynges
whiche you fhall tell, I
fhall remembre
the better.

TOXOPHI-
LVS. B.

¶ THE SECONDE BOOKE OF
the schole of shotyng.

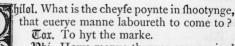 **P**hilol. What is the cheyfe poynte in shootynge, that euerye manne laboureth to come to ?

Tox. To hyt the marke.

Phi. Howe manye thynges are required to make a man euer more hyt the marke ?

Tox. Twoo.

Phi. Whiche twoo ?

Tox. Shotinge streyght and kepynge of a lengthe.

Phil. Howe shoulde a manne shoote strayght, and howe shulde a man kepe a length ?

Tox. In knowynge and hauynge thinges, belongynge to shootyng : and whan they be knowen and had, in well handlynge of them : whereof some belong to shotyng strayght, some to keping of a length, some commonly to them bothe, as shall be tolde seuerally of them, in place conuenient.

Phi. Thynges belongyng to shotyng, whyche be they ?

Tox. All thinges be outwarde, and some be instrumentes for euery sere archer to brynge with him, proper for his owne vse : other thynges be generall to euery man, as the place and tyme serueth.

Phi. Which be instrumentes ?

Tox. Bracer, shotynggloue, stryng, bowe and shafte.

Phi. Whiche be general to all men ?

Tox. The wether and the marke, yet the marke is euer vnder the rule of the wether.

Phi. Wherin standeth well handlynge of thynges ?

Tox. All togyther wythin a man him selfe, some handlynge is proper to instrumentes, some to the wether, somme to the marke, some is within a man hym selfe.

Phi. What handlyng is proper to the Instrumentes ?

Tox. Standynge, nockyng, drawyng, holdyng, low-sing, wherby commeth fayre shotynge, whiche neyther belong to wynde nor wether, nor yet to the marke, for in a rayne and at no marke, a man may shote a fayre shoote.

Phi. Well sayde, what handlynge belongeth to the wether ?

Tox. Knowyng of his wynde, with hym, agaynst hym, syde wynd, ful syde wind, syde wynde quarter with him, syde wynde quarter agaynste hym, and so forthe.

Phi. Well than go to, what handlynge belongeth to the marke ?

Tox. To marke his standyng, to shote compasse, to draw euermore lyke, to lowse euermore lyke, to con-syder the nature of the pricke, in hylles and dales, in strayte planes and winding places, and also to espy his marke.

Phi. Very well done. And what is onely within a man hym selfe ?

Tox. Good heede gyuynge, and auoydynge all affections: whiche thynges oftentymes do marre and make all. And these thynges spoken of me generally and brefely, yf they be wel knowen, had, and handled,

fhall brynge a man to fuche fhootynge, as fewe or none
euer yet came vnto, but furely yf he miffe in any one
of them, he can neuer hyt the marke, and in the more
he doth miffe, the farther he fhoteth from his marke.
But as in all other matters the fyrſt ſteppe or ſtayre to
be good, is to know a mannes faulte, and than to
amende it, and he that wyl not knowe his faulte, fhall
neuer amende it.

Phi. You fpeake now Toxophile, euen as I wold
haue you to fpeake : But lette vs returne agayne vnto
our matter, and thofe thynges whyche you haue packed
vp, in fo fhorte a roume, we wyll lowfe them forthe,
and take euery pyece as it were in our hande and looke
more narowlye vpon it.

Tox. I am content, but we wyll rydde them as faſt
as we can, bycaufe the funne goeth fo faſte downe, and
yet fomewhat muſte needes be fayde of euerye one of
them.

Phi. Well fayde, and I trowe we beganne wyth
thofe thynges whiche be inſtrumentes, whereof the
fyrſte, as I fuppofe, was the Braſer.

Tox. Litle is to be fayd of the brafer. A bracer
ferueth for two caufes, one to faue his arme from the
ſtrype of the ſtrynge, and his doublet from wearynge,
and the other is, that the ſtrynge glydynge fharpelye
and quicklye of the bracer, may make the fharper
fhoote. For if the ſtrynge fhoulde lyght vpon the bare
fleue, the ſtrengthe of the fhoote fhoulde ſtoppe and dye
there. But it is beſt by my iudgement, to gyue the
bowe fo muche bent, that the ſtrynge neede neuer touche
a mannes arme, and fo fhoulde a man nede no bracer
as I knowe manye good Archers, whiche occupye none.
In a bracer a man muſte take hede of. iii. thinges, yat it
haue no nayles in it, that it haue no bucles, that it be
faſt on with laces wythout agglettes. For the nayles
wyll fhere in funder, a mannes ſtring, before he be ware,
and fo put his bowe in ieopardy : Buckles and agglettes
at vnwares, fhall race hys bowe, a thinge bothe euyll to
the fyghte, and perilous for freatynge. And thus a

Bracer, is onely had for this purpofe, that the ftrynge maye haue redye paffage.

Phi. In my Bracer I am cunnyng ynough, but what faye you of the fhootyng gloue.

Tox. A fhootynge Gloue is chieflye, for to faue a mannes fyngers from hurtynge, that he maye be able to beare the fharpe ftryng to the vttermoft of his ftrengthe. And whan a man fhooteth, the might of his fhoote lyethe on the formoofte fynger, and on the Ringman, for the myddle fynger whiche is the longeft, lyke a lubber ftarteth backe, and beareth no weyghte of the ftrynge in a maner at all, therfore the two other fyngers, mufte haue thicker lether, and that mufte haue thickeft of all, where on a man lowfeth mofte, and for fure lowfyng, the formofte finger is mofte apte, bycaufe it holdeth beft, and for yat purpofe nature hath as a man woulde faye, yocked it with the thoumbe. Ledder, if it be nexte a mans fkynne, wyl fweat, waxe hard and chafe, therefore fcarlet for the foftnes of it and thick-neffe wyth all, is good to fewe wythin a mannes gloue. If that wylle not ferue, but yet youre finger hurteth, you mufte take a fearynge cloth made of fine virgin waxe, and Deres fewet, and put nexte your fynger, and fo on wyth youre gloue. If yet you fele your fynger pinched, leaue fhootyng both becaufe than you fhall fhoote nought, and agayn by litle and lytle, hurtynge your finger, ye fhall make it longe and longe to or you fhoote agayne. A newe gloue pluckes many fhootes bycaufe the ftringe goeth not freelye of, and therefore the fingers mufte be cut fhorte, and trimmed with fome ointment, that the ftring maye glyd wel awaye. Some wyth holdynge in the nocke of theyr fhafte too harde, rub the fkyn of there fingers. For this there be. ii. remedyes, one to haue a goofe quyll fplettyd and fewed againfte the nockynge, betwixt the lining and the ledder, whyche fhall helpe the fhoote muche to, the other waye is to haue fome roule of ledder fewed betwixt his fingers at the fetting on of the fingers, which fhall kepe his fingers fo in funder, that they

ſhal not hold the nock ſo faſt as they did. The
ſhootyng gloue hath a purſe whych ſhall ſerue to put
fine linen cloth and wax in, twoo neceſſary thynges for
a ſhooter, ſome men vſe gloues or other ſuche lyke thyng
on their bow hand for chafyng, becauſe they houlde ſo
harde. But that commeth commonlye, when a bowe
is not rounde, but ſomewhat ſquare, fine waxe ſhall do
verye well in ſuch a caſe to laye where a man holdeth
his bow : and thus muche as concernynge your gloue.
And theſe thynges althoughe they be trifles, yet bycauſe
you be but a yonge ſhoter, I woulde not leue them out.

Phi. And ſo you ſhal do me mooſt pleaſure : The
ſtring I trow be the next.

Tox. The nexte in dede. A thing though it be
lytle, yet not a litle to be regarded. But
here in you muſte be contente to put youre   Stringe.
truſte in honeſt ſtringers. And ſurely ſtringers ought
more diligently to be looked vpon by the officers than
ether bower or fletcher, bycauſe they may deceyue a
a ſimple man the more eaſelyer. And ill ſtringe
brekethe many a good bowe, nor no other thynge halfe
ſo many. In warre if a ſtring breke the man is loſte
and is no man, for his weapon is gone, and althoughe
he haue two ſtringes put one at once, yet he ſhall haue
ſmall leaſure and leſſe roume to bend his bow, therfore
god ſend vs good ſtringers both for war and peace.
Now what a ſtringe ought to be made on, whether of
good hempe as they do now a dayes, or of flaxe or of
ſilke, I leaue that to the iugemente of ſtringers, of
whome we muſte bye them on. Euſtathius
apon this verſe of homere.   Euſtathius.

Twang quoth the bow, and twang quoth the ſtring,
  out quicklie the ſhaft flue.   Iliad. 4.

doeth tel, that in oulde tyme they made theyr bowe
ſtrynges of bullox thermes, whiche they twyned togither as they do ropes, and therfore they made a
great twange. Bowe ſtrynges alſo hath bene made of
the heare of an horſe tayle called for the matter of

them Hippias as dothe appeare in manye good
authors of the Greke tongue. Great
ſtringes, and lytle ſtrynges be for diuerſe
purpoſes: the great ſtring is more ſurer for the bowe,
more ſtable to pricke wythal, but ſlower for the caſt,
the lytle ſtringe is cleane contrarye, not ſo ſure, therfore to be taken hede of leſſe, with longe tarienge on,
it breake your bowe, more fit to ſhoote farre, than apte
to pricke nere, therfore when you knowe the nature of
bothe bigge and, lytle you muſt fit your bow, according to the occaſion of your ſhootinge. In
ſtringinge of your bow (though this place belong rather
to the handlyng than to the thyng it ſelfe, yet bycauſe the thynge, and the handlynge of the thynge, be
ſo ioyned together, I muſt nede ſome tyme couple
the one wyth the other,) you muſt mark the fit length
of your bowe. For yf the ſtringe be to ſhort, the
bending wyll gyue, and at the laſt ſlyp and ſo put the
bowe in ieopardye. Yf it be longe, the bendynge
muſt nedes be in the ſmal of the ſtring, which beynge
ſore twined muſt nedes knap in ſunder to ye diſtruc-
tion of manye good bowes. Moreouer you muſt looke
that youre bowe be well nocked for fere the ſharpneſſe
of the horne ſhere a ſunder the ſtrynge. And that
chaunceth ofte when in bending, the ſtring hath but
one wap to ſtrengthe it wyth all : You muſt marke
alſo to ſet youre ſtringe ſtreygte on, or elles the one
ende ſhall wriethe contrary to the other, and ſo breke
your bowe. When the ſtringe begynnethe neuer ſo
lytle to were, truſt it not; but a waye with it for it is
an yll ſaued halpeny yat coſtes a man a crowne. Thus
you ſe howe many ieopardyes hangethe ouer the ſelye
poore bowe, by reaſon onlye of the ſtrynge. As when
the ſtringe is ſhorte, when it is longe, when eyther of
the nockes be nought, when it hath but one wap, and
when it taryethe ouer longe on.

Fauorinus.

Phi. I ſe wel it is no meruell, though ſo many
bowes be broken.

Tox. Bowes be broken twiſe as many wayes beſyde

thefe. But a gayne in ftringynge youre bowe, you muft loke for muche bende or lytle bende for they be cleane contrarye.

The lytle bende hath but one commoditie, whyche is in fhootyng fafter and farther fhoote, and ye caufe therof is, bycaufe the ftrynge hath fo far a paffage, or it parte wyth the fhafte. The greate bende hath many commodities : for it maketh eafyer fhootynge the bowe beyng halfe drawen afore. It needeth no bracer, for the ftrynge ftoppeth before it come at the arme. It wyl not fo fone hit a mannes fleue or other geare, by the fame reafon : It hurteth not the fhaft fedder, as the lowe bende doeth. It fuffereth a man better to efpye his marke. Therfore lette youre bowe haue good byg bend, a fhaftemente and. ii. fyngers at the leaft, for thefe which I haue fpoken of.

Phi. The brafer, gloue, and ftrynge, be done, nowe you mufte come to the bowe, the chefe inftrument of all. Bowe.

Tox. Dyuers countryes and tymes haue vfed alwayes dyuers bowes, and of dyuers fafhions.

Horne bowes are vfed in fome places nowe, and were vfed alfo in Homerus dayes, for Pandarus bowe, the beft fhooter among al the Iliad. 4. Troianes, was made of two Goete hornes ioyned togyther, the lengthe wherof fayth Homer, was. xvi handbredes, not far differing from the lengthe of our bowes.

Scripture maketh mention of braffe bowes. Iron bowes, and ftyle bowes, haue Psalm. 17. bene of longe tyme, and alfo nowe are vfed among the Turkes, but yet they muft nedes be vnprofitable. For yf braffe, yron or ftyle, haue theyr owne ftrength and pith in them, they be farre aboue mannes ftrength : yf they be made meete for mannes ftrengthe, theyr pithe is nothyng worth to fhoote any fhoote wyth all.

The Ethiopians had bowes of palme tre, whiche feemed to be very ftronge, but we haue none experience of them. The lengthe of Hero. in pol. them was. iiii. cubites. The men of Inde had theyr

bowes made of a rede, whiche was of a great ſtrengthe.
And no maruayle though bowe and ſhaftes were made
thereof, for the redes be ſo great in Inde, as Herodotus
ſayth, that of euery ioynte of a rede, a man
may make a fyſhers bote. Theſe bowes,   In Thalia.
ſayeth Arrianus in Alexanders lyfe, gaue ſo great a ſtroke,
that no harneys or buckler though it were
neuer ſo ſtrong, could wythſtand it. The   Arrianus. 8.
length of ſuche a bowe, was euen wyth the length of hym,
that vſed it. The Lycians vſed bowes made
of a tree, called in Latyn *Cornus*, (as con-   In Polym.
cernyng the name of it in Engliſh, I can ſoner proue
that other men call it falſe, than I can tell the right
name of it my ſelfe) this wood is as harde as horne
and very fit for ſhaftes, as ſhall be toulde after.

Ouid ſheweth that Syringa the Nymphe,
and one of the maydens of Diana, had a   Metamor. 1.
bowe of this wood whereby the poete meaneth, that it
was verye excellent to make bowes of.

As for braſell, Elme, Wych, and Aſſhe, experience
doth proue them to be but meane for bowes, and ſo to
conclude Ewe of all other thynges, is that, wherof
perfite ſhootyng woulde haue a bowe made.

Thys woode as it is nowe generall and common
amonges Englyſhe men, ſo hath it continewed from
longe tyme and had in mooſt price for bowes,
amonges the Romaynes, as doth apere in this halfe
verſe of Vyrgill.

> *Taxi torquentur in arcus.*   Virgilius.
>   i.
> *Ewe fit for a bowe to be made on.*

Nowe as I ſaye, a bowe of Ewe muſt be hadde for
perfecte ſhootinge at the prickes; whiche marke, bycauſe it is certayne, and moſte certaine rules may be
gyuen of it, ſhall ſerue for our communication, at this
time. A good bowe is knowen, much what as good
counſayle is knowen, by the ende and proofe of it,
and yet bothe a bowe and good counſell, maye be
made bothe better and worſe, by well or yll handlynge

of them: as oftentymes chaunceth. And as a man both mufte and wyll take counfell, of a wyfe and honefte man, though he fe not the ende of it, fo muft a fhooter of neceffitie, trufte an honeft and good bowyer for a bowe, afore he knowe the proofe of it. And as a wyfe man wyll take plentye of counfel afore hand what foeuer need, fo a fhooter fhulde haue alwayes. iii. or. iiii. bowes, in ftore, what fo euer chaunce.

Phi. But if I trufte bowyers alwayes, fometyme I am lyke to be deceyued.

Tox. Therefore fhall I tell you fome tokens in a bowe, that you fhal be the feeldomer deceyued. If you come into a fhoppe, and fynde a bowe that is fmall, long, heauy and ftrong, lyinge ft[r]eyght, not windyng, not marred with knot, gaule, wyndefhake, wem, freate or pynche, bye that bowe of my warrant. The befte colour of a bowe yat I fynde, is whan the backe and the bellye in woorkynge, be muche what after one maner, for such oftentymes in wearyng, do proue lyke virgin wax or golde, hauynge a fine longe grayne, euen from the one ende of the bowe, to the other: the fhort graine although fuche proue well fomtyme, are for ye moft parte, very brittle. Of the makynge of the bowe, I wyll not greatly meddle, lefte I fhoulde feeme to enter into an other mannes occupation, whyche I can no fkyll of. Yet I woulde defyre all bowyers to feafon theyr ftaues well, to woorke them and fynke them well, to giue them heetes conuenient, and tyllerynges plentye. For thereby they fhoulde bothe get them felues a good name, (And a good name encreafeth a mannes profyte muche) and alfo do greate commodite to the hole Realme. If any men do offend in this poynte, I am afrayde they be thofe iourny men whiche labour more fpedily to make manye bowes for theyr owne monye fake, than they woorke dilligently to make good bowes, for the common welth fake, not layinge before theyr eyes, thys wyfe prouerbe.

Sone ynough, if wel ynough.

Wherwyth euere honeſt handye craftes man ſhuld meaſure, as it were wyth a rule, his worke withal. He that is a iourney man, and rydeth vpon an other mannes horſe, yf he ryde an honeſt pace, no manne wyll dyſalowe hym: But yf he make Poſte haſte, bothe he that oweth the horſe, and he peraduenture alſo that afterwarde ſhal bye the horſe, may chaunce to curſe hym.

Suche haſtineſſe I am afrayde, maye alſo be found amonges ſome of them, whych through out ye Realme in diuerſe places worke ye kinges Artillarie for war, thinkynge yf they get a bowe or a ſheafe of arrowes to ſome faſhion, they be good ynough for bearynge gere. And thus that weapon whiche is the chiefe defence of the Realme, verye ofte doth lytle ſeruyce to hym that ſhoulde vſe it, bycauſe it is ſo negligentlye wrought of him that ſhuld make it, when trewlye I ſuppoſe that nether ye bowe can be to good and chefe woode, nor yet to well ſeaſoned or truly made, wyth hetynges and tillerynges, nether that ſhafte to good wood or to thorowely wrought, with the beſt pinion fedders that can be gotten, wherwith a man ſhal ſerue his prince, defende his countrie, and ſaue hym ſelfe frome his enemye. And I truſt no man wyll be angrye wyth me for ſpekynge thus, but thoſe which finde them ſelfe touched therin: which ought rather to be angrye wyth them ſelfe for doynge ſo, than to be miſcontent wyth me for ſaynge ſo. And in no caſe they ought to be diſpleaſed wyth me, ſeinge this is ſpoken alſo after that ſorte, not for the notynge of anye perſon ſeuerallye, but for the amendynge of euerye one generallye. But turne we agayne to knowe a good ſhootynge bowe for oure purpoſe.

Euerye bowe is made eyther of a boughe, of a plante or of the boole of the tree. The boughe commonlye is verye knotty, and full of pinnes, weak, of ſmall pithe, and ſone wyll folowe the ſtringe, and ſeldome werith to any fayre coloure, yet for chyldren and yonge beginners it maye ſerue well ynoughe. The plante proueth many times wel, yf it be of a good and clene groweth, and for the pith of it is quicke ynoughe of caſt, it wyll plye and bow far afore it breake, as al other yonge thinges do. The boole of ye tree is cleneſt without knot or pin, hauinge a faſte and harde woode by reaſonne of hys full groweth, ſtronge and myghtye of caſt, and beſt for a bow, yf the ſtaues be euen clouen, and be afterwarde wroughte not ouer[t]wharte the woode, but as the graine and ſtreyght growyng of the woode leadethe a man, or elles by all reaſon it muſt ſone breake, and that in many ſhiuers. This muſt be conſidered in the roughe woode, and when the bow ſtaues be ouerwrought and facioned. For in dreſſing and pikynge it vp for a bow, it is to late to loke for it. But yet in theſe poyntes as I ſayd before you muſte truſte an honeſt bowyer, to put a good bow in youre hand, ſomewhat lookinge your ſelfe to thoſe tokens whyche I ſhewed you. And you muſte not ſticke for a grote or. xii. d. more than a nother man would giue yf it be a good bowe. For a good bow twiſe paide for is better than an ill bowe once broken.

Thus a ſhooter muſte begyn not at the makynge of hys bowe lyke a bower, but at the byinge of hys bow lyke an Archere. And when his bow is bought and brought home, afore he truſte muche vpon it, let hym trye and trym it after thys ſorte.

Take your bow in to the feeld, ſhote in hym, ſinke hym wyth deade heauye ſhaftes, looke where he commethe mooſt, prouyde for that place betymes, leſte it pinche and ſo freate ; when you haue thus ſhot in him, and perceyued good ſhootynge woode in hym, you muſt haue hym agayne to a good cunnynge, and truſtie woorkeman, whyche ſhall cut hym ſhorter, and pike hym and dreſſe hym fytter, make hym comme rounde compace euery where, and whippyng at the endes, but with diſcretion, leſt he whyp in ſunder or els freete, ſoner than he is ware of, he muſt alſo lay hym ſtreght, if he be caſte or other-wiſe nede require, and if he be flatte made, gather hym rounde, and ſo ſhall he bothe ſhoote the faſter, for farre ſhootynge, and alſo the ſurer for nere pryckynge.

Phi. What yf I come into a ſhoppe, and ſpye oute

a bow, which fhal both than pleafe me very wel whan
I by him, and be alfo very fit and meete for me whan
I fhoote in hym: fo that he be both weake ynoughe
for eafye fhootynge, and alfo quycke and fpedye
ynoughe for farre caftynge, than I woulde thynke I
fhall nede no more bufineffe wyth him, but be contente wyth hym, and vfe hym well ynoughe, and fo by
that meanes, auoyde bothe great trouble, and alfo
fome coft whiche you cunnynge archers very often
put your felues vnto, beynge verye Englyfhe men, neuer
ceafynge piddelynge about your bowe and fhaftes
whan they be well, but eyther with fhortyng and pikynge your bowes, or els with newe fetheryng, peecynge and headinge your fhaftes, can neuer haue done
vntyll they be ftarke nought.

Tox. Wel *Philologe*, furelye if I haue any iudgement at all in fhootyng, it is no very great good token in
a bowe, whereof nothyng whan it is newe and freffhe,
nede be cutte away, euen as Cicero fayeth of a yonge
mannes wit and ftyle, which you knowe better than
I. For euerye newe thynge mufte alwayes haue more
than it neadeth, or elles it wyll not waxe better and
better, but euer decaye, and be worfe and worfe.
Newe ale if it runne not ouer the barrell whan it is
newe tunned, wil fone leafe his pith, and his head
afore he be longe drawen on.

And lyke wyfe as that colte whyche at the fyrfte
takynge vp, nedeth lytle breakyng and handlyng, but
is fitte and gentle ynoughe for the faddle, feeldome
or neuer proueth well, euen fo that bowe whyche
at the fyrfte byinge, wythout any more proofe and trim-
mynge, is fit and eafie to fhoote in, fhall neyther be
profitable to lafte longe nor yet pleafaunt to fhoote
well. And therfore as a younge horfe full of corage,
wyth handlynge and breakinge, is brought vnto a fure
pace and goynge, fo fhall a newe bowe freffhe and
quicke of cafte, by finkyng and cuttyng, be brought to
a ftedfaft fhootyng. And an eafie and gentle bow
whan it is newe, is not muche vnlyke a fofte fpirited

boye when he is younge. But yet as of an vnrulie
boye with right handlyng, proueth oftenest of al a
well ordered man ; fo of an vnfit and ftaffyſh bow
with good trimming, mufte nedes folowe alwayes a
ftedfaſt ſhotynge bowe.

And fuche a perfite bowe, whiche neuer wyll deceyue a man, excepte a man deceyue it, muſt be had
for that perfecte ende, whyche you looke for in ſhootinge.

Phi. Well Toxophile, I fee wel you be cunninger
in this gere than I : but put cafe that I haue thre
or fower fuche good bowes, pyked and dreſſed, as
you nowe ſpeke of, yet I do remembre yat manye
learned men do faye, that it is eaſier to gette a good
thynge, than to faue and keepe a good thyng, wherfore
if you can teache me as concernyng that poynte, you
haue fatiſſyed me plentifullye as concernynge a bowe.

Tox. Trulye it was the nexte thyng that I woulde
haue come vnto, for fo the matter laye.

Whan you haue broughte youre bowe to fuche a
poynte, as I ſpake of, than you muſt haue an herden or
wullen cloth waxed, wherwith euery day you muſt rubbe
and chafe your bowe, tyll it ſhyne and glytter withall.
Whyche thynge ſhall caufe it bothe to be cleane, well
fauoured, goodlye of coloure, and ſhall alfo bryng as it
were a cruſte, ouer it, that is to fay, ſhall make it
euery where on the outfyde, fo ſlyppery and harde,
that neyther any weete or wether can enter to hurte
it, nor yet any freat or pynche, be able to byte vpon
it : but that you ſhal do it great wrong before you
breake it. This muſt be done oftentimes but fpecially when you come from ſhootynge.

Beware alfo whan you ſhoote, of youre ſhaft hedes,
dagger, knyues, or agglettes, left they race your bowe,
a thing as I fayde before, bothe vnfemely to looke on,
and alfo daungerous for freates. Take hede alfo of
miſtie and dankyſhe dayes, whiche ſhal hurte a bowe,
more than any rayne. For then you muſte eyther
alway rub it, or els leaue ſhootynge.

Your bowecaſe (this I dyd not promiſe to ſpeake of,

bycaufe it is without the nature of shootynge, or els I shoulde truble me wyth
other thinges infinite more : yet feing it is a fauegarde
for the bowe, fomethynge I wyll faye of it) youre bowecafe I faye, yf you ryde forth, mufte neyther be
to wyde for youre bowes, for fo shall one clap vpon an
other, and hurt them, nor yet fo ftrayte that fcarfe they
can be thruft in, for that woulde laye them on fyde
and wynde them. A bowecafe of ledder, is not the
beft, for that is ofttymes moyfte which hurteth the
bowes very much. Therfore I haue fene good shooters
which would haue for euerye bowe, a fere cafe made
of wollen clothe, and than you maye putte. iii. or. iiii.
of them fo cafed, into a ledder cafe if you wyll. This
wollen cafe shall bothe kepe them in funder, and alfo
wylle kepe a bowe in his full ftrengthe, that it neuer
gyue for any wether. At home thefe wood cafes be
verye good for bowes to ftand in. But take hede yat
youre bowe ftande not to nere a ftone wall, for that
wyll make hym moyfte and weke, nor yet to nere any
fier for that wyll make him fhorte and brittle. And
thus muche as concernyng the fauyng and keping of
our bowe; nowe you shall heare what thynges ye muft
auoyde, for feare of breakyng your bowe.

A shooter chaunfeth to breake his bowe commonly.
iiii. wayes, by the ftrynge, by the fhafte, by drawyng to far, and by freates ; By the ftryng as I fayde
afore, whan the ftrynge is eyther to shorte, to long,
not furely put on, wyth one wap, or put croked on, or
fhorne in fundre wyth an euell nocke, or fuffered to
tarye ouer longe on. Whan the ftryng fayles the bowe
mufte nedes breake, and fpecially in the myddes ;
becaufe bothe the endes haue nothyng to ftop them ;
but whippes fo far backe, that the belly muft nedes
violentlye rife vp, the whyche you shall well perceyue
in bendyng of a bowe backward. Therfore a bowe
that foloweth the ftrynge is leaft hurt with breakyng of
ftrynges. By the fhafte a bowe is broken ether when
it is to fhort, and fo you fet it in your bow or when

Bowcase.

the nocke breakes for lytleneſſe, or when the ſtrynge
ſlyppes wythoute the nocke for wydeneſſe, than you
poule it to your eare and lettes it go, which muſt
nedes breake the ſhafte at the leaſte, and putte ſtringe
and bowe and al in ieopardy, bycauſe the ſtrength of the
bowe hath nothynge in it to ſtop the violence of it.

Thys kynde of breakynge is mooſte perilouſe for the
ſtanders by, for in ſuch a caſe you ſhall ſe ſometyme
the ende of a bow flye a hoole ſcore from a man, and
that mooſt commonly, as I haue marked oft the vpper
ende of the bowe. The bowe is drawne to far. ii.
wayes. Eyther when you take a longer ſhafte then
your owne, or els when you ſhyfte your hand to low or
to hye for ſhootynge far. Thys waye pouleth the backe
in ſunder, and then the bowe fleethe in manye peces.

So when you ſe a bowe broken, hauynge the bellye
riſen vp both wayes or tone, the ſtringe brake it.
When it is broken in twoo peces in a maner euen of and
ſpecyallye in the vpper ende, the ſhafte nocke brake it.

When the backe is pouled a ſunder in manye peeces
to farre drawynge, brake it.

Theſe tokens eyther alwayes be trewe or els verye
ſeldome myſſe.

The fourthe thyng that breketh a bow is fretes,
whych make a bowe redye and apte to
breake by any of the. iii. wayes afore   Freates.
ſayde. Freetes be in a ſhaft as well as in a bowe,
and they be muche lyke a Canker, crepynge and en-
creaſynge in thoſe places in a bowe, whyche be
weaker then other. And for thys purpoſe muſt your
bowe be well trymmed and piked of a conning man
that it may come rounde in trew compaſſe euery
where. For freetes you muſt beware, yf youre bow
haue a knot in the backe, leſt the places whyche be
nexte it, be not alowed ſtrong ynoughe to bere with
the knotte, or elles the ſtronge knotte ſhall freate the
weake places nexte it. Freates be fyrſt litle pincheſe,
the whych when you perceaue, pike the places about
the pinches, to make them ſomewhat weker, and as

well commynge as where it pinched, and fo the pinches
fhall dye, and neuer encreafe farther in to great freates.

Freates begynne many tymes in a pin, for there the
good woode is corrupted, that it mufte nedes be weke,
and bycaufe it is weake, therfore it freates.

Good bowyers therfore do rayfe euery pyn and
alowe it moore woode for feare of freatynge.

Agayne bowes mooft commonlye freate vnder the
hande, not fo muche as fome men fuppofe for the
moiftneffe of the hande, as for the heete of the hand :
the nature of heate fayeth Ariftotle is to lowfe, and not
to knyt faft, and the more lowfer the more weaker, the
weaker, the redier to freate.

A bowe is not well made, whych hath not wood
plentye in the hande. For yf the endes of the bowe
be ftaffyfhe, or a mans hande any thynge hoote the
bellye muft nedes fone frete. Remedie for fretes to
any purpofe I neuer hard tell of any, but onelye to
make the freated place as ftronge or ftronger then any
other. To fill vp the freate with lytle fheuers of a quill
and glewe (as fome fay wyll do wel) by reafon muft be
ftarke nought.

For, put cafe the freete dyd ceafe then, yet the caufe
which made it freate a fore (and that is weakeneffe of
the place) bicaufe it is not taken away muft nedes
make it freate agayne. As for cuttyng out of freates
wythe all maner of pecynge of bowes I wyll cleane ex-
clude from perfite fhootynge. For peced bowes be
muche lyke owlde houfen, whyche be more chargeable
to repayre, than commodioufe to dwell in. Agayne
to fwadle a bowe much about wyth bandes, verye
feldome dothe anye good, excepte it be to kepe downe
a fpel in the backe, otherwyfe bandes eyther nede not
when the bow is any thinge worthe, or els boote not
when it is marde and paft beft. And although I
knowe meane and poore fhooters, wyll vfe peced and
banded bowes fometyme bycaufe they are not able to
get better when they woulde, yet I am fure yf they
confyder it well, they fhall fynde it, bothe leffe charge

and more pleafure to ware at any tyme a couple of
fhyllynges of a new bowe than to beftowe. x. d. of
peacynge an olde bowe. For better is cofte vpon
fomewhat worth, than fpence vpon nothing worth.
And thys I fpeke alfo bycaufe you woulde haue me
referre all to perfitneffe in fhootynge.

Moreouer there is an other thynge, whyche wyl fone
caufe a bowe be broken by one of the. iii. wayes
whych be firft fpoken of, and that is fhotyng in winter,
when there is any frofte. Frofte is wherefoeuer is any
waterifh humour, as is in al woodes, eyther more or leffe,
and you knowe that al thynges frofen and Ifie, wyl
rather breke than bende. Yet if a man muft nedes
fhoote at any fuche tyme, lette hym take hys bowe,
and brynge it to the fyer, and there by litle and litle,
rubbe and chafe it with a waxed clothe, whiche fhall
bring it to that poynt, yat he maye fhote fafelye ynough
in it. This rubbyng with waxe, as I fayde before, is
a great fuccour, agaynft all wete and moyftneffe.

In the fyeldes alfo, in goyng betwyxt the pricks
eyther wyth your hande, or elles wyth a clothe you
mufte keepe your bowe in fuche a temper. And thus
muche as concernynge youre bowe, howe fyrfte to
knowe what wood is beft for a bowe, than to chofe
a bowe, after to trim a bowe, agayne to keepe it in
goodneffe, lafte of al, howe to faue it from al harm
and euylneffe.

And although many men can faye more of a bow
yet I truft thefe thynges be true, and almofte fufficient
for the knowlege of a perfecte bowe.

𝕻𝖍𝖎. Surelye I beleue fo, and yet I coulde haue
hearde you talke longer on it: althogh I can not fe,
what maye be fayd more of it. Therfore excepte you
wyll paufe a whyle, you may go forwarde to a fhafte.

𝕿𝖔𝖝. What fhaftes were made of, in oulde tyme
authours do not fo manifeftlye fhewe, as
of bowes. Herodotus doth tel, that in the　　Hero. eutep.
flood of Nilus, ther was a beaft, called a water horfe,
of whofe fkinne after it was dried, the Egyptians made

shaftes, and dartes on. The tree called   Sen. Hipp.
Cornus was so common to make shaftes of, that in good
authours of ye latyn tongue, *Cornus* is taken for a shafte,
as in Seneca, and that place of Virgill,   Virg. enei. 9.

> *Volat Itala Cornus.*

Yet of all thynges that euer I warked of olde authours,
either greke or latin, for shaftes to be made of, there
is nothing so common as reedes. Herodotus in des-
cribynge the mightie hooft of Xerxes doth   In Polym.
tell that thre great contries vsed shaftes
made of a rede, the Aethiopians, the Lycians (whose
shaftes lacked fethers, where at I maruayle moste of
all) and the men of Inde. The shaftes in
Inde were verye longe, a yarde and an   Arrianus. 8.
halfe, as Arrianus doth saye, or at the
leaft a yarde. as Q. Curtius doth saye, and   Q. Curt. 8.
therfore they gaue ye greater ftrype, but yet bycause
they were so long, they were the more vnhanfome, and
lesse profitable to the men of Inde, as Curtius doeth tell.

In Crete and Italie, they vsed to haue their shaftes
of rede also. The best reede for shaftes grewe in
Inde, and in Rhenus a flood of Italy.   Plin. 16. 36.

But bycause suche shaftes be neyther
easie for Englishe men to get, and yf they were gotten
scarse profitable for them to vse, I wyll lette them
passe, and speake of those shaftes whyche Englysh
men at this daye moste commonly do approue and
allowe.

A shaft hath three principall partes, the stele, the
fethers, and the head: whereof euerye one muste be
feuerallye spoken of.

❡ Steles be made of dyuerse woodes. as.

> Brafell.
> Turkie wood.
> Fufticke.
> Sugercheste.
> Hardbeame.
> Byrche.

Affhe.
Ooke.
Seruis tree.
Hulder.
Blackthorne.
Beche.
Elder.
Afpe.
Salow.

These wooddes as they be moſt commonly vſed, ſo
they be mooſte fit to be vſed : yet ſome one fytter
then an other for diuers mennes ſhotinge, as ſhalbe
toulde afterwarde. And in this pointe as in a bowe
you muſte truſte an honeſt fletcher. Neuertheleſſe al
thoughe I can not teache you to make a bowe or a
ſhafte, whiche belongeth to a bowyer and a fletcher to
comme to theyr lyuyng, yet wyll I ſhewe you ſome
tokens to knowe a bowe and a ſhafte, whiche per-
tayneth to an Archer to come to good ſhootynge.

A ſtele muſte be well ſeaſoned for Caſtinge, and it
muſt be made as the grayne lieth and as it groweth or
els it wyl neuer flye clene, as clothe cut ouertwhart and
agaynſte the wulle, can neuer hooſe a manne cleane.
A knottye ſtele maye be ſuffered in a bygge ſhafte,
but for a lytle ſhafte it is nothynge fit, bothe bycauſe it
wyll neuer flye far, and beſydes that it is euer in
danger of breakynge, it flieth not far bycauſe the
ſtrengthe of the ſhoote is hindred and ſtopped at the
knotte, euen as a ſtone caſt in to a plaine euen ſtil
water, wyll make the water moue a greate ſpace, yet
yf there be any whirlynge plat in the water, the
mouynge ceaſethe when it commethe at the whyrlynge
plat, whyche is not muche vnlyke a knotte in a ſhafte
yf it be conſidered wel. So euery thyng as it is plaine
and ſtreight of hys owne nature ſo is it fitteſt for far
mouynge. Therfore a ſtele whyche is harde to ſtande
in a bowe, without knotte, and ſtreighte (I meane not
artificiallye ſtreyghte as the fletcher dothe make it, but

naturally ftreight as it groweth in the wood) is beft to make a fhaft of, eyther to go cleane, fly far or ftand furely in any wedder. Now howe big, how fmall, how heuye, how lyght, how longe, how fhort, a fhafte fhoulde be particularlye for euerye man (feynge we muft taulke of the generall nature of fhootyng) can not be toulde no more than you Rhethoricians can appoynt any one kynde of wordes, of fentences, of fygures fyt for euery matter, but euen as the man and the matter requyreth fo the fytteft to be vfed. Therfore as concernynge thofe contraryes in a fhafte, euery man mufte auoyde them and draw to the meane of them, whyche meane is beft in al thynges. Yet yf a man happen to offende in any of the extremes it is better to offend in want and fcantneffe, than in to muche and outragioufe exceedynge. As it is better to haue a fhafte a lytle to fhorte than ouer longe, fomewhat to lyght, than ouer lumpyffhe, a lytle to fmall, than a greate deale to big, whiche thyng is not onely trewlye fayde in fhootynge, but in all other thynges that euer man goeth aboute, as in eatynge, taulkynge, and all other thynges lyke, whych matter was onfe excellentlye difputed vpon, in the Scooles, you knowe when.

And to offend, in thefe contraryes commeth much yf men take not hede, throughe the kynd of wood, wherof the fhaft is made: Ffor fome wood belonges to ye excedyng part, fome to ye fcant part, fome to ye meane, as Brafell, Turkiewood, Fufticke, Sugar chefte, and fuch lyke, make deade, heuy lumpifh, hobblyng fhaftes. Againe Hulder, black thorne, Serues tree, Beche, Elder, Afpe, and Salowe, eyther for theyr wekenes or lyghteneffe, make holow, ftarting, ftudding, gaddynge fhaftes. But Birche, Hardbeme, fome Ooke, and fome Affhe, beynge bothe ftronge ynoughe to ftande in a bowe, and alfo lyght ynoughe to flye far, are beft for a meane, whiche is to be foughte oute in euery thinge. And althoughe I knowe that fome men fhoote fo ftronge, that the deade woodes be lyghte ynoughe for them, and other fome fo weeke, that the lowfe woodes be lykewyfe for them bigge ynoughe yet generally for the mooft parte of men, the meane is the beft. And fo to conclude that, is alwayes befte for a man, whiche is meteft for him. Thus no wood of his owne nature, is eyther to lyght or to heuy, but as the fhooter is him felfe whyche dothe vfe it. For that fhafte whiche one yeare for a man is to lyghte and fcuddinge, for the fame felfe man the next yeare may chaunce be to heuy and hobblynge. Therfore can not I expreffe, excepte generally, what is beft wood for a fhaft, but let euery man when he knoweth his owne ftrength and the nature of euery wood, prouyde and fyt himfelfe there-after. Yet as concerning fheaffe Arroufe for war (as I fuppofe) it were better to make them of good Affhe, and not of Afpe, as they be now a dayes. For of all other woodes that euer I proued Affhe being big is fwifteft and agayne heuy to giue a greate ftripe with all, whyche Afpe fhall not doo. What heuynes doth in a ftripe euery man by experience can tell, therfore Affhe being both fwyfter and heuier is more fit for fheafe Arroes then Afpe, and thus muche for the beft wood for fhaftes.

Agayne lykewyfe as no one wood can be greatlye meet for all kynde of fhaftes, no more can one facion of the ftele be fit for euery fhooter. For thofe that be lytle brefted and big toward the hede called by theyr lykeneffe taperfafhion, refhe growne, and of fome merrye fellowes bobtayles, be fit for them whiche fhote vnder hande bycaufe they fhoote wyth a fofte lowfe, and ftreffes not a fhaft muche in the brefte where the weyghte of the bowe lyethe as you maye perceyue by the werynge of euery fhafte.

Agayne the bygge brefted fhafte is fytte for hym, which fhoteth right afore him, or els the breft being weke fhoulde neuer wythftande that ftrong piththy kynde of fhootynge, thus the vnderhande muft haue a fmall brefte, to go cleane awaye oute of the bowe, the forehande mufte haue a bigge brefte to bere the great myghte of the bowe. The ſhafte muſt be made rounde nothynge flat wyth out gal or wemme, for thys purpoſe. For bycauſe roundneſſe (whether you take example in heauen or in earthe) is fitteſt ſhappe and forme both for faſt mouing and alſo for ſone percynge of any thynge. And therfore Ariſtotle ſaythe that nature hath made the raine to be round, bycauſe it ſhoulde the eaſelyer enter throughe the ayre.

The nocke of the ſhafte is dyuerſly made, for ſome be greate and full, ſome hanſome and lytle, ſome wyde, ſome narow, ſome depe, ſome ſhalowe, ſome round, ſome lonſe, ſome wyth one nocke, ſome wyth a double nocke, wherof euery one hathe hys propertye.

The greate and full nocke, maye be well felte, and many wayes they ſaue a ſhafte from brekynge. The hanſome and lytle nocke wyll go clene awaye frome the hand, the wyde nocke is noughte, both for breakyng of the ſhafte and alſo for ſoden ſlyppynge oute of the ſtrynge when the narrowe nocke doth auoyde bothe thoſe harmes. The depe and longe nocke is good in warre for ſure kepyng in of the ſtrynge. The ſhalow, and rownde nocke is beſt for our purpoſe in prickyng for cleane delyueraunce of a ſhoote. And double nockyng is vſed for double ſuerty of the ſhaft. And thus far as concernynge a hoole ſtele.

Peecynge of a ſhafte with braſell and holie, or other heauy woodes, is to make the ende compaſſe heauy with the fethers in fliyng, for the ſtedfaſter ſhotyng. For if the ende were plumpe heauy wyth lead and the wood nexte it lyghte, the head ende woulde euer be downwardes, and neuer flye ſtrayght.

Two poyntes in peecing be ynough, leſt the moyſtnes of the earthe enter to moche into the peecinge, and ſo leuſe the glue. Therefore many poyntes be more pleaſaunt to the eye, than profitable for the vſe.

Summe vſe to peece theyr ſhaftes in the nocke wyth braſel, or holye, to counterwey, with the head, and I haue ſene ſumme for the ſame purpoſe, bore an hole a lytle bineth the nocke, and put leade in it. But yet none of thefe wayes be anye thing needful at al, for ye nature of a fether in flying, if a man marke it wel, is able to bear vp a wonderful weyght : and I thinke fuche peecing came vp firft, thus : whan a good Archer hath broken a good fhafte, in the fethers, and for the fantafie he hath had to it, he is lothe to leefe it, and therfore doeth he peece it. And than by and by other eyther bycaufe it is gaye, or elles becaufe they wyll haue a fhafte lyke a good archer, cuttethe theyre hole fhaftes, and peeceth them agayne : A thynge by my iudgement, more coftlye than nedefull.

And thus haue you heard what wood, what faffhion, what nockynge, what peecynge a ftele mufte haue : Nowe foloweth the fetherynge.

Phi. I woulde neuer haue thought you could haue fayd halfe fo muche of a ftele, and I thynke as concernyng the litle fether and the playne head, there is but lytle to faye.

Tox. Lytle, yes trulye : for there is no one thing, in al fhoting, fo moche to be loked on as the fether. For fyrfte a queftion maye be afked, whether any other thing befyde a fether, be fit for a fhaft or no ? if a fether onelye be fit, whether a goofe fether onely, or no ? yf a goofe fether be beft, then whether there be any difference, as concernynge the fether of an oulde goofe, and a yonge goofe : a gander, or a goofe : a fennye goofe, or an vplandifh goofe. Againe which is beft fether in any goofe, the ryght wing or the left wing, the pinion fether, or any other fether : a whyte, blacke, or greye fether ? Thirdly, in fettyng on of your fether, whether it be pared or drawen with a thicke rybbe, or a thinne rybbe (the rybbe is ye hard quill whiche deuydeth the fether) a long fether better or a fhorte, fet on nere the nocke, or farre from the nocke, fet on ftreight, or fom what bowyng ? and whether one or two fethers runne on the bowe. Fourthly in couling or fheryng, whether high or lowe, whether fomewhat fwyne backed (I mufte vfe

ſhoters wordes) or ſadle backed, whether rounde, or
ſquare ſhorne? And whether a ſhaft at any tyme ought
to be plucked, and how to be plucked.

Phi. Surely Toxophile, I thynke manye fletchers
(although daylye they haue theſe thinges in vre) if
they were aſked ſodeynly, what they coulde ſaye of a
fether, they could not ſaye ſo moch. But I praye you
let me heare you more at large, expreſſe thoſe thynges
in a fether, the whiche you packed vp in ſo narrowe a
rowme. And fyrſt whether any other thyng may be
vſed for a fether or not.

Tox. That was ye fyrſte poynte in dede, and
bycauſe there foloweth many after, I wyll hye apace
ouer them, as one that had manye a myle to ride.
Shaftes to haue had alwayes fethers Plinius   Pl. 16. 36.
in Latin, and Iulius Pollux in Greke, do   I. Pol 1. 10.
playnlye ſhewe, yet onely the Lycians I   Her. Polym.
reade in Herodotus to haue vſed ſhaftes without
fedders. Onelye a fedder is fit for a ſhafte for. ii.
cauſes, fyrſte bycauſe it is leathe weake to giue
place to the bowe, than bycauſe it is of that
nature, that it wyll ſtarte vp after ye bow. So, Plate,
wood or horne can not ſerue, bycauſe the[y] wil
not gyue place. Againe, Cloth, Paper, or Parchment
can not ſerue, bycauſe they wyll not ryſe after the
bowe, therfore a fedder is onely mete, bycauſe it onelye
wyl do bothe. Nowe to looke on the fedders of all maner
of birdes, you ſhal ſe ſome ſo lowe weke and ſhorte,
ſome ſo courſe, ſtoore and harde, and the rib ſo brickle,
thin and narrow, that it can nether be drawen, pared,
nor yet well ſet on, that except it be a ſwan for a dead
ſhafte (as I knowe ſome good Archers haue vſed) or a
ducke for a flyghte whiche laſtes but one ſhoote, there
is no fether but onelye of a gooſe that hath all commodities in it. And trewelye at a ſhort but, which
ſome man doth vſe, ye Pecock fether doth ſeldome
kepe vp ye ſhaft eyther ryght or leuel, it is ſo roughe
and heuy, ſo that many men which haue taken them
vp for gayeneſſe, hathe layde them downe agayne ſor

I

profyte, thus for our purpofe, the Goofe is beft fether, for the beft fhoter.

Phi. No that is not fo, for the beft fhoter that euer was vfed other fethers.

Tox. Ye are fo cunninge, in fhootynge I praye you who was that.

Phi. Hercules whyche had hys fhaftes fethered with Egles fethers as Hefiodus dothe faye.   Hefiod. in Scuto. Her.

Tox. Well as for Hercules, feynge nether water nor lande, heauen nor hell, coulde fcarfe contente hym to abyde in, it was no meruell thoughe a fely poore goufe fether could not plefe him to fhoote wythal, and agayne as for Egles they flye fo hye and builde fo far of, yat they be very hard to come by. Yet welfare the gentle goufe which bringeth to a man euen to hys doore fo manye excedynge commodities.   A Goufe.
For the goufe is mans comforte in war and in peace flepynge and wakynge. What prayfe fo euer is gyuen to fhootynge the goufe may chalenge the befte parte in it. How well dothe fhe make a man fare at his table? Howe eafelye dothe fhe make a man lye in hys bed? How fit euen as her fethers be onelye for fhootynge, fo be her quylles fytte onelye for wrytyng.

Philo. In deade Toxophyle that is the befte prayfe you gaue to a goufe yet, and furelye I would haue fayde you had bene to blame yf you had ouerfkypte it.

Tox. The Romaynes I trowe Philologe not fo muche bycaufe a goufe wyth cryinge faued theyr Capitolium and head toure wyth their golden Iupiter as Propertius doth fay very pretely in thys verfe.

Anferis et tutum uoce fuiffe Iouem.   Propertius
Id eft.
Theues on a night had ftolne Iupiter, had a goufe not a kekede.

Dyd make a golden goufe and fet hir in the top of ye Capitolium, and appoynted alfo the Cen-
fores to alow out of ye common hutche   Liuius 1. Dec. 5.
yearly ftipendes for ye findinge of certayne Geefe, ye Romaynes did not I faye giue al thys honor to a goufe

for yat good dede onely, but for other infinit mo which
comme dayly to a man byn Geefe, and furely yf I
fhould declame in ye prayfe of any maner of befte
lyuyng, I would chofe a goufe, But the goufe hath
made vs flee to farre from oure matter. Nowe fir
ye haue hearde howe a fether muft be had, and that a
goofe fether onely. It foloweth of a yong gofe and
an oulde, and the refidue belonging to a fether:
which thing I wyll fhortlye courfe ouer: wherof,
when you knowe the properties, you maye fitte your
fhaftes accordyng to your fhotyng, which rule you
muft obferue in all other thynges too, bycaufe no one
fafhion or quantitie can be fitte for euery man, no
more than a fhooe or a cote can be. The oulde goofe
fether is ftyffe and ftronge, good for a wynde, and
fytteft for a deed fhaft: the yonge goofe fether is
weake and fyne, beft for a fwyfte fhaft, and it muft be
couled at the firft fhering, fomewhat hye, for with
fhoting, it wyll fattle and faule very moche. The
fame thing (although not fo moche) is to be con-
fydered in a goofe and a gander. A fenny goofe,
euen as her flefh is blacker, ftoorer, vnholfomer, fo is
her fether for the fame caufe courfer ftoorer and
rougher, and therfore I haue heard very good fletchers
faye, that the feconde fether in fome place is better
then the pinion in other fome. Betwixt the winges is
lytle difference, but that you muft haue diuerfe fhaftes
of one flight, fethered with diuerfe winges, for
diuerfe windes: for if the wynde and the fether go
both one way the fhaft wyl be caryed to moche.
The pinion fethers as it hath the firfte place in the
winge, fo it hath the fyrft place in good fetheringe.
You maye knowe it afore it be pared, by a bought
whiche is in it, and agayne when it is colde, by the
thinneffe aboue, and the thickneffe at the grounde, and
alfo by the ftifnes and fineffe which wyll cary a fhaft
better, fafter and further, euen as a fine fayle cloth
doth a fhyppe.

The coulour of the fether is lefte to be regarded,

yet fommewhat to be looked on: for a good whyte, you haue fometyme an yll greye. Yet furelye it ftandeth with good reafon to haue the cocke fether black or greye, as it were to gyue a man warning to nocke ryght. The cocke fether is called that which ftandeth aboue in ryght nocking, which if you do not obferue the other fethers muft nedes run on the bowe, and fo marre your fhote. And thus farre of the goodneffe and choyfe of your fether: now foloweth the fetting on. Wherin you muft looke that your fethers be not drawen for haftineffe, but pared euen and ftreyghte with diligence. The fletcher draweth a fether when he hath but one fwappe at it with his knyfe, and then playneth it a lytle, with rubbynge it ouer his knyfe. He pareth it when he taketh leyfure and hede to make euery parte of the ryb apt to ftand ftreight, and euen on vpon the ftele. This thing if a man take not heede on, he maye chaunce haue caufe to faye fo of his fletcher, as in dreffinge of meate is communelye fpoken of Cookes: and that is, that God fendeth vs good fethers, but the deuyll noughtie Fletchers. Yf any fletchers heard me faye thus, they wolde not be angrye with me, excepte they were yll fletchers: and yet by reafon, thofe fletchers too, ought rather to amend them felues for doing yll, then be angry with me for faying truth. The ribbe in a ftyffe fether may be thinner, for fo it wyll ftande cleaner on: but in a weake fether you muft leaue a thicker ribbe, or els yf the ryb which is the foundacion and grounde, wherin nature hath fet euerye clefte of the fether, be taken to nere the fether, it mufte nedes folowe, that the fether fhall faule, and droupe downe, euen as any herbe doeth whyche hath his roote to nere taken on with a fpade. The lengthe and fhortneffe of the fether, ferueth for diuers fhaftes, as a long fether for a long heauy, or byg fhafte, the fhorte fether for the contrary. Agayne the fhorte may ftande farther, the longe nerer the nocke. Youre fether mufte ftande almoofte ftreyght on, but yet after that forte, yat it maye turne

rounde in flyinge. And here I confider the wonderfull nature of fhootynge, whiche ftandeth all togyther by
that fafhion, which is mofte apte for quicke mouynge,
and that is by roundeneffe. For firfte the bowe muft be
gathered rounde, in drawyng it muft come rounde compaffe, the ftrynge mufte be rounde, the ftele rounde, the
beft nocke rounde, the feather fhorne fomwhat rounde,
the fhafte in flyenge, mufte turne rounde, and if it flye
far, it flyeth a rounde compace. For eyther aboue
or benethe a rounde compace, hyndereth the flyinge.
Moreouer bothe the fletcher in makynge your fhafte,
and you in nockynge your fhafte, mufte take heede
that two fethers equallye runne on the bowe. For
yf one fether runne alone on the bowe, it fhal
quickely be worne, and fhall not be able to matche
with the other fethers, and agayne at the lowfe, yf the
fhafte be lyght, it wyl ftarte, if it be heuye, it wil hoble.
And thus as concernyng fettyng on of your fether.
Nowe of coulynge.

To fhere a fhafte hyghe or lowe, mufte be as the
fhafte is, heauy or lyght, great or lytle, long or fhort.
The fwyne backed fafhion, maketh the fhaft deader,
for it gathereth more ayer than the faddle backed, and
therfore the faddle backe is furer for daunger of
wether, and fitter for fmothe fliing. Agayn to fhere
a fhaft rounde, as they were wount fomtime to do, or
after the triangle fafhion, whyche is muche vfed nowe
a dayes, bothe be good. For roundneffe is apte for
fliynge of his owne nature, and al maner of triangle
fafhion, (the fharpe poynte goyng before) is alfo
naturally apte for quycke entrynge, and therfore fayth
Cicero, that cranes taught by nature, ob-
ferue in flyinge a triangle fafhion alwayes,   De nat. deor.
bycaufe it is fo apte to perce and go thorowe the
ayer wythall. Lafte of all pluckynge of fethers is
noughte, for there is no fuerty in it, therfore let euery
archer haue fuch fhaftes, that he maye bothe knowe
them and truft them at euery chaunge of wether. Yet
if they muft nedes be plucked, plucke them as litle as

can be, for fo fhal they be the leffe vnconftante. And thus I haue knit vp in as fhorte a roume as I coulde, the beft fethers fetheringe and coulinge of a fhafte.

Phi. I thynke furelye you haue fo taken vp the matter wyth you, yat you haue lefte nothynge behinde you. Nowe you haue brought a fhafte to the head, whiche if it were on, we had done as concernyng all inftrumentes belongyng to fhootynge.

Tox. Neceffitie, the inuentour of all goodneffe (as all authours in a maner, doo faye) amonges all other thinges inuented a fhaft heed, firfte to faue the ende from breakyng, then it made it fharpe to ftycke better, after it made it of ftrong matter, to laft better: Laft of all experience and wyfedome of men, hathe brought it to fuche a perfitneffe, that there is no one thing fo profitable, belongyng to artillarie, either to ftryke a mannes enemye forer in warre, or to fhoote nerer the marke at home, then is a fitte heed for both purpofes. For if a fhaft lacke a heed, it is worth nothynge for neither vfe. Therfore feinge heedes be fo neceffary, they muft of neceffitie, be wel looked vpon. Heedes for warre, of longe tyme haue ben made, not onely of diuers matters, but alfo of diuers fafhions. The Troians had heedes of yron, as this verfe fpoken of Pandarus, fheweth :

Vp to the pappe his ftring did he pull, his fhaft to the harde yron.

Iliados. 4

The Grecians had heedes of braffe, as Vlyffes fhaftes were heeded, when he flewe Antinous, and the other wowers of Penelope.

Quite through a dore, flewe a fhafte with a braffe head.

Odysse. 21.

It is playne in Homer, where Menelaus was wounded of Pandarus fhafte, yat the heedes were not glewed on, but tyed on with a ftring, as the commentaries in Greke playnelye tell.

Iliados. 4.

And therfore fhoters at that tyme to carry their fhaftes withoute heedes, vntill they occupyed them, and than

fet on an heade as it apereth in Homer the. xxi.
booke *Odyffei*, where Penelope brought Vlixes bowe
downe amonges the gentlemen, whiche came on wow-
ing to her, that he whiche was able to bende it and
drawe it, might inioye her, and after her
folowed a mayde fayth Homer, carienge   Odyffe. 21.
a bagge full of heades, bothe of iron and braffe.

The men of Scythia, vfed heades of braffe.   The
men of Inde vfed heades of yron.   The Ethiopians
vfed heades of a harde fharpe ftone, as   Clio.
bothe Herodotus and Pollux do tel.   Hero
The Germanes as Cornelius Tacitus doeth   Polym
faye, had theyr fhaftes headed with bone, and many
countryes bothe of olde tyme and nowe, vfe heades
of horne, but of all other yron and ftyle mufte nedes
be the fitteft for heades.

Iulius Pollux calleth otherwyfe than we doe, where
the fethers be the head, and that whyche   I. Pol. 1 : 10.
we call the head, he calleth the poynte.

Fafhion of heades is diuers and that of olde tyme :
two maner of arrowe heades fayeth Pollux, was vfed
in olde tyme.   The one he calleth ὄγκινος defcrybynge
it thus, hauyng two poyntes or barbes, lookyng backewarde to the ftele and the fethers, which furely we call
in Englifhe a brode arrowe head or a fwalowe tayle.
The other he calleth γλωχὶς, hauing. ii. poyntes ftretch-
yng forwarde, and this Englyfh men do call a forke-
head : bothe thefe two kyndes of heades, were vfed in
Homers dayes, for Teucer vfed forked heades, fayinge
thus to Agamemnon.

Eighte good fhaftes haue I fhot fithe I came, eche one wyth a forke
heade.   Iliad. 8.

Pandarus heades and Vlyffes heades were broode
arrow heades, as a man maye learne in Homer that
woulde be curioufe in knowyng that matter. Hercules
vfed forked heades, but yet they had thre pointes or
forkes, when other mennes had but twoo.   Plutarchus
The Parthyans at that great battell where   in Craffo.

they slewe ritche Crassus and his sonne vsed brode
Arrowe heades, whyche stacke so sore that the
Romaynes could not poule them out agayne. Commodus the Emperoure vsed forked heades,
whose facion Herodiane doeth lyuely and   Herodia. 1
naturally descrybe, sayinge that they were lyke the shap
of a new mone wherwyth he would smite of the heade of
a birde and neuer misse, other facion of heades haue not
I red on.   Our Englyshe heades be better in war than
eyther forked heades, or brode arrowe heades.   For
firste the ende beynge lyghter they flee a great deele
the faster, and by the same reason gyueth a far sorer
stripe.   Yea and I suppose if ye same lytle barbes
whiche they haue, were clene put away, they shuld
be far better.   For thys euery man doth graunt, yat a
shaft as long as it flyeth, turnes, and whan it leueth
turnyng it leueth goyng any farther.   And euery
thynge that enters by a turnynge and boring facion,
the more flatter it is, the worse it enters, as a knife
thoughe it be sharpe yet becaufe of the edges, wil not
bore so wel as a bodkin, for euery rounde thynge
enters beste and therefore nature, sayeth Aristotle, made
the rayne droppes rounde for quicke percynge the
ayer.   Thus, eyther shaftes turne not in flyeng, or els
our flatte arrowe heades stoppe the shafte in entrynge.

Phi. But yet Toxophile to holde your communication a lytle I suppose the flat heade is better, bothe
bycaufe it maketh a greter hoole, and alfo bycaufe it
sticks faster in.

Tox. Thefe two reasons as they be bothe trewe, so
they be both nought.   For fyrft the leffe hoole, yf it
be depe, is the worft to heale agayn : when a man
shoteth at hys enemy, he defyreth rather yat it should
enter far, than stick faft.   For what remedye is it I
praye you for hym whych is smitten with a depe
wounde to poull out the shaft quickely, except it be to
hafte his death spedely? thus heades whyche make a
lytle hole and depe, be better in war, than thofe which
make a great hole and sticke faft in.

Iulius Pollux maketh mencion of cer- Pollux. 7.
tayne kindes of heades for war which beare Psal. 7.
fyre in them, and fcripture alfo fpeaketh fomwhat of
the fame. Herodotus doth tell a won- Hero. Vran.
derfull pollicy to be done by Xerxes what
tyme he befeged the great Toure in Athenes : He
made his Archers binde there fhafte heades aboute
wyth towe, and than fet it on fyre and fhoote them,
whych thyng done by many Archers fet all the places
on fyre, whych were of matter to burne; and befydes
that dafed the men wythin, fo yat they knewe not
whyther to turne them. But to make an ende of all
heades for warre I woulde wyfhe that the head makers
of Englande fhoulde make their fheafe arrowe heades
more harder poynted then they be : for I my felfe haue
fene of late fuch heades fet vpon fheafe Arrowes, as ye
officers yf they had fene them woulde not haue bene
content wyth all.

Now as concernyng heades for pryckyng, which is
oure purpofe, there be dyuerfe kyndes, fome be blonte
heades, fome fharpe, fome both blonte and fharpe.
The blont heades men vfe bycaufe they perceaue
them to be good, to kepe a lengthe wyth all, they
kepe a good lengthe, bycaufe a man poulethe them no
ferder at one tyme than at another. For in felynge
the plompe ende alwayes equallye he may lowfe them.
Yet in a winde, and agaynfte the wynd the wether hath
fo much power on the brode end, yat no man can
kepe no fure lengthe, wyth fuch a heade. Therfore a
blont hede in a caulme or downe a wind is very good,
otherwyfe none worfe.

Sharpe heades at the ende wythout anye fhoulders
(I call that the fhoulder in a heade whyche a mans
finger fhall feele afore it come to the poynte) wyll
perche quycklye throughe a wynde, but yet it hath. ii.
difcommodities, the one that it wyll kepe no lengthe,
it kepeth no lengthe, bycaufe no manne can poule it
certaynly as far one tyme as at an other : it is not
drawen certaynlye fo far one tyme as at an other,

bycaufe it lackethe fhouldrynge wherwyth as wyth a
fure token a man myghte be warned when to lowfe,
and alfo bycaufe menne are afrayde of the fharpe
poynt for fettyng it in ye bow. The feconde incom-
moditie is when it is lyghted on ye ground, ye fmal
poynte fhall at euery tyme be in ieopardye of hurtynge,
whyche thynge of all other wyll fonreft make the fhafte
lefe the lengthe. Now when blonte heades be good
to kepe a lengthe wythall, yet noughte for a wynde,
fharpe heades good to perche the wether wyth al,
yet nought for a length, certayne heademarkers
dwellyng in London perceyuynge the commoditie of
both kynde of heades ioyned wyth a difcommoditie,
inuented newe files and other inftrumentes where wyth
[t]he[y] broughte heades for pryckynge to fuch a perfitneffe, that all the commodities of the twoo other
heades fhould be put in one heade wyth out anye difcommoditie at all. They made a certayne kynde of
heades whyche men call hie rigged, creafed, or fhoul-
dred heades, or fyluer fpone heades, for a certayne
lykeneffe that fuche heades haue wyth the knob ende
of fome fyluer fpones.

Thefe heades be good both to kepe a length withal
and alfo to perche a wynde wythal, to kepe a length
wythall bycaufe a man maye certaynly poule it to the
fhouldrynge euery fhoote and no farther, to perche a
wynde wythall bycaufe the pointe from the fhoulder
forwarde, breketh the wether as al other fharpe thynges
doo. So the blonte fhoulder feruethe for a fure lengthe
kepynge, the poynte alfo is euer fit, for a roughe and
greate wether percyng. And thus much as fhortlye as
I could, as concernyng heades both for war and peace.

Phi. But is there no cunning as concerning fetting
on of ye head?

Tox. Wel remembred. But that poynt belongeth to
fletchers, yet you may defyre hym to fet youre heade,
full on, and clofe on. Ful on is whan the wood is
be[n]t hard vp to the ende or ftoppynge of the heade,
clofe on, is when there is lefte wood on euerye fyde

the fhafte, ynoughe to fyll the head withall, or when it
is neyther to little nor yet to greate. If there be any
faulte in any of thefe poyntes, ye head whan it lyghteth
on any hard ftone or grounde wil be in ieoperdy.
eyther of breakynge, or els otherwyfe hurtynge. Stop-
pynge of heades eyther wyth leade, or any thynge els,
fhall not nede now, bycaufe euery filuer fpone, or
fhowldred head is ftopped of it felfe. Shorte heades be
better than longe : For firfte the longe head is worfe
for the maker, to fyle ftrayght compace euery waye :
agayne it is worfe for the fletcher to fet ftrayght on :
thyrdlye it is alwayes in more ieoperdie of breakinge,
whan it is on. And nowe I trowe Philologe, we haue
done as concernynge all Inftrumentes belongyng to
fhootynge, whiche euery fere archer ought, to prouyde for
hym felfe. And there remayneth. ii. thynges behinde,
whiche be generall or common to euery man the
Wether and the Marke, but bicaufe they be fo knit
wyth fhootynge ftrayght, or kepynge of a lengthe, I
wyll deferre them to that place, and now we will come,
(God wyllyng) to handle oure inftrumentes, the thing
that euery man defireth to do wel.

Phi. If you can teache me fo well to handle thefe
inftrumentes as you haue defcribed them, I fuppofe I
fhalbe an archer good ynough.

Tox. To learne any thing (as you knowe better than
I Philologe) and fpeciallye to do a thing with a mannes
handes, muft be done if a man woulde be excellent, in
his youthe. Yonge trees in gardens, which lacke al
fenfes, and beaftes without reafon, when they be yong,
may with handling and teaching, be brought to wonderfull thynges. And this is not onely true in natural
thinges, but in artificiall thinges to, as the potter moft
connyngly doth caft his pottes whan his claye is fofte
and workable, and waxe taketh printe when it is
warme, and leathie weke, not whan claye and waxe be
hard and oulde : and euen fo, euerye man in his youthe,
bothe with witte and body is mofte apte and pliable
to receyue any cunnyng that fhulde be taught hym.

This communication of teaching youthe, maketh me to remembre the right worſhipfull and my ſinguler good mayſter, Sir Humfrey Wingfelde, to whom nexte God, I ought to refer for his manifolde benefites beſtowed on me, the poore talent of learnyng, whiche god hath lent me : and for his ſake do I owe my ſeruice to all other of the name and noble houſe of the Wyngfeldes, bothe in woord and dede. Thys worſhypfull man hath euer loued and vſed, to haue many children brought vp in learnynge in his houſe amonges whome I my ſelfe was one. For whom at terme tymes he woulde bryng downe from London bothe bowe and ſhaftes. And when they ſhuld playe he woulde go with them him ſelfe in to the fyelde, and ſe them ſhoote, and he that ſhot fayreſt, ſhulde haue the beſt bowe and ſhaftes, and he that ſhot ilfauouredlye, ſhulde be mocked of his felowes, til he ſhot better.

Woulde to god all Englande had vſed or wolde vſe to lay the foundacion of youth, after the example of this worſhipful man in bringyng vp chyldren in the Booke and the Bowe : by whiche two thynges, the hole common welth both in peace and warre is chefelye ruled and defended wythall.

But to our purpoſe, he that muſte come to this high perfectnes in ſhootyng which we ſpeake of, muſte nedes begin to learne it in hys youthe, the omitting of whiche thinge in Englande, both maketh fewer ſhooters, and alſo euery man that is a ſhoter, ſhote warſe than he myght, if he were taught.

Phi. Euen as I knowe that this is true, whiche you ſaye, euen ſo Toxophile, haue you quyte diſcouraged me, and drawen my minde cleane from ſhootynge, ſeinge by this reaſon, no man yat hath not vſed it in his youthe can be excellent in it. And I ſuppoſe the ſame reſon woulde diſcourage many other mo, yf they hearde you talke after this forte.

Tox. This thyng Philologe, ſhall diſcourage no man that is wyſe. For I wyll proue yat wiſdome may worke the ſame thinge in a man, that nature doth in a chylde.

A chylde by thre thinges, is brought to excellencie. By Aptneſſe, Deſire, and Feare : Aptneſſe maketh hym pliable lyke waxe to be formed and faſhioned, euen as a man woulde haue hym. Deſyre to be as good or better, than his felowes : and Feare of them whome he is vnder, wyl cauſe hym take great labour and payne with diligent hede, in learnynge any thinge, wherof procedeth at the laſte excellency and perfectneſſe.

A man maye by wiſdome in learnyng any thing, and ſpecially to ſhoote, haue thre lyke commodities alſo, wherby he maye, as it were become younge agayne, and ſo attayne to excellencie. For as a childe is apte by naturall youth, ſo a man by vſyng at the firſte weake bowes, far vnderneth his ſtrength, ſhal be as pliable and readye to be taught fayre ſhotyng as any chylde : and daylye vſe of the ſame, ſhal both kepe hym in fayer ſhotyng, and alſo at ye laſt bryng hym to ſtronge ſhootynge.

And in ſtede of the feruente deſyre, which pro-uoketh a chylde to be better than hys felowe, lette a man be as muche ſtirred vp with ſhamefaſtnes to be worſe than all other. And the ſame place that feare hathe in a chylde, to compell him to take peyne, the ſame hath loue of ſhotyng in a man, to cauſe hym forſake no labour, withoute whiche no man nor chylde can be excellent. And thus whatſoeuer a chylde may be taught by Aptneſſe, Deſire, and Feare, the ſame thing in ſhootynge, maye a man be taughte by weake bowes, Shamefaſtneſſe and Loue.

And hereby you may ſe that that is true whiche Cicero ſayeth, that a man by vſe, may be broughte to a newe nature. And this I dare be bould to ſaye, that any man whiche will wiſely begynne, and conſtantlye perſeuer in this trade of learnyng to ſhote, ſhall attayne to perfectneſſe therein.

Phi. This communication Toxophile, doeth pleaſe me verye well, and nowe I perceyue that moſte gene-rally and chefly youthe muſte be taughte to ſhoote, and ſecondarilye no man is debarred therfrom excepte it be more thorough his owne negligence for bicaufe he wyll not learne, than any difabilitie, bicaufe he can not lerne.

Therfore seyng I wyll be glad to folowe your counfell in chofynge my bowe and other inftrumentes, and alfo am afhamed that I can fhote no better than I can, moreouer hauynge fuche a loue toward fhotynge by your good reafons to day, that I wyll forfake no labour in the exercife of the fame, I befeche you imagyn that we had bothe bowe and fhaftes here, and teache me howe I fhould handle them, and one thynge I defyre you, make me as fayre an Archer as you can.

For thys I am fure in learnynge all other matters, nothynge is broughte to the mooft profytable vfe, which is not handled after the mooft cumlye fafhion. As mafters of fence haue no ftroke fit ether to hit an other or elfe to defende hym felfe, whyche is not ioyned wyth a wonderfull cumlineffe. A Cooke can not chop hys herbes neither quickelye nor hanfomlye excepte he kepe fuche a mefure with hys choppynge kniues as woulde delyte a manne both to fe hym and heare hym.

Euerye hand craft man that workes beft for hys owne profyte, workes mooft femelye to other mens fight. Agayne in buyldynge a houfe, in makynge a fhyppe, euery parte the more hanfomely, they be ioyned for profyt and lafte, the more cumlye they be fafhioned to euery mans fyght and eye. Nature it felfe taught men to ioyne alwayes welfauouredneffe with profytableneffe. As in man, that ioynt or pece which is by anye chaunce depriued of hys cumlyneffe the fame is alfo debarred of hys vfe and profytableneffe.

As he that is gogle eyde and lokes a fquinte hath both hys countenaunce clene marred, and hys fight fore blemmyfhed, and fo in all other members lyke. Moreouer what tyme of the yeare bryngeth moofte profyte wyth it for mans vfe, the fame alfo couereth and dekketh bothe earthe and trees wyth mooft cumlyneffe for mans pleafure. And that tyme whych takethe

awaye the pleafure of the grounde, carieth wyth hym
alfo the profyt of the grounde, as euery man by experience knoweth in harde and roughe winters.　Some
thynges there be whych haue no other ende, but onely
cumlyneffe, as payntyng, and Daunfing.　And vertue it
felfe is nothynge eles but cumlyneffe, as al Philofophers do agree in opinion, therfore feynge that whych
is beft done in anye matters, is alwayes mooft cumlye
done as both Plato and Cicero in manye places
do proue, and daylye experience dothe teache in other
thynges, I praye you as I fayde before teatche me to
fhoote as fayre, and welfauouredly as you can imagen.

𝕿𝔬𝔵. Trewlye Philologe as you proue verye well in
other matters, the beft fhootynge, is alwayes the mooft
cumlye fhootynge but thys you know aswell as I that
Craffus fhewethe in Cicero that as cumlineffe is the
chefe poynt, and moft to be fought for in all thynges,
fo cumlyneffe onlye, can neuer be taught by any Arte
or craft.　But maye be perceyued well when it is done,
not defcribed wel how it fhould be done.

Yet neuertheleffe to comme to it there be manye
waye whych wayes men haue affayde in other matters,
as yf a man would folowe in learnynge to fhoote
faire, the noble paynter Zeuxes in payntyng Helena,
whyche to make his Image bewtifull dyd chofe out. v.
of the fayreft maydes in al the countrie aboute, and in
beholdynge them conceyued and drewe out fuche an
Image that it far exceded al other, bycaufe the comelineffe of them al was broughte in to one mooft periyte
comelineffe: So lykewyfe in fhotynge yf a man, woulde
fet before hys eyes. v. or. vi. of the fayreft Archers that
euer he faw fhoote, and of one learne to ftande, of a
nother to drawe, of an other to lowfe, and fo take of
euery man, what euery man coulde do beft, I dare faye
he fhoulde come to fuche a comlyneffe as neuer man
came to yet.　As for an example, if the mooft comely
poynte in fhootynge that Hewe Prophete the Kynges
feruaunte hath and as my frendes Thomas and Raufe
Cantrell doth vfe with the mooft femelye facyons that.

iii. or iiii. excellent Archers haue befide, were al ioyned
in one, I am fure all men woulde wonder at ye excellencie
of it. And this is one waye to learne to fhoote fayre.

Phi. This is very wel truly, but I praye you teache
me fomewhat of fhootyng fayre youre felfe.

Tox. I can teache you to fhoote fayre, euen as
Socrates taught a man ones to knowe God, for when
he axed hym what was God : naye fayeth he I can tell
you better what God is not, as God is not yll, God is
vnfpeakeable, vnfearcheable and fo forth : Euen lykewyfe can I faye of fayre fhootyng, it hath not this dif-
commodite with it nor that difcommoditie, and at laft
a man maye fo fhifte all the difcommodities from
fhootynge that there fhall be left no thynge behynde
but fayre fhootynge. And to do this the better you
muft remember howe that I toulde you when I de-
fcrybed generally the hole nature of fhootyng that
fayre fhotyng came of thefe thynges, of ftandynge,
nockynge, drawynge, howldynge and lowfynge, the
whych I wyll go ouer as fhortly as I can, defcribynge
the difcommodities that men commonly vfe in all
partes of theyr bodies, that you yf you faulte in any
fuch maye knowe it and fo go about to amend it.
Faultes in Archers do excede the number of Archers,
whyche come wyth vfe of fhootynge wythoute teachynge. Vfe and cuftome feparated from knowlege
and learnynge, doth not onely hurt fhootynge, but the
mooft weyghtye thynges in the worlde befide : And
therfore I maruayle moche at thofe people whyche
be the mayneteners of vfes withoute knowlege hauynge
no other worde in theyr mouthe but thys vfe, vfe, cuftome, cuftome. Suche men more wylful than wyfe,
befide other difcommodities, take all place and occafion
from al amendment. And thys I fpeake generally of
vfe and cuftome.

Whych thynge yf a learned man had it in hande
yat woulde applye it to anye one matter, he myght
handle it wonderfullye. But as for fhootyng, vfe is the
onely caufe of all fautes in it and therfore chylderne

more eaſly and ſoner maye be taught to ſhote excellentlye then men, bycauſe chylderne may be taught
to ſhoote well at the fyrſte, men haue more payne to
vnlearne theyr yll vſes, than they haue laboure afterwarde to come to good ſhootynge.

All the diſcommodities whiche ill cuſtome hath
graffed in archers, can neyther be quycklye poulled
out, nor yet ſone reckened of me, they be ſo manye.

Some ſhooteth, his head forwarde as though he
woulde byte the marke : an other ſtareth wyth hys
eyes, as though they ſhulde flye out : An other
winketh with one eye, and loketh with the other :
Some make a face with writhing theyr mouthe and
countenaunce ſo, as though they were doyng you wotte
what : An other blereth out his tonge : An other
byteth his lyppes : An other holdeth his necke a wrye.
In drawyng ſome ſet ſuche a compaſſe, as thoughe
they woulde tourne about, and blyſſe all the feelde :
Other heaue theyr hand nowe vp nowe downe, that a
man can not decerne wherat they wolde ſhote, an
other waggeth the vpper ende of his bow one way,
the neyther ende an other waye. An other wil ſtand
poyntinge his ſhafte at the marke a good whyle and by
and by he wyll gyue hym a whip, and awaye or a man
wite. An other maketh ſuche a wreſtling with his
gere, as thoughe he were able to ſhoote no more as
longe as he lyued. An other draweth ſoftly to ye middes, and by and by it is gon, you can not knowe howe.

An other draweth his ſhafte lowe at the breaſte,
as thoughe he woulde ſhoote at a rouynge marke, and
by and by he lifteth his arme vp pricke heyghte. An
other maketh a wrynchinge with hys backe, as though
a manne pynched hym behynde.

An other coureth downe, and layeth out his but-
tockes, as though he ſhoulde ſhoote at crowes.

An other ſetteth forwarde hys lefte legge, and draweth backe wyth head and ſhowlders, as thoughe he
pouled at a rope, or els were afrayed of ye marke.
An other draweth his ſhafte well, vntyll wythin. ii.

fyngers of the head, and than he ſtayeth a lyttle, to looke at hys marke, and that done, pouleth it vp to the head, and lowſeth : whych waye although ſumme excellent ſhoters do vſe, yet ſurely it is a faulte, and good mennes faultes are not to be folowed.

Summe men drawe to farre, ſumme to ſhorte, ſumme to ſlowlye, ſumme to quickely, ſumme holde ouer longe, ſumme let go ouer ſone.

Summe ſette theyr ſhafte on the grounde, and fetcheth him vpwarde. An other poynteth vp towarde the ſkye, and ſo bryngeth hym downewardes.

Ones I ſawe a manne whyche vſed a braſar on his cheke, or elles he had ſcratched all the ſkynne of the one ſyde, of his face, with his drawynge hand.

An other I ſawe, whiche at euerye ſhoote, after the looſe, lyfted vp his ryght legge ſo far, that he was euer in ieoperdye of faulyng.

Summe ſtampe forwarde, and ſumme leape backwarde. All theſe faultes be eyther in the drawynge, or at the looſe : with many other mo whiche you may eaſelye perceyue, and ſo go about to auoyde them.

Nowe afterwarde whan the ſhafte is gone, men haue manye faultes, whyche euell Cuſtome hath broughte them to, and ſpecially in cryinge after the ſhafte, and ſpeakynge woordes ſcarce honeſt for ſuche an honeſt paſtyme.

Suche woordes be verye tokens of an ill mynde, and manifeſte ſignes of a man that is ſubiecte to inmeaſurable affections. Good mennes eares do abhor them, and an honeſt man therfore wyl auoyde them. And beſydes thoſe whiche muſte nedes haue theyr tongue thus walkynge, other men vſe other fautes as ſome will take theyr bowe and writhe and wrinche it, to poule in his ſhafte, when it flyeth wyde, as yf he draue a carte. Some wyll gyue two or. iii. ſtrydes forwarde, daunſing and hoppynge after his ſhafte, as long as it flyeth, as though he were a madman. Some which feare to be to farre gone, runne backewarde as it were to poule his ſhafte backe. Another runneth forwarde, whan he feareth to be ſhort, heau-

ynge after his armes, as though he woulde helpe his
shafte to flye. An other writhes or runneth a syde, to
poule in his shafte strayght. One lifteth vp his heele,
and so holdeth his foote still, as longe as his shafte
flyeth. An other casteth his arme backewarde after
the lowse. And an other swynges hys bowe aboute
hym, as it were a man with a staffe to make roume in
a game place. And manye other faultes there be,
whiche nowe come not to my remembraunce. Thus
as you haue hearde, manye archers wyth marrynge
theyr face and countenaunce, wyth other partes, of
theyr bodye, as it were menne that shoulde daunce an-
tiques, be farre from the comelye porte in shootynge,
whiche he that woulde be excellent muste looke for.

Of these faultes I haue verie many my selfe, but I
talke not of my shootynge, but of the generall nature
of shootynge. Nowe ymagin an Archer that is cleane
wythout al these faultes and I am sure euerye man
would be delyted to se hym shoote.

And althoughe suche a perfyte cumlynesse can not
be expressed wyth any precepte of teachyng, as Cicero
and other learned menne do saye, yet I wyll speake
(accordyng to my lytle knowlege) that thing in it,
whych yf you folowe, althoughe you shall not be
wythout fault, yet your fault shal neyther quickly be
perceued, nor yet greatly rebuked of them that stande
by. Standyng, nockyng, drawyng, holdyng, lowsyng,
done as they shoulde be done, make fayre shootynge.

The fyrste poynte is when a man shoulde shote, to
take suche footyng and standyng as shal be
both cumlye to the eye and profytable to   Standynge.
hys vse, settyng hys countenaunce and al the other partes
of hys bodye after suche a behauiour and porte, that
bothe al hys strengthe may be employed to hys owne
moost a[d]uantage, and hys shoot made and handled
to other mens pleasure and delyte. A man must not
go to hastely to it, for that is rashnesse, nor yet make
to much to do about it, for yat is curiositie, ye one
fote must not stande to far from the other, leste he
stoupe to muche whyche is vnsemelye, nor yet to nere

together, lefte he ftande to ftreyght vp, for fo a man fhall neyther vfe hys ftrengthe well, nor yet ftande ftedfaftlye.

The meane betwyxt bothe muft be kept, a thing more pleafaunte to behoulde when it is done, than eafie to be taught howe it fhoulde be done.

To nocke well is the eafieft poynte of all, and there in is no cunninge, but onelye dylygente hede   *Nockynge.* gyuyng, to fet hys fhafte neyther to hye nor to lowe, but euen ftreyght ouertwharte hys bowe, Vnconftante nockynge maketh a man leefe hys lengthe.

And befydes that, yf the fhafte hande be hye and the bowe hande lowe, or contrarie, bothe the bowe is in ieopardye of brekynge, and the fhafte, yf it be lytle, wyll ftart : yf it be great it wyll hobble. Nocke the cocke fether vpward alwayes as I toulde you when I defcribed the fether. And be fure alwayes yat your ftringe flip not out of the nocke, for then al is in ieopardye of breakynge.

Drawynge well is the beft parte of   *Drawynge.* fhootyng. Men in oulde tyme vfed other maner of drawynge than we do. They vfed to drawe low at the breft, to the ryght pap and no farther, and this to be trew is playne in Homer, where he defcrybeth Pandarus fhootynge.   *Iliad. 4.*

Vp to the pap his ftringe dyd he pul, his fhafte to the hard heed.

The noble women of Scythia vfed the fame fafhyon of fhootyng low at the breft, and bicaufe there lefte pap hindred theyr fhootynge at the lowfe they cut it of when they were yonge, and therfore be they called in lackynge theyr pap Amazones. Nowe a dayes contrarye wyfe we drawe to the ryghte eare and not to the pap. Whether the olde waye in drawynge low to the pap, or the new way to draw a loft to   *Procopius* the eare be better, an excellente wryter in   *Hift. Pers.* Greke called Procopius doth faye hys mynde, fhewyng yat the oulde fafhyon in drawing to ye pap was nought of no pithe, and therfore faith Procopius: is Artyllarye difprayfed in Homer whych calleth it ἀβληχρόν. I. Weake and able to do no good. Draw-

yng to the eare he prayſeth greatly, whereby men
ſhoote bothe ſtronger and longer : drawynge therfore
to the eare is better than to drawe at the breſte.
And one thyng commeth into my remembraunce nowe
Philologe when I ſpeake of drawyng, that I neuer
red of other kynde of ſhootyng, than drawing wyth a
mans hand ether to the breſte or eare : This thyng
haue I ſought for in Homer Herodotus and Plutarch,
and therfore I meruayle how croſbowes came fyrſt vp,
of the which I am ſure a man ſhall finde
lytle mention made on in any good Authour.   Crosbowes..

Leo the Emperoure woulde haue hys ſouldyers
drawe quycklye in warre, for that maketh a ſhaft flie
a pace.   In ſhootynge at the pryckes, haſty and quicke
drawing is neyther ſure nor yet cumlye.   Therfore to
drawe eaſely and vniformely, that is for to ſaye not
waggyng your hand, now vpwarde, now downewarde, but
alwayes after one faſhion vntil you come to the rig or
ſhouldring of ye head, is beſt both for profit and ſemeli-
neſſe, Holdynge muſt not be longe, for it
bothe putteth a bowe in ieopardy, and alſo   Holding.
marreth a mans ſhoote, it muſt be ſo lytle yat it may be
perceyued better in a mans mynde when it is done, than
ſeene with a mans eyes when it is in doyng.   Lowsynge.

Lowſynge muſte be muche lyke. So
quycke and hard yat it be wyth oute all girdes, ſo
ſofte and gentle that the ſhafte flye not as it were
ſente out of a bow caſe.   The meane betwixte bothe,
whyche is perſyte lowſynge is not ſo hard to be
folowed in ſhootynge as it is to be deſcrybed in
teachyng.   For cleane lowſynge you muſt take hede of
hyttynge any thynge aboute you.   And for
the ſame purpoſe Leo the Emperour would   Leo.
haue al Archers in war to haue both theyr heades
pouled, and there berdes ſhauen lefte the heare of theyr
heades ſhuld ſtop the ſyght of the eye, the heere of
theyr berdes hinder the courſe of the ſtrynge.

And theſe preceptes I am ſure Philologe yf you folowe
in ſtandyng, nockyng, drawynge, holdynge, and lowſynge,
ſhal bryng you at the laſt to excellent fayre ſhootynge.

Phi. All thefe thynges Toxophile althoughe I bothe nowe perceyue them thorowlye, and alfo wyll remember them dilligently: yet to morowe or fome other day when you haue leafure we wyll go to the pryckes, and put them by lytle and lytle in experience. For teachynge not fol-owed, doeth euen as muche good as bookes neuer looked vpon. But nowe feing you haue taught me to fhote fayre, I praye you tel me fomwhat, how I fhould fhoote nere lefte that prouerbe myght be fayd iuftlye of me fome-tyme. He fhootes lyke a gentle man fayre and far of.

Tox. He that can fhoote fayre, lacketh nothyng but fhootyng ftreyght and kepyng of a length wherof commeth hyttynge of the marke, the ende both of fhootyng and alfo of thys our communication. The handlyng of ye wether and the mark bicaufe they belong to fhootyng ftreyghte, and kepynge of a lengthe, I wyll ioyne them togyther, fhewinge what thinges belonge to kepynge of a lengthe, and what to fhootynge ftreyght.

The greateft enemy of fhootyng is the wynde and the wether, wherby true kepyng a lengthe is chefely hindred. If this thing were not, men by teaching might be brought to wonderful neare fhootynge. It is no maruayle if the litle poore fhafte being fent alone, fo high in to the ayer, into a great rage of wether, one wynde toffinge it that waye, an other thys waye, it is no maruayle I faye, thoughe it leefe the lengthe, and miffe that place, where the fhooter had thought to haue founde it. Greter matters than fhotynge are vnder the rule and wyll of the wether, as faylynge on the fea. And lykewife as in fayling, the chefe poynt of a good mafter, is to knowe the tokens of chaunge of wether, the courfe of the wyndes, that therby he maye the better come to the Hauen: euen fo the beft propertie of a good fhooter, is to knowe the nature of the wyndes, with hym and agaynfte hym, that thereby he maye the nerer fhote at hys marke. Wyfe mayfters whan they canne not winne the befte hauen, they are gladde of the nexte: Good fhooters alfo, yat can not whan they would hit

Wynde and wether.

the marke, wil labour to come as nigh as they can. All thinges in this worlde be vnperfite and vnconftant, therfore let euery man acknowlege hys owne weake-neffe, in all matters great and fmal, weyghtye and merye, and glorifie him, in whome only perfyte perfit-neffe is. But nowe fir, he that wyll at all aduentures vfe the feas knowinge no more what is to be done in a tempeft than in a caulme, fhall foone becumme a marchaunt of Eele fkinnes : fo that fhoter whiche putteth no difference, but fhooteth in all lyke, in rough wether and fayre, fhall alwayes put his wyn-ninges in his eyes.

Lytle botes and thinne boordes, can not endure the rage of a tempeft. Weake bowes, and lyght fhaftes can not ftande in a rough wynde. And lykewyfe as a blynde man which fhoulde go to a place where he had neuer ben afore, that hath but one ftrayghte waye to it, and of eyther fyde hooles and pyttes to faule into, nowe falleth in to this hole and than into that hole, and neuer commeth to his iourney ende, but wandereth alwaies here and there, farther and farther of : So that archer which ignoruntly fhoteth confidering neyther fayer nor foule, ftandynge nor nockynge, fether nor head, drawynge nor lowfyng, nor yet any compace, fhall alwayes fhote fhorte and gone, wyde and farre of, and neuer comme nere, excepte perchaunce he ftumble fumtyme on the marke. For ignoraunce is nothynge elles but mere blyndeneffe.

A mayfter of a fhippe firft learneth to knowe the cummyng of a tempeft, the nature of it, and howe to behaue hym felfe in it, eyther with chaungynge his courfe, or poullynge downe his hye toppes and brode fayles, beyng glad to efchue as muche of the wether as he can : Euen fo a good archer wyl fyrft wyth dilligent vfe and markynge the wether, learne to knowe the nature of the wynde, and wyth wyfedome, wyll meafure in hys mynde, howe muche it wyll alter his fhoote, eyther in lengthe kepynge, or els in ftreyght fhotynge, and fo with chaunging his ftandynge, or takynge an other fhafte, the whiche he knoweth perfytlye to be fitter for his pourpofe, eyther bycaufe it is lower fethered, or els bycaufe it is of a better wyng, wyll fo handle wyth difcretion hys fhoote, that he fhall feeme rather to haue the wether vnder hys rule, by good hede gyuynge, than the wether to rule hys fhafte by any fodayne chaungyng.

Therefore in fhootynge there is as muche difference betwixt an archer that is a good wether man, and an other that knoweth and marketh nothynge, as is betwixte a blynde man and he that can fe.

Thus, as concernynge the wether, a perfyte archer mufte firfte learne to knowe the fure flyghte of his fhaftes, that he may be boulde alwayes, to truft them, than mufte he learne by daylye experience all maner of kyndes of wether, the tokens of it, whan it wyl cumme, the nature of it when it is cumme, the diuerfitie and alterynge of it, whan it chaungeth, the decreafe and diminifhing of it, whan it ceafeth. Thirdly, thefe thinges knowen, and euery fhoote diligentlye marked, than mufta man compare alwayes, the wether and his footyng togyther, and with difcretion meafure them fo, that what fo euer the roughe wether fhall take awaye from hys fhoote the fame fhall iufte footynge reftore agayne to hys fhoote.

Thys thynge well knowen, and difcretelye handeled in fhootynge, bryngeth more profite and commendation and prayfe to an Archer, than any other thynge befydes.

He that woulde knowe perfectly the winde and wether, mufte put differences betwixte tymes. For diuerfitie of tyme caufeth diuerfitie of wether, as in the whole yeare, Sprynge tyme, Somer, Faule of the leafe, and Winter; Lykewyfe in one day Mornynge, Noonetyme, After noone, and Euentyde, bothe alter the wether, and chaunge a mannes bowe wyth the ftrength of man alfo. And to knowe that this is fo, is ynough for a fhoter and artillerie, and not to ferche the caufe, why it fhoulde be fo: whiche belongeth to a learned man and Philofophie.

In confyderinge the tyme of the yeare, a wyfe Archer wyll folowe a good Shipman. In Winter and rough

wether, fmall bootes and lytle pinkes forfake the feas :
And at one tyme of the yeare, no Gallies come
abrode ; So lykewyfe weake Archers, vfyng fmall and
holowe fhaftes, with bowes of litle pith, mufte be content to gyue place for a tyme.

And this I do not faye, eyther to difcommende or
difcourage any weake fhooter : For lykewyfe, as there
is no fhippe better than Gallies be, in a fofte and a
caulme fea, fo no man fhooteth cumlier or nerer hys
marke, than fome weake archers doo, in a fayre and
cleare daye.

Thus euery archer muft knowe, not onelye what
bowe and fhafte is fitteft for him to fhoote withall, but
alfo whattyme and feafon is beft for hym to fhote in.
And furely, in al other matters to, amonge al degrees
of men, there is no man which doth any thing eyther
more difcretely for his commendation, or yet more
profitable for his aduauntage, than he which wyll knowe
perfitly for what matter and for what tyme he is
mooft apte and fit. Yf men woulde go aboute matters whych they fhould do and be fit for, and not
fuche thynges whyche wylfullye they defyre and yet
be vnfit for, verely greater matters in the common
welthe than fhootyng fhoulde be in better cafe than
they be. This ignorauncie in men whyche know
not for what tyme, and to what thynge they be fit,
caufeth fome wyfhe to be riche, for whome it were
better a greate deale to be poore : other to be
medlynge in euery mans matter, for whome it were
more honeftie to be quiete and ftyll. Some to defire
to be in the Courte, whiche be borne and be fitter
rather for the carte. Somme to be mayfters and rule
other, whiche neuer yet began to rule them felfe : fome
alwayes to iangle and taulke, whych rather fhoulde
heare and kepe filence. Some to teache, which
rather fhould learne. Some to be preftes, whiche
were fytter to be clerkes. And thys peruerfe iudgement of ye worlde, when men mefure them felfe a
miffe, bringeth muche myforder and greate vnfemely-
neffe to the hole body of the common wealth, as yf

a manne fhould were his hoofe vpon his head, or a
woman go wyth a fworde and a buckeler euery man
would take it as a greate vncumlyneffe although it be
but a tryfle in refpecte of the other.

Thys peruerfe iudgement of men hindreth no thynge
fo much as learnynge, bycaufe commonlye thofe whych
be vnfitteft for learnyng, be cheyfly fet to learnynge.

As yf a man nowe a dayes haue two fonnes, the one
impotent, weke, fickly, lifpynge, ftuttynge, and
ftamerynge, or hauynge any miffhape in hys bodye :
what doth the father of fuche one commonlye faye ?
This boye is fit for nothynge els, but to fet to
lernyng and make a preft of, as who would fay, yat
outcaftes of the worlde, hauyng neyther countenaunce
tounge nor wit (for of a peruerfe bodye cummeth commonly a peruerfe mynde) be good ynough to make
thofe men of, whiche fhall be appoynted to preache
Goddes holye woorde, and minifter hys bleffed
facramentes, befydes other mooft weyghtye matters in
the common welthe put ofte tymes, and worthelye to
learned mennes difcretion and charge : whan rather
fuche an offyce fo hygh in dignitie, fo godlye in adminiftration, fhulde be committed to no man, whiche
fhulde not haue a countenaunce full of cumlyneffe to
allure good menne, a bodye full of manlye authoritie to
feare ill men, a witte apte for al learnynge with tongue
and voyce, able to perfwade all men. And although
fewe fuche men as thefe can be founde in a common
wealthe, yet furelye a godly difpofed man, will bothe
in his mynde thyncke fit, and with al his ftudie labour to
get fuch men as I fpeke of, or rather better, if better
can be gotten for fuche an hie adminiftration, whiche
is moft properlye appoynted to goddes owne matters
and bufineffes.

This peruerfe iugement of fathers as concernynge
the fitneffe and vnfitneffe of theyr chyldren caufeth the
common wealthe haue many vnfit minifters : And
feyng that minifters be, as a man woulde fay, inftrumentes wherwith the common wealthe doeth worke
all her matters withall, I maruayle howe it chaunceth

yat a pore fhomaker hath fo much wit, yat he will prepare no inftrument for his fcience neither knyfe nor
aule, nor nothing els whiche is not very fitte for him :
the common wealthe can be content to take at a fonde
fathers hande, the rifraffe of the worlde, to make thofe
inftrumentes of, wherwithal fhe fhoulde worke ye
hieft matters vnder heauen.   And furely an aule of
lead is not fo vnprofitable in a fhomakers fhop, as
an vnfit minifter, made of groffe metal, is vnfemely in ye
common welth.   Fathers in olde time among ye noble
Perfians might not do with theyr children as they
thought good, but as the iudgement of the common
wealth al wayes thought beft.   This fault of fathers
bringeth many a blot with it, to the great deformitie of
the common wealthe : and here furely I can prayfe
gentlewomen which haue alwayes at hande theyr
glaffes, to fe if any thinge be amiffe, and fo will
amende it, yet the common wealth hauing ye glaffe of
knowlege in euery mans hand, doth fe fuch vncumlines
in it : and yet winketh at it.   This faulte and many
fuche lyke, myght be fone wyped awaye, yf fathers
woulde beftow their children on yat thing alwayes,
whervnto nature hath ordeined them mofte apte and
fit.   For if youth be grafted ftreyght, and not a wrye,
the hole common welth wil florifh therafter.   Whan
this is done, than mufte euery man beginne to be more
ready to amende hym felfe, than to checke an other,
meafuryng their matters with that wife prouerbe of
Apollo, *Knowe thy felfe* : that is to faye, learne to
knowe what thou arte able, fitte, and apt vnto, and
folowe that.

   This thinge fhulde be bothe cumlie to the common
wealthe, and mooft profitable for euery one, as doth
appere very well in all wife mennes deades, and
fpecially to turne to our communication agayne in
fhootynge, where wife archers haue alwayes theyr
inftrumentes fit for theyr ftrength, and wayte euermore fuche tyme and wether, as is mofte agreable to
their gere.   Therfore if the wether be to fore, and
vnfit for your fhootynge, leaue of for that daye, and

wayte a better feafon. For he is a foole yat wyl not
go, whome neceffitie driueth.

Phi, This communication of yours pleafed me fo
well Toxophile, that furelye I was not haftie to calle
you, to defcrybe forthe the wether but with all my
harte woulde haue fuffered you yet to haue ftande
longer in this matter. For thefe thinges touched of you
by chaunfe, and by the waye, be farre aboue the matter
it felfe, by whofe occafion ye other were broughte in.

Tox. Weyghtye matters they be in dede, and fit
bothe in an other place to be fpoken: and of an
other man than I am, to be handled. And bycaufe
meane men muft meddle wyth meane matters, I wyl
go forwarde in defcrybyng the wether, as concernynge
fhooting: and as I toulde you before, In the hole
yere, Spring tyme, Somer, Fal of the leafe, and
Winter: and in one day, Morning, Noone tyme,
After noone, and Euentyde, altereth the courfe of the
wether, the pith of the bowe, the ftrength of the man.
And in euery one of thefe times the wether altereth,
as fumtyme wyndie, fumtyme caulme, fumtyme cloudie,
fumtyme clere, fumtyme hote, fumtyme coulde, the
wynde fumtyme moiftye and thicke, fumtyme drye and
fmothe. A litle winde in a moyftie day, ftoppeth a
fhafte more than a good whifkynge wynde in a clere
daye. Yea, and I haue fene whan there hath bene no
winde at all, the ayer fo miftie and thicke, that both
the markes haue ben wonderfull great. And ones,
whan the Plage was in Cambrige, the downe winde
twelue fcore marke for the fpace of. iii. weekes, was.
xiii. fcore, and an halfe, and into the wynde, beynge
not very great, a great deale aboue. xiiii. fcore.

The winde is fumtyme playne vp and downe,
whiche is commonly mofte certayne, and requireth
leaft knowlege, wherin a meane fhoter with meane
geare, if he can fhoote home, maye make beft fhifte.
A fyde wynde tryeth an archer and good gere verye
muche. Sumtyme it bloweth a lofte, fumtyme hard
by the grounde: Sumtyme it bloweth by blaftes. and
fumtyme it continueth al in one : Sumtyme ful fide

wynde, fumtyme quarter with hym and more, and lykewyfe agaynft hym, as a man with caftynge vp lyght
graffe, or els if he take good hede, fhall fenfibly learne
by experience. To fe the wynde, with a man his eyes,
it is vnpoffible, the nature of it is fo fyne, and fubtile,
yet this experience of the wynde had I ones my felfe,
and that was in the great fnowe that fell. iiii. yeares
agoo : I rode in the hye waye betwixt Topcliffe vpon
Swale, and Borowe bridge, the waye beyng fumwhat
trodden afore, by waye fayrynge men. The feeldes
on bothe fides were playne and laye almoft yearde
depe with fnowe, the nyght afore had ben a litle frofte,
fo yat the fnowe was hard and crufted aboue. That
morning the fun fhone bright and clere, the winde was
whiftelinge a lofte, and fharpe accordynge to the tyme
of the yeare. The fnowe in the hye waye laye lowfe
and troden wyth horfe feete : fo as the wynde blewe,
it toke the lowfe fnow with it, and made it fo flide
vpon the fnowe in the felde whyche was harde and
crufted by reafon of the froft ouer nyght, that therby
I myght fe verye wel, the hole nature of the wynde as
it blewe yat daye. And I had a great delyte and
pleafure to marke it, whyche maketh me now far
better to remember it. Sometyme the wynd would
be not paft. ii. yeardes brode, and fo it would carie
the fnowe as far as I could fe. An other tyme the
fnow woulde blowe ouer halfe the felde at ones.
Sometyme the fnowe woulde tomble foftly, by and
by it would flye wonderfull faft. And thys I perceyued alfo that ye wind goeth by ftreames and
not hole togither. For I fhould fe one ftreame
wyth in a Score on me, than the fpace of. ii. fcore
no fnow would ftirre, but after fo muche quantitie of
grounde, an other ftreame of fnow at the fame very
tyme fhould be caryed lykewyfe, but not equally. For
the one would ftande ftyll when the other flew a pace,
and fo contynewe fomtyme fwiftlyer fometime flowlyer,
fometime broder, fometime narrower, as far as I coulde
fe. Nor it flewe not ftreight, but fometyme it crooked
thys waye fometyme that waye, and fomtyme it ran

round aboute in a compafe. And fomtyme the
fnowe wold be lyft clene from the ground vp in to the
ayre, and by and by it would be al clapt to the grounde
as though there had bene no winde at all, ftreightway
it woulde rife and flye agayne.

And that whych was the mooft meruayle of al, at
one tyme. ii. driftes of fnowe flewe, the one out of the
Weft into ye Eaft, the other out of the North in to ye
Eaft : And I faw. ii. windes by reafon of ye fnow the
one croffe ouer the other, as it had bene two hye
wayes. And agayne I fhoulde here the wynd blow in
the ayre, when nothing was ftirred at the ground.
And when all was ftill where I rode, not verye far from
me the fnow fhould be lifted wonderfully. This experience made me more meruaile at ye nature of the
wynde, than it made me conning in ye knowlege of
ye wynd : but yet therby I learned perfitly that it is
no meruayle at al thoughe men in a wynde leafe theyr
length in fhooting, feying fo many wayes the wynde is
fo variable in blowynge.

But feynge that a Mayfter of a fhyp, be he neuer fo
cunnynge, by the vncertayntye of the wynde, leefeth
many tymes both lyfe and goodes, furelye it is no
wonder, though a ryght good Archer, by the felf fame
wynde fo variable in hys owne nature, fo vnfenfyble to
oure nature, leefe manye a fhoote and game.

The more vncertaine and difceyuable the wynd is,
the more hede muft a wyfe Archer gyue to know the
gyles of it.

He yat doth miftruft is feldome begiled. For
although therby he fhall not attayne to that which
is beft, yet by thefe meanes he fhall at leafte auoyde
yat whyche is worft. Befyde al thefe kindes of windes
you muft take hede yf you fe anye cloude apere and
gather by lytle and litle agaynft you, or els yf a fhowre
of raine be lyke to come vpon you : for than both the
dryuing of the wether and the thyckynge of the ayre
increafeth the marke, when after ye fhowre al thynges
are contrary clere and caulme, and the marke for the
moft parte new to begyn agayne. You muft take

hede alſo yf euer you ſhote where one of the markes
or both ſtondes a lytle ſhort of a hye wall, for there
you may be eaſlye begyled. Yf you take graſſe and
caſte it vp to ſe howe the wynde ſtandes, manye tymes
you ſhal ſuppoſe to ſhoote downe the wynde, when you
ſhote cleane agaynſt the wynde. And a good reaſon
why. For the wynd whych commeth in dede againſt
you, redoundeth bake agayne at the wal, and whyrleth
backe to the prycke and a lytle farther and than
turneth agayne, euen as a vehement water doeth
agaynſte a rocke or an hye braye whyche example of
water as it is more ſenſible to a mans eyes, ſo it is
neuer a whyt the trewer than this of the wynde. So
that the graſſe caſte vp ſhall flee that waye whyche in
dede is the longer marke and deceyue quycklye a
ſhooter that is not ware of it.

This experience had I ones my ſelfe at Norwytch in
the chapel felde wythin the waulles. And thys waye
I vſed in ſhootynge at thoſe markes.

When I was in the myd way betwixt the markes
whyche was an open place, there I toke a fether or a
lytle lyght graſſe and ſo as well as I coulde, learned
how the wynd ſtoode, that done I wente to the prycke
as faſte as I coulde, and according as I had founde ye
wynde when I was in the mid waye, ſo I was fayne
than to be content to make the beſt of my ſhoote that
I coulde. Euen ſuche an other experience had I in a
maner at Yorke, at the prickes, lying betwixte the
caſtell and Ouſe ſyde. And although you ſmile
Philologe, to heare me tell myne owne fondenes:
yet ſeing you wil nedes haue me teach you ſomwhat
in ſhotyng, I muſt nedes ſomtyme tel you of myne
owne experience, and the better I may do ſo, by-
cauſe Hippocrates in teachynge phyſike,   Hippo. De
vſeth verye muche the ſame waye. Take   morb. vulg.
heede alſo when you ſhoote nere the ſea coſt,
although you be. ii. or. iii. miles from the ſea, for
there diligent markinge ſhall eſpie in the moſt
clere daye wonderfull chaunginge. The ſame is to
be conſidered lykewyſe by a riuer ſide ſpeciallie if

it ebbe and flowe, where he yat taketh diligent hede
of ye tide and wether, ſhal lightly take away al yat he
ſhooteth for.   And thus of ye nature of windes and
wether according to my marking you haue hearde
Philologe : and hereafter you ſhal marke farre mo
your ſelfe, if you take hede.   And the wether thus
marked as I tolde you afore, you muſte take hede,
of youre ſtanding, yat therby you may win as much
as you ſhal looſe by the wether.

Phi. I ſe well it is no maruell though a man miſſe
many tymes in ſhootyng, ſeing ye wether is ſo vncon-
ſtant in blowing, but yet there is one thing whiche
many archers vſe, yat ſhall cauſe a man haue leſſe
nede to marke the wether, and that is Ame gyuing.

Tox. Of gyuyng Ame, I can not tel wel, what I
ſhuld ſay.   For in a ſtraunge place it taketh away al
occaſion of foule game, which is ye only prayſe of it,
yet by my iudgement, it hindreth ye knowlege of
ſhotyng, and maketh men more negligente : ye which
is a diſprayſe.   Though Ame be giuen, yet take hede,
for at an other mans ſhote you can not wel take Ame,
nor at your owne neither, bycauſe the wether wil
alter, euen in a minute ; and at the one marke and not
at the other, and trouble your ſhafte in the ayer, when
you ſhal perceyue no wynde at the ground, as I my
ſelfe haue ſene ſhaftes tumble a lofte, in a very fayer
daye.   There may be a fault alſo, in drawing or lowſynge, and many thynges mo, whiche all togyther, are
required to kepe a iuſt length.   But to go forward the
nexte poynte after the markyng of your wether, is the
takyng of your ſtandyng.   And in a ſide winde you
muſt ſtand ſumwhat croſſe in to the wynde, for ſo
ſhall you ſhoote the ſurer.   Whan you haue taken
good footing, than muſt you looke at your ſhafte, yat
no earthe, nor weete be lefte vpon it, for ſo ſhould you
leeſe the lengthe.   You muſt loke at the head alſo,
left it haue had any ſtrype, at the laſt ſhoote.   A
ſtripe vpon a ſtone, many tymes will bothe marre
the head, croke the ſhafte, and hurte the fether,
wherof the left of them all, wyll cauſe a man leaſe

his lengthe. For fuche thinges which chaunce euery
fhoote, many archers vfe to haue fumme place made
in theyr cote, fitte for a lytle fyle, a ftone, a Hun-
fyfhfkin, and a cloth to dreffe the fhaft fit agayne at
all nedes. Thys muft a man looke to euer when
he taketh vp his fhaft. And the heade maye be made
to fmothe, which wil caufe it flye to far : when youre
fhafte is fit, than muft you take your bow euen in the
middes or elles you fhall both leafe your lengthe, and
put youre bowe in ieopardye of breakynge. Nockynge iufte is next, which is muche of the fame nature.
Than drawe equallye, lowfe equallye, wyth houldynge
your hande euer of one heighte to kepe trew compaffe. To looke at your fhafte hede at the lowfe, is
the greateft helpe to kepe a lengthe that can be,
whych thyng yet hindreth excellent fhotyng, bicaufe
a man can not fhote ftreight perfitlye excepte he
looke at his marke : yf I fhould fhoote at a line and
not at the marke, I woulde alwayes loke at my fhaft
ende, but of thys thyng fome what afterwarde. Nowe
if you marke the wether diligentlye, kepe your ftandynge iuftely, houlde and nocke trewlye, drawe and
lowfe equallye, and kepe your compace certaynelye,
you fhall neuer miffe of your lengthe.

Phi. Then there is nothyng behinde to make me
hit ye marke but onely fhooting ftreight.

Tox. No trewlye. And fyrfte I wyll tell you what
fhyftes Archers haue founde to fhoote ftreyght, than
what is the beft waye to fhoote ftreyght. As the
wether belongeth fpecially to kepe a lengthe (yet
a fide winde belongeth alfo to fhote ftreight) euen
in the nature of the pricke is to fhote ftreight. The
lengthe or fhortneffe of the marke is alwayes vnder
the rule of the wether, yet fumwhat there is in ye
marke, worthye to be marked of an Archer. Yf the
prickes ftand of a ftreyght plane ground they be ye
beft to fhote at. Yf ye marke ftand on a hyl fyde or
ye ground be vnequal with pittes and turninge wayes
betwyxte the markes, a mans eye fhall thynke that

to be ſtreight whyche is croked: The experience of
this thing is ſene in payntynge, the cauſe of it is
knowen by learnynge.

And it is ynoughe for an archer to marke it and
take hede of it. The cheife cauſe why men can not
ſhoote ſtreight, is bicauſe they loke at theyr ſhaft: and
this fault commeth bycauſe a man is not taught to
ſhote when he is yong. Yf he learne to ſhoote by himſelfe he is afrayde to pull the ſhafte throughe the
bowe, and therfore looketh alwayes at hys ſhafte: yll
vſe confirmeth thys faulte as it doth many mo.

And men continewe the longer in thys faulte bycauſe
it is ſo good to kepe a lengthe wyth al, and yet to ſhote
ſtreight, they haue inuented ſome waies, to eſpie a tree
or a hill beyonde the marke, or elles to haue ſumme
notable thing betwixt ye markes: and ones I ſawe a
good archer whiche did caſte of his gere, and layd his
quiuer with it, euen in the midway betwixt ye prickes.
Summe thought he dyd ſo, for ſauegarde of his gere:
I ſuppoſe he did it, to ſhoote ſtreyght withall. Other
men vſe to eſpie ſumme marke almooſt a bow wide
of ye pricke, and than go about to kepe him ſelfe on
yat hande that the prycke is on, which thing howe
much good it doth, a man wil not beleue, that doth
not proue it. Other and thoſe very good archers
in drawyng, loke at the marke vntill they come almoſt
to ye head, than they looke at theyr ſhafte, but at ye
very lowſe, with a ſeconde ſight they fynde theyr marke
agayne. This way and al other afore of me reherſed
are but ſhiftes and not to be folowed in ſhotyng
ſtreyght. For hauyng a mans eye alwaye on his marke,
is the only waye to ſhote ſtreght, yea and I ſuppoſe ſo
redye and eaſy a way yf it be learned in youth and
confirmed with vſe, yat a man ſhall neuer miſſe therin.
Men doubt yet in loking at ye mark what way is
beſt whether betwixt the bowe and the ſtringe, aboue
or beneth hys hand, and many wayes moo: yet it
maketh no great matter which way a man looke
at his marke yf it be ioyned with comly ſhotynge.
The diuerſitie of mens ſtandyng and drawyng cauſeth

diuerſe men [to] loke at theyr marke diuerſe wayes: yet
they al lede a mans hand to ſhoote ſtreight yf nothyng
els ſtoppe. So that cumlyneſſe is the only iudge of beſt
lokyng at the marke. Some men wonder why in caſting
a mans eye at ye marke, the hand ſhould go ſtreyght.
Surely ye he conſydered the nature of a mans eye, he
wolde not wonder at it: For this I am certayne of,
that no ſeruaunt to hys mayſter, no chylde to hys
father is ſo obedient, as euerye ioynte and pece of the
body is to do what ſoeuer the eye biddes. The eye is
the guide, the ruler and the ſuccourer of al the other
partes. The hande, the foote and other members
dare do nothynge without the eye, as doth appere on
the night and darke corners. The eye is the very
tonge wherwith wyt and reaſon doth ſpeke to euery
parte of the body, and the wyt doth not ſo ſone ſignifye
a thynge by the eye, as euery parte is redye to folow,
or rather preuent the byddyng of the eye. Thys is
playne in many thinges, but moſt euident in fence and
feyghtynge, as I haue heard men ſaye. There euery
parte ſtandynge in feare to haue a blowe, runnes to the
eye for helpe, as yonge chyldren do to ye mother: the
foote, the hand, and al wayteth vpon the eye. Yf the
eye byd ye hand either beare of, or ſmite, or the foote
ether go forward, or backeward, it doth ſo: And that
whyche is mooſt wonder of all the one man lookynge
ſtedfaſtly at the other mans eye and not at his hand,
wyl, euen as it were, rede in his eye where he
purpoſeth to ſmyte nexte, for the eye is nothyng els
but a certayne wyndowe for wit to ſhote oute hir
head at.

Thys wonderfull worke of god in makynge all the
members ſo obedient to the eye, is a pleaſaunte thynge
to remember and loke vpon: therfore an Archer maye
be ſure in learnyng to looke at hys marke when he is
yong, alwayes to ſhoote ſtreyghte. The thynges that
hynder a man whyche looketh at hys marke, to ſhote
ſtreyght, be theſe: A ſyde wynde, a bowe either to
ſtronge, or els to weake, an ill arme, whan the fether
runneth on the bowe to much, a byg breſted ſhafte, for

hym that fhoteth vnder hande, bycaufe it wyll hobble: a little brefted fhafte for hym yat fhoteth aboue ye hande, bicaufe it wyl ftarte: a payre of windynge prickes, and many other thinges mo, which you fhal marke your felfe, and as ye knowe them, fo learne to amend them. If a man woulde leaue to looke at his fhafte, and learne to loke at his marke, he maye vfe this waye, whiche a good fhooter tolde me ones that he did. Let him take his bowe on the nyght, and fhoote at. ii. lightes, and there he fhall be compelled to looke alwayes at his marke, and neuer at his fhafte: This thing ones or twyfe vfed wyl caufe hym forfake lokynge at hys fhafte. Yet let hym take hede of fettynge his fhafte in the bowe.

Thus Philologe to fhoote ftreyght is the leafte mayfterie of all, yf a manne order hym felfe thereafter, in hys youthe. And as for keypynge a lengthe, I am fure the rules whiche I gaue you, will neuer difceyue you, fo that there fhal lacke nothynge, eyther of hittinge the marke alwayes, or elles verye nere fhotynge, excepte the faulte be onely in youre owne felfe, whiche maye come. ii. wayes, eyther in hauing a faynt harte or courage, or elles in fufferynge your felfe ouer muche to be led with affection: yf a mans mynde fayle hym, the bodye whiche is ruled by the mynde, can neuer do his duetie, yf lacke of courage were not, men myght do mo maftries than they do, as doeth appere in leapynge and vaultinge.

All affections and fpecially anger, hurteth bothe mynde and bodye. The mynde is blynde therby: and yf the mynde be blynde, it can not rule the bodye aright. The body both blood and bone, as they fay, is brought out of his ryght courfe by anger: Wherby a man lacketh his right ftrengthe, and therfore can not fhoote wel. Yf thefe thynges be auoyded (wherof I wyll fpeake no more, both bycaufe they belong not properly to fhoting, and alfo you can teache me better, in them, than I you) and al the preceptes which I haue gyuen you, dilligently marked, no doubt ye fhal fhoote as well as euer man dyd yet, by the grace of God.

Thys communication handled by me Philologe, as I knowe wel not perfytly, yet as I fuppofe truelye you muft take in good worthe, wherin if diuers thinges do not all togyther pleafe you, thanke youre felfe, whiche woulde haue me rather faulte in mere follye, to take that thynge in hande whyche I was not able for to perfourme, than by any honefte fhamefaftnes withfay your requeft and minde, which I knowe well I haue not fatiffied. But yet I wyl thinke this labour of mine the better beftowed, if tomorow or fome other daye when you haue leyfour, you wyl fpende as much tyme with me here in this fame place, in entreatinge the queftion *De origine animæ.* and the ioynyng of it with the bodye, that I maye knowe howe far Plato, Ariftotle, and the Stoicians haue waded in it.

Phi. How you haue handeled this matter Toxophile I may not well tel you my felfe nowe, but for your gentleneffe and good wyll towarde learnyng and fhotyng, I wyll be content to fhewe you any pleafure whenfoeuer you wyll: and nowe the funne is doune therfor if it pleafe you, we wil go home and drynke in my chambre, and there I wyll tell you playnelye what I thinke of this communication and alfo, what daye we will appoynt at your requeft for the other matter, to mete here agayne.

Deo gratias.

LONDONI.

In œdibus Edouardi VVhytchurch.

Cum priuilegio ad impri-
mendum folum.

1545.

1. TOXOPHILUS, THE FOUNDATION OF ASCHAM'S AFTER-FORTUNES. In a humorous letter to Queen Elizabeth, on 10. Oct. 1567. (87.): Afcham divides his idea of her into two ; and afking her in one perfonality as his friend, to intercede with her other perfonality, as queen, to relieve him from his difficulties, recounts to her the hiftory of his penfion.

"I wrote once a little book of fhooting ; King HENRY, her moft noble father, did fo well like and allow it, as he gave me a living for it; when he loft his life I loft my living; but noble King EDWARD again did firft revive it by his goodnefs, then did increafe it by his liberality ; thirdly, did confirm it by his authority under the great feal of England, which patent all this time was both a great pleafure and profit to me, faving that one un-pleafant word in that patent, called "during pleafure," turned me after to great difpleafure; for when King EDWARD went, his pleafure went with him, and my whole living went away with them both. But behold God's goodnefs towards me, and his provi-dence over me, in Queen MARY, her highnefs' fifter's time, when I had loft all, and neither looked nor hoped for any thing again, all my friends being under foot, without any labour, without my knowledge I was fuddenly fent for to come to the council. I came with all will, and departed with much comfort, for there I was fworn fecretary for the Latin tongue, becaufe fome of them knew that King EDWARD had given me that office when I was abfent in Germany, by good Mr Secretary's procurement, and becaufe fome did think I was fitter to do that office than thofe were that did exercife it. When I faw other fo willing to do for me, I was the bolder fomewhat to fpeak for myfelf. I faw WINCHESTER did like well the manner of my writing ; I faw alfo that he only was *Dominus regit me* that time. I told him that my patent and living for my Book of Shooting was loft. Well, faid he, caufe it to be written again, and I will do what I can I did fo, and here I will open to your majefty a pretty fubtlety in doing happily a good turn to myfelf, whereat perchance your majefty will fmile ; for furely I have laughed at it twenty times myfelf, and that with good caufe, for I have lived fomewhat the better for it ever fince. I caufed the fame form of the patent to be written out, but I willed a vacant place to be left for the fum. I brought it fo written to the bifhop : he afked me why the old fum was not put in. Sir, quoth I, the fault is in the writer, who hath done very ill befide, to leave the vacant place fo great, for the old word *ten* will not half fill the room, and therefore furely, except it pleafe your lordfhip to help to put in twenty pounds, that would both fill up the vacant place well now and alfo fill my purfe the better hereafter, truly I fhall be put to new charges in caufing the patent to be new written again The bifhop fell in a laughter, and forthwith went to Queen MARY and told what I had faid, who, without any more speaking, before I had done her any service, of her own bountifull goodnesse made my patent twenty pounds by year during my life, for her and her successors."

That this account is but partially correct, and that he was making a telling story to amuse the Queen, appears from his letter to Gardiner, at the time of the renewal of his pension.

(170.)   TO BISHOP GARDINER.   [About April 1554.]

In writing out my patent I have left a vacant place for your wisdom to value the sum; wherein I trust to find further favour; for I have both good cause to ask it, and better hope to obtain it, partly in consideration of my unrewarded pains and undis-charged costs, in teaching King EDWARD'S person, partly for my three years' service in the Emperor's court, but chiefly of all when King HENRY first gave it me at Greenwich, your lordship in the gallery there asking me what the king had given me, and knowing the truth, your lordship said it was too little, and most gently offered me to speak to the king for me.   But then I most happily desired your lordship to reserve that goodnesse to another time, which time God hath granted even to these days, when your lordship may now perform by favour as much as then you wished by good will, being as easy to obtain the one as to ask the other.   And I beseech your lordship see what good is offered me in writing the patent : the space which is left by chance doth seem to crave by good luck some words of length, as *viginti* or *triginta*, yea, with the help of a little dash *quadraginta* would serve best of all.   But sure as for *decem* it is somewhat with the shortest : nevertheless I for my part shall be no less contented with the one than glad with the other, and for either of both more than bound to your lordship.   And thus God prosper your lordship.   Your lordship's most bounden to serve you.

R. ASKAM.

To the Rt Reverend Father in God,
My Lord Bishop of Winchester his Grace, these.

2.   The Byzantine Emperor LEO VI [b 865—ascended the throne 1. Mar. 886—d 911], surnamed in flattery the *Philosopher*, is reputed to have written, besides other works, one entitled Τῶν ἐν πολέμοις τακτικῶν συντομός παράδοσις, (A summary exposition of the art of war). Sir John Cheke's translation into Latin, of this book. in 1543 or 1544, was published at Basle in 1554, under the title of *Leonis Imperatoris. De bellico apparatu Liber, e græco in latinum conuersus*, IOAN CHECO *Cantrabrigensi Interp.*

3.   The Dutchman PETER NANNING, latinized NANNIUS, [b 1500—d 21 July 1557] was Professor of Latin, in college of ' the three languages ' in the University of Louvain. He wrote a short tract of 34 pp, *De milite peregrino :* in which, in a dialogue

between Olympius and Xenophon, he difcuffes Archery-*v*-Guns
This tract is attached to another entitled *Oratio de ob`idione`
Louanienfi Both were publifhed at Louvain in September 1543.

4. The Frenchman JOHN RAVISIUS TEXTOR [b about 1480
—d 3 Dec: 1524] : became Rector of the Univerfity of Paris.
His *Officina* was firft publifhed in 1522. The paffage that pro-
voked Afcham's ire is, *Crinitus ait Scotos (qui vicini funt Bri-
tannis) in dirigendis fagittis acres effe et egregios.* Fol 158. Ed.
1532.

5. The Florentine PETER RICCIO or latinized CRINITUS
[b 1465—d about 1504.], an Italian biographer and poet. In
December, 1504 was publifhed his *Commentarii de Honefta Dis-
ciplina.*

6. The French Chronicler, ROBERT GAGUIN [b about 1425
—d 22. July. 1502.] General of the Order of the Trinitarians,
and reputed the beft narrator of his age. The firft edition of his
Compendium fuper Francorum geftis was publifhed in Paris, in
1495.

7. The Scot IOHN MAJOR, latinized IOANNES MAJOR, D.D.
[b 1478—d 1540] was for many years Profeffor of Theology and
one of the Doctors of the Sorbonne, at Paris. He publifhed his
*Hiftoria Maioris Britanniæ, tam Angliæ quam Scotiæ, per
Ioannem Maiorem, nomine quidem Scotum, profeffione autem
Theologum, e veterum monumentis concinnata.* 4to Paris. 1521.
" This hiftory is divided into fix books wherein he gives a fum-
mary account of the affairs of Scotland from Fergus I. till the
marriage of King James III., in the year 1469, with which he
concludes his work." Mackenzie. *Writers of the Scottifh
Nation,* ii. 315.

8. HECTOR BOETHIUS, or ROECE, or BOEIS [b about 1470—
d about 1550] a native of Dundee, became Principal of King's
College, Aberdeen. wrote *Scotorum hiftoriæ a prima gentis
origine. &c.* in 17 books, firft publifhed in Paris in 1526, and
fubfequently enlarged in later editions.

9. Sir Thomas Elyot [d 1546.] The work referred to by
Afcham, does not appear ever to have been publifhed.

A List of WORKS

Edited by

Professor EDWARD ARBER

F.S.A. ; Fellow of King's College, London ; Hon. Member of the Virginia and Wisconsin Historical Societies ; late English Examiner at the London University ; and also at the Victoria University, Manchester ; Emeritus Professor of English Language and Literature, Mason College, Birmingham.

An English Garner

English Reprints

The War Library

The English Scholar's Library

The first Three English Books on America

The first English New Testament, 1526

The Paston Letters, 1422–1509.   Edited
    by JAMES GAIRDNER.   3 vols.

A List of 837 London Publishers, 1553–
    1640

All the Works in this Catalogue are published at net prices.

ARCHIBALD CONSTABLE AND CO.,

14, PARLIAMENT ST., WESTMINSTER.

NOTE

THE ENGLISH GARNER, THE ENGLISH REPRINTS, *and* THE
ENGLISH SCHOLAR'S LIBRARY *are now issued in a new style
of binding. A few copies in the old style are still to be had,
and will be supplied if specially ordered, as long as the stock
lasts. Some of Professor Arber's Publications can still be supplied on Large Paper. Prices on application to the Booksellers
or from the Publishers.*

ARCHIBALD CONSTABLE & CO.

An English Garner

INGATHERINGS FROM OUR HISTORY AND LITERATURE.

*** *Abridged Lists of the Texts ; many of which are very rare, and not obtainable in any other form.*

VOL I.

Large Crown 8vo, cloth, 5s. net.

English Political, Naval, and Military History, etc., etc.

1. The Expedition to Scotland in May, 1543.
2. R. PEEKE'S fight at Xerez with a quarter-staff against three Spaniards at once, armed with poniards and daggers ; when he killed one and put the other two to flight. 1625.
3. The Capture of Cris, in Galatia, by Captain QUAILE and 35 men. 1626.
4. Ranks in the British Army, about 1630.
5. The Return of CHARLES II. to Whitehall, 1660.
6. The Retaking of St. Helena, 1673.

English Voyages, Travels, Commerce, etc., etc.

7. The Beginnings of English Trade with the Levant, 1511–1570.
8. The Voyage from Lisbon to Goa of the first Englishman (THOMAS STEVENS, a Jesuit) known to have reached India by the Cape of Good Hope. 1572.
9. The extraordinary captivity, for nineteen years, of Captain ROBERT KNOX in Ceylon ; with his singular deliverance. 1660–1679.

English Life and Progress.

10. The Benefits of observing Fish Days. 1594.
11. The Great Frost. Cold doings in London. 1608.
12. The Carriers of London, and the Inns they stopped at, in 1637.
13. A Narrative of the Draining of the Fens. 1661.

English Literature, Literary History, and Biography.

14. Sir HENRY SIDNEY. A Letter to his son PHILIP, when at Shrewsbury School.

English Poetry.

15. Love Posies. Collected about 1590.
16. Sir PHILIP SIDNEY. ASTROPHEL and STELLA [Sonnets] 1591. With the story of his affection for Lady PENELOPE DEVEREUX, afterwards RICH.
17. EDMUND SPENSER *and others.* ASTROPHEL. A Pastoral Elegy on Sir PHILIP SIDNEY. 1591.
18. JOHN DENNIS. The Secrets of Angling [*i.e. Trout Fishing*], 1613. Forty years before WALTON'S *Angler.*
19. Many other single Poems by various Authors.

VOL II.

Large Crown 8vo, cloth, 5s. net.

English Political, Naval, and Military History, etc., etc.

1. The Triumph at Calais and Boulogne of HENRY VIII. [with ANNE BOLEYN] and FRANCIS I. November, 1532.
2. The Coronation Procession of Queen ANNE [BOLEYN] from the Tower through London to Westminster. June, 1533.
3. English Army Rations in 1591.
4. Rev. T. PRINCE. A History of New England in the form of Annals, from 1602 to 1633. Published at Boston, N.E., in 1736–1755. This is the most exact condensed account in existence of the foundation of our first Colonies in America.

English Voyages, Travels, Commerce, etc., etc.

5. Captain T. SANDERS. The unfortunate voyage of the *Jesus* to Tripoli, where the crew were made slaves. 1584–1585.
6. N. H. The Third Circumnavigation of the Globe, by THOMAS CAVENDISH, in the *Desire*. 1586–1588.
7. The famous fight of the *Dolphin* against Five Turkish Men-of-War off Cagliari. 1617.

English Life and Progress.

8. Dr. J. DEE. The Petty Navy Royal. [Fisheries]. 1577.
9. Captain HITCHCOCK. A Political Plat [*Scheme*], etc. [Herring Fisheries.]
10. D. DEFOE. The Education of Women. 1692.

English Literature, Literary History, and Biography.

11. F. MERES. A Sketch of English Literature, etc., up to September, 1598. This is the most important contemporary account of SHAKESPEARE'S Works to this date; including some that have apparently perished.
12. J. WRIGHT. The Second Generation of English Actors, 1625-1670. This includes some valuable information respecting London Theatres during this period.

English Poetry.

13. Sir P. SIDNEY. Sonnets and Poetical Translations. Before 1587.
14. H. CONSTABLE, *and others.* DIANA. [Sonnet.] 1594.
15. Madrigals, Elegies, and Poems, by various other Poets.

VOL. III.

Large Crown 8vo, cloth, 5s. net.

English Political, Naval, and Military History, etc., etc.

1. W. PATTEN. The Expedition into Scotland : with the Battle of Pinkie Cleugh or Musselburgh, 1547. This was the "Rough Wooing of MARY, Queen of Scots," whom the English wanted to marry EDWARD VI.

English Voyages, Travels, Commerce, etc., etc.

2. J. H. VAN LINSCHOTEN. Voyage to Goa and back, in Portuguese carracks. 1583-1592.

This work showed the way to the East, and led to the formation of the Dutch and the English East India Companies. For nearly three years this Dutchman, returning in charge of a cargo of pepper, spices. etc., was pinned up in the Azores by the English ships ; of whose daring deeds he gives an account.

3. E. WRIGHT. The voyage of the Earl of CUMBERLAND to the Azores in 1589. This is a part of LINSCHOTEN'S story re-told more fully from an English point of view.

4. The first Englishmen—JOHN NEWBERY and RALPH FITCH —that ever reached India overland, *viâ* Aleppo and the Persian Gulf, in 1583-1589. They met with LINSCHOTEN there ; and also T. Stevens, the Jesuit, see vol. i. p. 130.

English Life and Progress.

5. J. CAIUS, M.D. Of English Dogs. 1536. Translated from the Latin by A. FLEMING in 1576.

6. Britain's Buss. A Computation of the Cost and Profit of a Herring Buss or Ship. 1615.

English Literature, Literary History, and Biography.

7. T. ELLWOOD. Relations with J. MILTON. This young Quaker rendered many services to the Poet ; amongst which was the suggestion of *Paradise Regained.*

8. J. DRYDEN. Of Dramatic Poesy. An Essay. This charming piece of English Prose was written in 1665 and published in 1668. With it is given the entire Controversy between DRYDEN and Sir R. HOWARD on this subject.

English Poetry.

9. S. DANIEL. DELIA. [Sonnets.] 1594.

10. T. CAMPION, M.D. Songs and Poems. 1601-1613.

11. Lyrics, Elegies, etc., by other Poets.

VOL IV.

Large Crown 8vo, cloth, 5s. *net*.

English Political, Naval, and Military History, etc., etc.

1. E. UNDERHILL, "the Hot Gospeller," Imprisonment in 1553, with Anecdotes of Queen MARY's Coronation Procession, WYATT's Rebellion, the Marriage of PHILIP and MARY, etc.

2. J. FOX. The Imprisonment of the Princess ELIZABETH. 1554-1555.

3. Texts relating to the Winning of Calais and Guisnes by the French in January, 1556.

4. The Coronation Procession of Queen ELIZABETH. January, 1559.

5. Sir THOMAS OVERBURY. Observations of Holland, Flanders, and France, in 1609. A most sagacious Political Study.

6. JAMES I. The Book of Sports. 1618.

7. Abp. G. ABBOTT. Narrative of his Sequestration from Office in 1627 by CHARLES I., at the instigation of BUCKINGHAM and LAUD.

8. Major-General Sir T. MORGAN. Progress [*i.e. March*] in France and Flanders, with the 6,000 "Red Coats" at the taking of Dunkirk, etc., in 1657-8.

English Voyages, Travels, Commerce, etc., etc.

9. The first Britons who ever reached the city of Mexico : T. BLAKE, a Scotchman, before 1536; and J. FIELD and R. TOMSON, 1556.

10. The wonderful recovery of the *Exchange* from forty-five Turkish pirates of Algiers by J. RAWLINS and twenty-four other slaves. February, 1622.

English Life and Progress.

11. T. GENTLEMAN. England's Way to Win Wealth. [Fisheries.] The Dutch obtained more wealth from their Herring Fishery *along the English shores* than the Spaniards did from their American gold mines.

English Poetry.

12. ? T. OCCLEVE. The Letter of CUPID. 1402.

13. L. SHEPPARD. JOHN BON and Mast[er] PARSON. [A Satire on the Mass.] 1551.

14. Rev. T. BRICE. A Register of the Tormented and Cruelly Burned within England. 1555-1558. These verses give the names of most of the Marian Martyrs.

15. J. C. ALCILIA ; PHILOPARTHEN's loving folly ! [Love Poems.] 1595.

16. G. WITHER. Fair VIRTUE, the Mistress of PHIL'ARETE. 1622. This is WITHER's masterpiece. Over 6,000 lines of verse in many metrical forms.

17. The Songs that JOHN DOWLAND, the famous Lutenist, set to music.

VOL. VI.

Large Crown 8vo, cloth, 5s. net.

English Political, Naval, and Military History, etc., etc.

1. The Examination, at Saltwood Castle, Kent, of WILLIAM of THORPE, by Abp. T. ARUNDELL, 7 August, 1407. Edited by W. TYNDALE, 1530. This is the best account of Lollardism from the inside, given by one who was the leader of the second generation of Lollards.

English Voyages, Travels, Commerce, etc., etc.

2. J. CHILTON. Travels in Mexico. 1568–1575.
3. J. BION. An Account of the Torments, etc. 1708.

English Life and Progress.

4. The most dangerous Adventure of R. FERRIS, A. HILL, and W. THOMAS; who went in a boat by sea from London to Bristol. 1590.
5. Leather. A Discourse to Parliament. 1629.
6. H. PEACHAM. The Worth of a Penny, or a Caution to keep Money. 1641. With all the variations of the later Editions.
7. Sir W. PETTY. Political Arithmetic. [Written in 1677.] 1690. One of the earliest and best books on the Science of Wealth.

English Literature, Literary History, and Biography.

8. ISAAC BICKERSTAFF, Esq. [Dean J. Swift.] Predictions for the year 1708. [One of these was the death of J. PARTRIDGE, the *Almanack* Maker, on 29 March, 1708.] Other tracts of this laughable controversy follow.
9. [J. GAY.] The Present State of Wit. 3 May, 1711. [A Survey of our Periodical Literature at this date; including the *Review, Tatler,* and *Spectator.*]
10. [Dr. J. ARBUTHNOT.] Law [*i.e. War*] is a Bottomless Pit, exemplified in the Case of the Lord STRUTT [*the Kings of Spain*], JOHN BULL [*England*] the Clothier, NICHOLAS FROG [*Holland*] the Linendraper, and LEWIS BABOON [LOUIS XIV. of Bourbon= *France*]. In four parts. 1712.
This famous Political Satire on the War of the Spanish Succession was designed to prepare the English public for the Peace of Utrecht, signed on 11 April, 1713. In part I., on 28 February, 1712, first appeared in our Literature, the character of JOHN BULL, for an Englishman.
11. T. TICKELL. The life of ADDISON. 1721.
12. Sir R. STEELE. Epistle to W. CONGREVE [in reply]. 1722.

English Poetry.

13. The first printed *Robin Hood* Ballad. Printed about 1510.
14. W. PERCY. COELIA. [Sonnets.] 1594.
15. G. WITHER. FIDELIA. [This is WITHER's second master-

piece. The *Lament of a Woman thinking that she is forsaken in love.*] 1615.

16. M. DRAYTON. IDEA. [Sonnets.] 1619.

17. The Interpreter. [A Political Satire interpreting the meaning of the Protestant, The Puritan, The Papist.] 1622.

VOL. VII.
Large Crown 8vo, cloth, 5s. net.

English Political, Naval, and Military History, etc., etc.

1. Sir F. VERE, *General of the English troops in the Dutch service.* Commentaries of his Services : at (1) the Storming of Cadiz in 1596, (2) the Action at Turnhout in 1597, (3) The Battle of Nieuport in 1600 ; but especially (4) the Siege of Ostend, of which place he was Governor from 11 June, 1601, to 7 June, 1602.

2. The retaking of *The Friends' Adventure* from the French by R. LYDE and a boy. 1693.

English Voyages, Travels, Commerce, etc., etc.

3. H. PITMAN. Relation, etc. For doing noble Red Cross work at the Battle of Sedgemoor this surgeon was sent as a White Slave to Barbadoes, etc. 1689.

English Life and Progress.

4. W. KEMP's [SHAKESPEARE'S fellow Actor] Nine Days' Wonder ; performed in a Morris Dance from London to Norwich. April, 1600.

5. A series of Texts on the indignities offered to the Established Clergy, and especially the Private Chaplains, in the Restoration Age, by the Royalist laity ; including

Dr. J. EACHARD's witty 'Grounds of the Contempt of the Clergy and Religion.' 1670.

English Literature, Literary History and Biography.

6. Another Series of Tracts, in prose and verse, illustrating the great Public Services rendered by D. DEFOE, up to the death of Queen Anne ; including :

D. DEFOE. An Appeal to Honour and Justice, etc. 1715.

D. DEFOE. The *True* Born Englishman. 1701.

D. DEFOE. The History of *Kentish Petition.* 1701.

D. DEFOE. LEGION'S *Memorial.* 1701.

D. DEFOE. The Shortest Way with the Dissenters, etc. 1702.

D. DEFOE. A Hymn to the Pillory. 1703.

D. DEFOE. Prefaces to the *Review.* 1704–1710.

English Poetry.

7. T. DELONEY. Three Ballads on the Armada fight. August, 1588.

8. R. L. (1) DIELLA [Sonnets] ; (2) The Love of DOM DIEGO and GYNEURA. 1596. *

VOL. VIII.

Large Crown 8vo, cloth, 5s. net.

This Index Volume will, if possible, contain the following :—

English Political, Naval, and Military History, etc., etc.

English Voyages, Travels, Commerce, etc., etc.

English Life and Progress.

English Poetry.

Chronological List of Works included in the Series.

Index.

English Reprints.

(For full titles, etc., see pp. 10-19.)

1. JOHN MILTON.
Areopagitica. 1644.

(*a*) AREOPAGITICA : *A Speech of Mr.* JOHN MILTON *For the Liberty of Unlicenc'd Printing, To the Parliament of England.*

(*b*) A Decree of Starre-Chamber, concerning Printing, made the eleuenth of July last past, 1637.

(*c*) An Order of the Lords and Commons assembled in Parliament for the Regulating of Printing, &c. 1643.

LORD MACAULAY. He attacked the licensing system in that sublime treatise which every statesman should wear as a sign upon his hand, and as frontlets between his eyes.—*Edinburgh Review, p.* 344, *August,* 1825.

H. HALLAM. Many passages in this famous tract are admirably eloquent : an intense love of liberty and truth flows through it ; the majestic soul of MILTON breathes such high thoughts as had not been uttered before.—*Introduction to the Literature of Europe,* iii. 660. *Ed.* 1839.

W. H. PRESCOTT. The most splendid argument perhaps the world had then witnessed on behalf of intellectual liberty.—*History of FERDINAND ant ISABELLA,* iii. 391. *Ed.* 1845.

2. HUGH LATIMER.
Ex-Bishop of Worcester.
The Ploughers. 1549.

A notable Sermon of ye reuerende Father Master HUGHE LATIMER, *whiche he preached in ye Shrouds at paules churche in London on the xviii daye of Januarye.*

SIR R. MORISON. Did there ever any one (I say not in England only, but among other nations) flourish since the time of the Apostles, who preached the gospel more sincerely, purely, and honestly, than HUGH LATIMER, Bishop of *Worcester?*—*Apomaxis Calumniarum . . quibus* JOANNES COCLEUS &c., f. 78. *Ed.* 1537.

It was in this Sermon, that LATIMER (himself an ex-Bishop) astonished his generation by saying that the Devil was the most diligent Prelate and Preacher in all England. "Ye shal neuer fynde him idle I warraunte you."

3. STEPHEN GOSSON.
Stud. Oxon.
The School of Abuse. 1579.

(*a*) *The Schoole of Abuse. Conteining a pleasaunt inuectiue against Poets, Pipers, Plaiers, Jesters, and such like Caterpillers of a Commonwealth ; Setting up the Flagge of Defiance to their mischieuous exercise and ouerthrowing their Bulwarkes, by Prophane Writers, Naturall reason and common experience.* 1579.

(*b*) *An Apologie of the Schoole of Abuse, against Poets, Pipers, Players, and their Excusers.* [*Dec.*] 1579.

⁂ This attack is thought to have occasioned SIR PHILIP SIDNEY'S writing of the following *Apologie for Poesie.*

GOSSON was, in succession, Poet, Actor, Dramatist, Satirist, and a Puritan Clergyman.

4. Sir PHILIP SIDNEY.

An Apology for Poetry. [? 1580.]

An Apologie for Poetrie. Written by the right noble, vertuous, and learned Sir PHILIP SIDNEY, Knight. 1595.

H. W. LONGFELLOW. The defence of Poetry is a work of rare merit. It is a golden little volume, which the scholar may lay beneath his pillow, as CHRYSOSTOM did the works of ARISTOPHANES.—*North American Review*, p. 57. *January, 1832.*

The Work thus divides itself :—

The Etymology of Poetry.
The Anatomy of the Effects of Poetry.
The Anatomy of the Parts of Poetry.
Objections to Poetry answered.
Criticism of the existing English Poetry.

5. EDWARD WEBBE,

A Chief Master Gunner.

Travels. 1590.

The rare and most vvonderful thinges which EDWARD WEBBE an Englishman borne, hath seene and passed in his troublesome trauailes, in the Citties of Ierusalem, Damasko, Bethelem and Galely : and in all the landes of Iewrie, Egipt, Grecia, Russia, and in the Land of Prester John.

Wherein is set foorth his extreame slauerie sustained many yeres togither, in the Gallies and wars of the great Turk against the Landes of Persia, Tartaria, Spaine, and Portugall, with the manner of his releasement and coming to England. [1590.]

6. JOHN SELDEN.

Table Talk. [1634-1654.]

Table Talk : being the Discourses of JOHN SELDEN, Esq. ; or his Sence of various Matters of weight and high consequence, relating especially to Religion and State. 1689.

S. T. COLERIDGE. There is more weighty bullion sense in this book than I ever found in the same number of pages of any uninspired writer. . . . O ! to have been with SELDEN over his glass of wine, making every accident an outlet and a vehicle of wisdom.—*Literary Remains*, iii. 361-2. *Ed.* 1836.

H. HALLAM. This very short and small volume gives, perhaps, a more exalted notion of SELDEN's natural talents than any of his learned writings. —*Introduction to the Literature of Europe*, iii. 347. *Ed.* 1836.

Above all things, Liberty.

7. ROGER ASCHAM.

Toxophilus. 1544.

Toxophilus, the Schole of Shootinge, conteyned in two bookes.
To all Gentlemen and yomen of Englande, pleasaunte for theyr
pastime to rede, and profitable for theyr use to follow both in war
and peace.

In a dialogue between *TOXOPHILUS* and *PHILOLOGUS*, ASCHAM not
only gives us one of the very best books on Archery in our language ; but
as he tells King Henry VIII., in his Dedication, "this litle treatise was
purposed, begon, and ended of me, onelie for this intent, that Labour,
Honest pastime, and Vertu might recouer againe that place and right, that
Idlenesse, Unthriftie Gaming, and Vice hath put them fro."

8. JOSEPH ADDISON.

Criticism on *Paradise Lost.* 1711–1712.

From the *Spectator*, being its Saturday issues between 31 December, 1711,
and 3 May, 1712.   In these papers, which constitute a Primer to *Paradise
Lost*, ADDISON first made known, and interpreted to the general English
public, the great Epic poem, which had then been published nearly half a
century.

After a general discussion of the *Fable*, the *Characters*, the *Sentiments*,
the *Language*, and the *Defects* of MILTON'S Great Poem ; the Critic devotes
a Paper to the consideration of the *Beauties* of each of its Twelve Books.

9. JOHN LYLY,

Novelist, Wit, Poet, and Dramatist.

Euphues. 1579–1580.

EUPHVES, *the Anatomy af Wit.   Very pleasant for all
Gentlemen to reade, and most necessary to remember.*

*VVherein are contened the delights that Wit followeth in his
youth, by the pleasantnesse of loue, and the happinesse he reapeth
in age by the perfectnesse of Wisedome.* 1579.

EUPHUES *and his England.   Containing his voyage and
aduentures, myxed with sundry pretie discourses of honest Loue,
the description of the countrey, the Court, and the manners of
that Isle.* 1580.

Of great importance in our Literary History.

10. GEORGE VILLIERS,

Second Duke of BUCKINGHAM.

The Rehearsal. 1671.

The Rehearsal, as it was Acted at the Theatre Royal.

Many of the passages of anterior plays that were parodied in this famous Dramatic Satire on DRYDEN in the character of *BAYES*, are placed on opposite pages to the text. BRIAN FAIRFAX'S remarkable life of this Duke of BUCKINGHAM is also prefixed to the play.

The Heroic Plays, first introduced by Sir W. D'AVENANT, and afterwards greatly developed by DRYDEN, are the object of this laughable attack. LACY, who acted the part of *BAYES*, imitated the dress and gesticulation of DRYDEN.

The Poet repaid this compliment to the Duke of BUCKINGHAM, in 1681, by introducing him in the character of *ZIMRA* in his *ABSOLOM and ACHITOPHEL.*

11. GEORGE GASCOIGNE,

Soldier and Poet.

The Steel Glass, &c. 1576.

(a) *A Remembrance of the wel imployed life, and godly end, of* GEORGE GASKOIGNE, *Esquire, who deceassed at Stalmford in Lincoln shire, the 7 of October,* 1577. *The reporte of* GEOR. WHETSTONS, *Gent.* 1577.

There is only one copy of this metrical Life. It is in the Bodleian Library.

(b) *Certaine notes of instruction concerning the making of verse or ryme in English.* 1575.

This is our First printed piece of Poetical Criticism.

(c) *The Steele Glas.*

Written in blank verse.

Probably the fourth printed English Satire : those by BARCLAY, ROY, and Sir T. WYATT being the three earlier ones.

(d) *The complaynt of* PHILOMENE. *An Elegie.* 1576.

12. JOHN EARLE,

Afterwards Bishop of SALISBURY.

Microcosmographie. 1628.

Micro-cosmographie, or a Peece of the World discovered ; in Essays and Characters.

This celebrated book of Characters is graphically descriptive of the English social life of the time, as it presented itself to a young Fellow of Merton College, Oxford ; including *A She precise Hypocrite, A Sceptic in Religion, A good old man, etc.*

This Work is a notable specimen of a considerable class of books in our Literature, full of interest : and which help Posterity much better to understand the Times in which they were written.

13. HUGH LATIMER,
Ex-Bishop of WORCESTER.

Seven Sermons before Edward VI. 1549.

The fyrste [—seuenth] Sermon of Mayster HUGHE LATIMER, whiche he preached before the Kynges Maiestie wythin his graces palayce at Westminster on each Friday in Lent. 1549.

Sir JAMES MACKINTOSH. LATIMER, . . . brave, sincere, honest, inflexible, not distinguished as a writer or a scholar, but exercising his power over men's minds by a fervid eloquence flowing from the deep conviction which animated his plain, pithy, and free-spoken Sermons.—*History of England*, ii. 291. *Ed.* 1831.

14. Sir THOMAS MORE.
Translation of Utopia. 1516–1557.

A frutefull and pleasaunt worke of the best state of a publique weale, and of the new yle called Utopia: VVritten in Latine by Sir THOMAS MORE, Knyght, and translated into Englyshe by RALPH ROBYNSON.

LORD CAMPBELL. Since the time of PLATO there had been no composition given to the world which, for imagination, for philosophical discrimination, for a familiarity with the principles of government, for a knowledge of the springs of human action, for a keen observation of men and manners, and for felicity of expression, could be compared to the *Utopia.—Lives of the Lord Chancellors* (*Life of Sir. T. More*), i. 583. *Ed.* 1845.

In the imaginary country of Utopia, MORE endeavours to sketch out a State based upon two principles—(1) community of goods, no private property; and consequently (2) no use for money.

15. GEORGE PUTTENHAM,
A Gentleman Pensioner to Queen ELIZABETH.

The Art of English Poesy. 1589.

The Arte of English Poesie.
Contriued into three Bookes : The first of POETS and POESIE, the second of PROPORTION, the third of ORNAMENT.

W. OLDYS. It contains many pretty observations, examples, characters, and fragments of poetry for those times, now nowhere else to be met with.—*Sir WALTER RALEIGH*, liv. *Ed.* 1736.

O. GILCHRIST. On many accounts one of the most curious and entertaining, and intrinsically one of the most valuable books of the age of QUEEN ELIZABETH. The copious intermixture of contemporary anecdote, tradition, manners, opinions, and the numerous specimens of coeval poetry nowhere else preserved, contribute to form a volume of infinite amusement, curiosity, and value.—*Censura Literaria*, i. 339. *Ed.* 1805.

This is still also an important book on Rhetoric and the Figures of Speech.

16. JAMES HOWELL,

Clerk of the Council to CHARLES I.; afterwards Historiographer to CHARLES II.

Instructions for Foreign Travel. 1642.

Instructions for forreine travelle. Shewing by what cours, and in what compasse of time, one may take an exact Survey of the Kingdomes and States of Christendome, and arrive to the practical knowledge of the Languages, to good purpose.

The *MURRAY, BÆDEKER,* and *Practical Guide* to the Grand Tour of Europe, which, at that time, was considered the finishing touch to the complete education of an English Gentleman.

The route sketched out by this delightfully quaint Writer, is France, Spain, Italy, Switzerland, Germany, the Netherlands, and Holland. The time allowed is 3 years and 4 months : the months to be spent in travelling, the years in residence at the different cities.

17. NICHOLAS UDALL,

Master, first of Eton College, then of Westminster School.

Roister Doister. [1553–1566.]

This is believed to be the first true English Comedy that ever came to the press.

From the unique copy, which wants a title-page, now at Eton College ; and which is thought to have been printed in 1566.

Dramatis Personæ.

RALPH ROISTER DOISTER.
MATTHEW MERRYGREEK.
GAWIN GOODLUCK, *affianced to Dame* CUSTANCE.
TRISTRAM TRUSTY, *his friend.*
DOBINET DOUGHTY, *" boy" to* ROISTER DOISTER.
TOM TRUEPENNY, *servant to Dame* CUSTANCE.
SIM SURESBY, *servant to* GOODLUCK.
Scrivener.
Harpax.
DAME CHRISTIAN CUSTANCE, *a widow.*
MARGERY MUMBLECRUST, *her nurse.*
TIBET TALKAPACE ⎱ *her maidens.*
ANNOT ALYFACE ⎰

18. A Monk of Evesham,

The Revelation, &c. 1186[–1410]. 1485.

¶ *Here begynnyth a marvellous reuelacion that was schewyd of almighty god by sent Nycholas to a monke of Euyshamme yn the days of Kynge Richard the fyrst. And the yere of owre lord, M.C.Lxxxxvi.*

One of the rarest of English books printed by one of the earliest of English printers, WILLIAM DE MACLINIA ; who printed this text about 1485, *in the lifetime of* CAXTON.

The essence of the story is as old as it professes to be ; but contains later additions, the orthography, being of about 1410. It is very devoutly written, and contains a curious Vision of Purgatory.

The writer is a prototype of BUNYAN ; and his description of the Gate in the Crystal Wall of Heaven, and of the solemn and marvellously sweet Peal of the Bells of Heaven that came to him through it, is very beautiful.

19.   JAMES I.

A Counterblast to Tobacco.   1604.

(a) *The Essays of a Prentise, in the Diuine Art of Poesie.*

Printed while JAMES VI. of Scotland, at Edinburgh in 1585 ; and includes *Ane Short treatise, conteining some Reulis and Cautelis to be obseruit and eschewit in Scottis Poesie*, which is another very early piece of printed Poetical Criticism.

(b) *A Counterblaste to Tobacco.*   1604.

To this text has been added a full account of *the Introduction and Early use of Tobacco in England*. The herb first came into use in Europe as a medicinal leaf for poultices : smoking it was afterwards learnt from the American Indians.

Our Royal Author thus sums up his opinion :—

"A custome lothsome to the eye, hateful to the nose, harmefull to the braine, dangerous to the lungs, and in the blacke stinking fume thereof, nearest resembling the horrible Stigian smoke of the pit that is bottomless."

20.   Sir ROBERT NAUNTON,

Master of the Court of Wards.

Fragmenta Regalia.   1653.

Fragmenta Regalia : or Observations on the late Queen ELIZABETH, *her Times and Favourites.* [1630.]

Naunton writes :—

"And thus I have delivered up this my poor Essay ; a little Draught of this great Princess, and her Times, with the Servants of her State and favour."

21.   THOMAS WATSON,

Londoner, Student-at-Law.

Poems.   1582–1593.

(a) *The Ἑκατομπαθια or Passionate Centurie of Loue.*

Divided into two parts : whereof, the first expresseth the Author's sufferance in Loue : the latter, his long farwell to Loue and all his tyrannie.   1582.

(b) MELIBŒUS, *Sive Ecloga in obitum Honoratissimi Viri Domini* FRANCISCI WALSINGHAMI.   1590.

(c) *The same translated into English, by the Author.*   1590.

(d) *The Tears of Fancie, or Loue disdained.*   1593.

From the *unique* copy, wanting *Sonnets* 9–16, in the possession of S. CHRISTIE MILLER, Esq., of Britwell.

22. WILLIAM HABINGTON,

Castara. 1640.

CASTARA. *The third Edition. Corrected and augmented.*

CASTARA was Lady LUCY HERBERT, the youngest child of the first Lord POWIS ; and these Poems were chiefly marks of affection during a pure courtship followed by a happy marriage. With these, are also Songs of Friendship, especially those referring to the Hon. GEORGE TALBOT.

In addition to these Poems, there are four prose Characters ; on *A Mistress, A Wife, A Friend,* and *The Holy Man.*

23. ROGER ASCHAM,

The Schoolmaster. 1570.

The Scholemaster, or plane and perfite way of teachyng children to understand, write, and speake, in Latin tong, but specially purposed for the priuate bryngyng up of youth in Ientleman and Noble mens houses, &c.

This celebrated Work contains the story of Lady JANE GREY's delight in reading *PLATO*, an attack on the *Italianated* Englishman of the time, and much other information not specified in the above title.

In it, ASCHAM gives us very fully his plan of studying Languages, which may be described as *the double translation of a model book.*

24. HENRY HOWARD,
Earl of SURREY.
Sir THOMAS WYATT.
NICHOLAS GRIMALD.
Lord VAUX.

Tottel's Miscellany. 5 June, 1557.

Songes and Sonettes, vvritten by the right honourable Lorde HENRY HOWARD *late Earle of* SURREY, *and other.*

With 39 additional Poems from the second edition by the same printer, RICHARD TOTTEL, of 31 July, 1557.

This celebrated Collection is the First of our Poetical Miscellanies, and also the first appearance in print of any considerable number of English Sonnets.

TOTTEL in his *Address to the Reader*, says : —

"That to haue wel written in verse, yea and in small parcelles, deserueth great praise, the workes of diuers Latines, Italians, and other, doe proue sufficiently. That our tong is able in that kynde to do as praiseworthely as ye rest, the honorable stile of the noble earle of Surrey, and the weightinesse of the depewitted Sir Thomas Wyat the elders verse, with seuerall graces in sondry good Englishe writers, doe show abundantly."

25. Rev. THOMAS LEVER,

Fellow and Preacher of St. John's College, Cambridge.

Sermons. 1550.

(*a*) *A fruitfull Sermon in Paules church at London in the Shroudes.*

(*b*) *A Sermon preached the fourth Sunday in Lent before the Kynges Maiestie, and his honourable Counsell.*

(*c*) *A Sermon preached at Pauls Crosse.* 1550.

These Sermons are reprinted from the original editions, which are of *extreme* rarity. They throw much light on the communistic theories of the Norfolk rebels; and the one at Paul's Cross contains a curious account of Cambridge University life in the reign of EDWARD VI.

26. WILLIAM WEBBE,

Graduate.

A Discourse of English Poetry. 1586.

A Discourse of English Poetrie. Together with the Authors iudgement, touching the reformation of our English Verse.

Another of the early pieces of Poetical Criticism, written in the year in which SHAKESPEARE is supposed to have left Stratford for London.

Only two copies of this Work are known, one of these was sold for £64.

This Work should be read with STANYHURST'S *Translation of Æneid, I.-IV.*, 1582, see p. 64. WEBBE was an advocate of English Hexameters; and here translates VIRGIL'S first two Eglogues into them. He also translates into Sapphics COLIN'S Song in the Fourth Eglogue of SPENSER'S *Shepherd's Calendar.*

27. FRANCIS BACON.

afterwards Lord VERULAM Viscount ST. ALBANS.

A Harmony of the *Essays*, &c. 1597–1626.

And after my manner, I alter ever, when I add. So that nothing is finished, till all be finished.—Sir FRANCIS BACON, 27 Feb., 1610-[11].

(*a*) *Essays, Religious Meditations, and Places of perswasion and disswasion.* 1597.

(*b*) *The Writings of Sir* FRANCIS BACON *Knight the Kinges Sollicitor General in Moralitie, Policie, Historie.*

(*c*) *The Essaies of Sir* FRANCIS BACON *Knight, the Kings Solliciter Generall.*

(*d*) *The Essayes or Counsells, Civill and Morall of* FRANCIS *Lord* VERULAM, *Viscount* ST. ALBAN. 1625.

28. WILLIAM ROY. JEROME BARLOW.

Franciscan Friars.

Read me, and be not wroth! [1528.]

(a) *Rede me and be nott wrothe,*
     For I saye no thynge but trothe.
     I will ascende makynge my state so hye,
     That my pompous honoure shall never dye.
     O Caytyfe when thou thynkest least of all,
     With confusion thou shalt have a fall.

This is the famous satire on Cardinal WOLSEY, and is the First English *Protestant* book ever printed, not being a portion of Holy Scripture. See *p.* 22 for the Fifth such book.

The next two pieces form one book, printed by HANS LUFT, at Marburg, in 1530.

(b) *A proper dyaloge, betwene a Gentillman and a husband-man, eche complaynynge to other their miserable calamite, through the ambicion of the clergye.*

(c) *A compendious old treatyse, shewynge, how that we ought to have the scripture in Englysshe.*

29. Sir WALTER RALEIGH. GERVASE MARKHAM. J. H. VAN LINSCHOTEN.

The Last Fight of the "Revenge." 1591.

(a) *A Report of the truth of the fight about the Iles of Acores, this last la Sommer. Betwixt the* REUENGE, *one of her Maiesties Shippes, and an* ARMADA *of the King of Spaine.*

[By Sir W. RALEIGH.]

(b) *The most honorable Tragedie of Sir* RICHARD GRINUILE, *Knight.* 1595.

[By GERVASE MARKHAM.]

(c) [*The Fight and Cyclone at the Azores.*

[By JAV HUYGHEN VAN LINSCHOTEN.]

Several accounts are here given of one of the most extraordinary Sea fights in our Naval History.

30. BARNABE GOOGE.

Eglogues, Epitaphs, and Sonnets. 1563.

Eglogs, Epytaphes, and Sonettes Newly written by BARNABE GOOGE.

Three copies only known. Reprinted from the *Huth* copy.

In the prefatory *Notes of the Life and Writings of B. GOOGE,* will be found an account of the trouble he had in winning MARY DARELL for his wife.

A new Literature generally begins with imitations and translations. When this book first appeared, Translations were all the rage among the "young England" of the day. This Collection of *original* Occasional Verse is therefore the more noticeable. The Introduction gives a glimpse of the principal Writers of the time, such as the Authors of the *Mirror for Magistrates,* the Translators of SENECA's *Tragedies,* etc., and including such names as BALDWIN, BAVANDE, BLUNDESTON, NEVILLE, NORTH, NORTON, SACKVILLE, and YELVERTON.

The English Scholar's Library.

16 Parts are now published, in Cloth Boards, £2 1s.
Any part may be obtained separately.

The general character of this Series will be gathered
from the following pages :—21-26.

1. William Caxton,
our first Printer.

Translation of REYNARD THE FOX. 1481.

[COLOPHON.] *I haue not added ne mynussshed but haue folowed as nyghe as I can my copye which was in dutche | and by me* WILLIAM CAXTON *translated in to this rude and symple englyssh in th[e] abbey of westmestre.*

Interesting for its own sake ; but especially as being translated as well as printed by CAXTON, who finished the printing on 6 June, 1481.

The Story is the History of the Three fraudulent Escapes of the Fox from punishment, the record of the Defeat of Justice by flattering lips and dishonourable deeds. It also shows the struggle between the power of Words and the power of Blows, a conflict between Mind and Matter. It was necessary for the physically weak to have Eloquence : the blame of REYNARD is in the frightful misuse he makes of it.

The author says, "There is in the world much seed left of the Fox, which now over all groweth and cometh sore up, though they have no red beards."

2. John Knox,
the Scotch Reformer.

THE FIRST BLAST OF THE TRUMPET, &C.
1558.

(*a*) *The First Blast of a Trumpet against the monstrous Regiment of Women.*

(*b*) *The Propositions to be entreated in the Second* BLAST.

This work was wrung out of the heart of JOHN KNOX, while, at Dieppe, he heard of the martyr fires of England, and was anguished thereby. At that moment the liberties of Great Britain, and therein the hopes of the whole World, lay in the laps of four women—MARY of Loraine, the Regent of Scotland ; her daughter MARY (the Queen of Scots); Queen MARY TUDOR ; and the Princess ELIZABETH.

The Volume was printed at Geneva.

(*c*) KNOX'S *apologetical Defence of his* FIRST BLAST, &C., *to Queen* ELIZABETH. 1559.

3. Clement Robinson,
and divers others.

A HANDFUL OF PLEASANT DELIGHTS.
1584.

A Handeful of pleasant delites, Containing sundrie new Sonets and delectable Histories, in diuers kindes of Meeter. Newly deuised to the newest tunes that are now in vse, to be sung : euerie Sonet orderly pointed to his proper Tune. With new additions of certain Songs, to verie late deuised Notes, not commonly knowen, nor vsed heretofore.

OPHELIA quotes from *A Nosegaie, &c.*, in this Poetical Miscellany ; of which only one copy is now known.

It also contains the earliest text extant of the *Ladie Greensleeues*, which first appeared four years previously.

This is the Third printed Poetical Miscellany in our language.

4. [Simon Fish,

of Gray's Inn.]

A SUPPLICATION FOR THE BEGGARS.

[? 1529.]

A Supplicacyon for the Beggars.

Stated by J. Fox to have been distributed in the streets of London on Candlemas Day [2 Feb., 1529].

This is the Fifth Protestant book (not being a portion of Holy Scripture that was printed in the English Language.

The authorship of this anonymous tract, is fixed by a passage in Sir T. MORE'S *Apology*, of 1533, quoted in the Introduction.

5. [Rev. John Udall,

Minister at Kingston on Thames.]

DIOTREPHES. [1588.]

The state of the Church of Englande, laid open in a conference betweene DIOTREPHES *a Byshopp*, TERTULLUS *a Papiste*, DE-METRIUS *an vsurer*, PANDOCHUS *an Innekeeper, and* PAULE *a preacher of the word of God.*

This is the forerunning tract of the *MARTIN MARPRELATE Contro-versy.* For the production of it, ROBERT WALDEGRAVE, the printer, was ruined ; and so became available for the printing of the Martinist invectives.

The scene of the Dialogue is in PANDOCHUS'S Inn, which is in a posting-town on the high road from London to Edinburgh.

6. [?]

THE RETURN FROM PARNASSUS.

[Acted 1602.] 1606.

The Returne from Pernassus : or The Scourge of Simony. Publiquely acted by the Students in Saint Iohns Colledge in Cambridge.

This play, written by a University man in December, 1601, brings WILLIAM KEMP and RICHARD BURBAGE on to the Stage, and makes them speak thus :

"KEMP. Few of the vniuersity pen plaies well, they smell too much of that writer *Ouid* and that writer *Metamorphosis*, and talke too much of *Proserpina* and *Iuppiter.* Why herees our fellow *Shakespeare* puts them all downe, I [*Ay*] and *Ben Ionson* too. O that *Ben Ionson* is a pestilent fellow, he brought vp *Horace* giuing the Poets a pill, but our fellow *Shake-speare* hath given him a purge that made him beray his credit :

"BURBAGE. It's a shrewd fellow indeed :"

What this controversy between SHAKESPEARE and JONSON was, has not yet been cleared up. It was evidently recent, when (in Dec., 1601) this play was written.

7. Thomas Decker,
The Dramatist.

THE SEVEN DEADLY SINS OF LONDON, &c. 1606.

The seuen deadly Sinnes of London : drawn in seuen seuerall Coaches, through the seuen seuerall Gates of the Citie, bringing the Plague with them.

A prose Allegorical Satire, giving a most vivid picture of London life, in October, 1606.

The seven sins are—

> FRAUDULENT BANKRUPTCY.
> LYING.
> CANDLELIGHT (*Deeds of Darkness*).
> SLOTH.
> APISHNESS (*Changes of Fashion*).
> SHAVING (*Cheating*), and CRUELTY.

Their chariots, drivers, pages, attendants, and followers, are all allegorically described.

8. *The Editor.*

AN INTRODUCTORY SKETCH TO THE MARTIN MARPRELATE CONTROVERSY. 1588–1590.

(*a*) *The general Episcopal Administration, Censorship, &c.*
(*b*) *The Origin of the Controversy.*
(*c*) *Depositions and Examinations.*
(*d*) *State Documents.*
(*e*) *The Brief held by Sir* JOHN PUCKERING, *against the Martinists.*

The REV. J. UDALL (who was, however, *not* a Martinist) ; Mrs. CRANE, of Molesey, Rev. J. PENRY, Sir R. KNIGHTLEY, of Fawsley, near Northampton ; HUMPHREY NEWMAN, the London cobbler ; JOHN HALES, Esq., of Coventry ; Mr. and Mrs. WEEKSTON, of Wolston : JOB THROCKMORTON, Esq. ; HENRY SHARPE, bookbinder of Northampton, and the four printers.

(*f*) *Miscellaneous Information.*
(*g*) *Who were the Writers who wrote under the name of* MARTIN MARPRELATE?

9. [Rev. John Udall,
Minister at Kingston on Thames.]

A DEMONSTRATION OF DISCIPLINE. 1588.

A Demonstration of the trueth of that discipline which CHRISTE *hath prescribed in his worde for the gouernement of his Church, in all times and places, vntil the ende of the worlde.*

Printed with the secret Martinist press, at East Molesey, near Hampton Court, in July, 1588 ; and secretly distributed with the *Epitome* in the following November.

For this Work, UDALL lingered to death in prison.

It is perhaps the most complete argument, in our language, for Presbyterian Puritanism, as it was then understood. Its author asserted for it, the infallibility of a Divine Logic : but two generations had not passed away, before (under the teachings of Experience) much of this Church Polity had been discarded.

10.   Richard Stanyhurst,
the Irish Historian.

Translation of ÆNEID I.–IV.   1582.

Thee first fovre Bookes of VIRGIL *his Æneis translated intoo English heroical [i.e., hexameter] verse by* RICHARD STANY-HURST, *wyth oother Poëtical diuises theretoo annexed.*

Imprinted at Leiden in Holland by IOHN PATES, *Anno M.D.LXXXII.*

This is one of the oddest and most grotesque books in the English language ; and having been printed in Flanders, the original Edition is of *extreme* rarity.

The present text is, by the kindness of Lord ASHBURNHAM and S. CHRISTIE-MILLER, Esq., reprinted from the only two copies known, neither of which is quite perfect.

GABRIEL HARVEY desired to be epitaphed, *The Inventor of the English Hexameter* ; and STANYHURST, in imitating him, went further than any one else in maltreating English words to suit the exigencies of Classical feet.

11.   *Martin Marprelate.*

THE EPISTLE.   1588.

Oh read ouer D. JOHN BRIDGES, *for it is a worthy worke : Or an epitome of the fyrste Booke of that right worshipfull volume, written against the Puritanes, in the defence of the noble cleargie, by as worshipfull a prieste,* JOHN BRIDGES, *Presbyter, Priest or Elder, doctor of Diuillitie, and Deane of Sarum.*

The Epitome [p. 26] is not yet published, but it shall be, when the Byshops are at convenient leysure to view the same.   In the meane time, let them be content with this learned Epistle.

Printed oversea, in Europe, within two furlongs of a Bounsing Priest, at the cost and charges of M. MARPRELATE, *gentleman.*

12.   Robert Greene, M.A.

MENAPHON.   1589.

MENAPHON.   CAMILLAS *alarum to slumbering* EUPHUES, *in his melancholie Cell at Silexedra.   VVherein are deciphered the variable effects of Fortune, the wonders of Loue, the triumphes of inconstant Time.   Displaying in sundrie conceipted passions (figured in a continuate Historie) the Trophees that Vertue carrieth triumphant, maugre the wrath of Enuie, or the resolution of Fortune.*

One of GREENE's novels with TOM NASH's Preface, so important in reference to the earlier *HAMLET*, before SHAKESPEARE's tragedy.

GREENE's "love pamphlets" were the most popular Works of Fiction in England, up to the appearance of Sir P. SIDNEY's *Arcadia* in 1590.

13. George Joy,
an early Protestant Reformer.

AN APOLOGY TO TINDALE. 1535.

An Apologye made by GEORGE JOYE *to satisfye (if it may be)*
W. TINDALE : *to pourge and defende himself ageinst so many
sclaunderouse lyes fayned vpon him in* TINDAL'S *vncharitable
and unsober* Pystle *so well worthye to be prefixed for the Reader to
induce him into the understanding of hys* new Testament *diligently corrected and printed in the yeare of our Lorde,* 1534, *in*
Nouember [Antwerp, 27 Feb., 1535.

This almost lost book is our only authority in respect to the surreptitious
editions of the English *New Testament,* which were printed for the English
market with very many errors, by Antwerp printers who knew not English,
in the interval between TINDALE'S first editions in 1526, and his revised Text
(above referred to) in 1534.

14. Richard Barnfield.
of Darlaston, Staffordshire.

POEMS. 1594–1598.

The affectionate Shepherd. Containing the Complaint of
DAPHNIS *for the Loue of* GANYMEDE.

In the following Work, BARNFIELD states that this is "an imitation of
Virgill, in the second Eglogue of *Alexis."*

CYNTHIA. *With Certaine Sonnets, and the Legend of* CAS-
SANDRA. 1595.

The Author thus concludes his Preface : "Thus, hoping you will beare
with my rude conceit of *Cynthia* (if for no other cause, yet, for that it is the
First Imitation of the verse of that excellent Poet, Maister *Spencer,* in his
Fayrie Queene), I leaue you to the reading of that, which I so much desire
may breed your delight."

The Encomion of Lady PECUNIA : *or, The Praise of Money.*
1598.

Two of the Poems in this Text have been wrongly attributed to SHAKE-
SPEARE. The disproof is given in the Introduction.

15. T[homas] C[ooper].
[*Bishop of* WINCHESTER.]

ADMONITION TO THE PEOPLE OF ENGLAND.

*An admonition to the people of England· VVherein are an-
svvered, not onley the slaunderous vntruethes, reprochfully vttered
by* MARTIN *the Libeller, but also many other Crimes by some of
his broode, objected generally against all Bishops, and the chiefe of
the Cleargie, purposely to deface and discredit the present state of
the Church.* [*Jan.* 1589].

This is the official reply on the part of the Hierarchy, to MARTIN MAR-
PRELATE's *Epistle of* [Nov.] 1508 : see No. 11. on *p.* 24.

It was published between the appearance of the *Epistle* and that of the
Epitome.

16. Captain John Smith,

President of Virginia, and Admiral of New England.

WORKS.—1608-1631. 2 *vols.* 12*s.* 6*d.*

A complete edition, with six facsimile plates.

Occasion was taken, in the preparation of this Edition, dispassionately to test the Author's statements. The result is perfectly satisfactory. The Lincolnshire Captain is to be implicitly believed in all that he relates of his own personal knowledge.

The following are the chief Texts in this Volume :—

(1.) **A true Relation of Occurrences in Virginia.** 1608.
(2.) **A Map of Virginia.** 1612.
(3.) **A Description of New England.** 1616.
(4.) **New England's Trials.** 1620 and 1622.
(5.) **The History of Virginia, New England, and Bermuda.** 1624.
(6.) **An Accidence for young Seamen.** 1626.
(7.) **His true Travels, Adventures, and Observations.** 1630.
(8.) **Advertisements for Planters in New England, or anywhere.** 1631.

The first Three English Books on America. [? 1511]–1555.

This work is a perfect Encyclopædia respecting the earliest Spanish and English Voyages to America.

Small Paper Edition, 456 *pp., in One Volume, Demy 4to,* £1 1*s.*

Large Paper Edition in One Volume, Royal 4to, £3 3*s.*

The Three Books are—

(1.) **Of the new landes, etc.** Printed at Antwerp about **1511.** *This is the first English book in which the word* America [*i.e.* Armonica] *occurs.*

(2.) **A Treatise of the new India, etc.** Translated by RICHARD EDEN from SEBASTIAN MUENSTER'S *Cosmography :* and printed in 1553. *The Second English Book on America.*

(3.) **The Decades of the New World, etc.,** by PIETRO MARTIRE [PETRUS MARTYR], translated by RICHARD EDEN, and printed in 1555. *The Third English Book on America.* SHAKESPEARE obtained the character of CALIBAN from this Work.

A List of 837 London Publishers, 1553–1640.

This Master Key to English Bibliography for the period also gives the approximate period that each Publisher was in business.

Demy 4to, 32 *pp.,* 10*s.* 6*d. net.*

Fcap. 4to, Cloth, Gilt, 10s. 6d. *net.*

THE ONLY KNOWN FRAGMENT OF

The First printed
English New Testament, in Quarto.
By W. TINDALE AND W. ROY.

Sixty photo-lithographed pages ; preceded by a critical PREFACE.

BRIEFLY told, the story of this profoundly interesting work is as follows :—

In 1524 TINDALE went from London to Hamburgh ; where remaining for about a year, he journeyed on to Cologne ; and there, assisted by WILLIAM ROY, subsequently the author of the satire on WOLSEY, *Rede me and be nott wrothe* [see *p.* 19], he began this first edition in 4to, *with glosses*, of the English New Testament.

A virulent enemy of the Reformation, COCHLÆUS, at that time an exile in Cologne, learnt, through giving wine to the printer's men, that P. QUENTAL the printer had in hand a secret edition of three thousand copies of the English New Testament. In great alarm, he informed HERMAN RINCK, a Senator of the city, who moved the Senate to stop the printing ; but COCHLÆUS could neither obtain a sight of the Translators, nor a sheet of the impression.

TINDALE and ROY fled with the printed sheets up the Rhine to Worms ; and there completing this edition, produced also another in 8vo, *without glosses*. Both editions were probably in England by March, 1526.

Of the six thousand copies of which they together were composed, there remain but this fragment of the First commenced edition, in 4to ; and of the Second Edition, in 8vo, one complete copy in the Library of the Baptist College at Bristol, and an imperfect one in that of St. Paul's Cathedral, London.

In the *Preface*, the original documents are given intact, in connection with

Evidence connected with the first Two Editions of the English New Testament, viz., in Quarto and Octavo—

I. WILLIAM TINDALE'S antecedent career.
II. The Printing at Cologne.
III. The Printing at Worms.
IV. WILLIAM ROY's connection with these Editions.
V. The landing and distribution in England.
VI. The persecution in England.

Typographical and Literary Evidence connected with the present Fragment—

I. It was printed for TINDALE by PETER QUENTAL at Cologne, before 1526.
II. It is not a portion of the separate Gospel of *Matthew* printed previous to that year.
III. It is therefore certainly a fragment of the Quarto.

Is the Quarto a translation of LUTHER'S *German Version ?*
Text. The prologge. Inner Marginal References. Outer Marginal Glosses.

⁎⁎ For a continuation of this Story see G. Joy's *Apology* at *p.* 25.

Captain WILLIAM SIBORNE.

The Waterloo Campaign. 1815.

4th Ed. Crown 8vo. 832 *pages.* 13 *Medallion Portraits of Generals.* 15 *Maps and Plans.*

Bound in Red Cloth, uncut edges. FIVE SHILLINGS, Net.

The Work is universally regarded to be the best general Account in the English language of the Twenty Days' War : including the Battles of Quatre Bras, Ligny, Waterloo, and Wavre ; and the subsequent daring March on Paris. It is as fair to the French as it is to the Allies.

WILLIAM BEATTY, M.D., Surgeon of H.M.S. Victory.

An Authentic Narrative of the Death of Lord Nelson.

21st October, 1805.

2nd Ed. Crown 8vo. 96 *pages. Two Illustrations :*

(1) Of Lord NELSON in the dress he wore when he received his mortal wound.

(2) Of the Bullet that killed him.

Bound in Blue Cloth, uncut edges. HALF-A-CROWN, Net.

The Paston Letters.

1422—1509.

A NEW EDITION, containing upwards of 400 letters, etc., hitherto unpublished.

EDITED BY

JAMES GAIRDNER,

Of the Public Record Office.

3 Vols. Fcap. 8vo, Cloth extra, 15s. *net.*

" *The Paston Letters* are an important testimony to the progressive condition of Society, and come in as a precious link in the chain of moral history of England, which they alone in this period supply. They stand, indeed, singly, as far as I know, in Europe ; for though it is highly probable that in the archives of Italian families, if not in France or Germany, a series of merely private letters equally ancient may be concealed ; I do not recollect that any have been published. They are all written in the reigns of HENRY VI. and EDWARD IV., except a few that extend as far as HENRY VII., by different members of a wealthy and respectable, but not noble, family ; and are, therefore, pictures of the life of the English gentry of that age."— HENRY HALLAM, *Introduction to the Literature of Europe,* i. 228, *Ed.* 1837.

These Letters are the genuine correspondence of a family in Norfolk during the Wars of the Roses. As such, they are altogether unique in character ; yet the language is not so antiquated as to present any serious difficulty to the modern reader. The topics of the letters relate partly to the private affairs of the family, and partly to the stirring events of the time : and the correspondence includes State papers, love letters, bailiff's accounts, sentimental poems, jocular epistles, etc.

Besides the public news of the day, such as the Loss of Normandy by the English ; the indictment, and subsequent murder at sea of the Duke of SUFFOLK ; and all the fluctuations of the great struggle of YORK and LANCASTER ; we have the story of JOHN PASTON'S first introduction to his wife ; incidental notices of severe domestic discipline, in which his sister frequently had her head broken ; letters from Dame ELIZABETH BREWS, a match-making Mamma, who reminds the youngest JOHN PASTON that Friday is "Saint Valentine's Day," and invites him to come and visit her family from the Thursday evening till the Monday, etc., etc.

Every Letter has been exhaustively annotated ; and a Chronological Table, with most copious Indices, conclude the Work.

THE "WHITEHALL EDITION" OF THE WORKS OF WILLIAM SHAKESPEARE.

Edited from the Original Texts by H. ARTHUR DOUBLEDAY, with the assistance of T. GREGORY FOSTER and ROBERT ELSON.

In 12 volumes, imperial 16mo.

The special features to which the publishers would call attention are the TYPE, which is large enough to be read with comfort by all; the NUMBERING of the LINES, for convenience of reference; the ARRANGEMENT of the PLAYS in chronological order; and the GLOSSARY which is given at the end of each play. The text has been carefully edited from the original editions, and follows as nearly as possible that of the Folio of 1623. A few notes recording the emendations of modern Editors which have been adopted are printed at the end of each play.

The volumes are handsomely bound in buckram and in cloth, 5s. per volume. Also in half-parchment, gilt top, 6s. per volume.

SOME PRESS OPINIONS OF "THE WHITEHALL SHAKESPEARE."

"The print is clear, the paper good, the margin sufficient, and the volume not too cumbersome."—*Times*.

"The text gives every evidence of being edited with care and scholarship. . . . On the whole, *The Whitehall Shakespeare* promises to be one of the most generally attractive among the many editions of the bard which compete for public favour."—*Scotsman*.

"The general effect is excellent . . . it deserves a great success."—*National Observer*.

"*The Whitehall Shakespeare* commends itself by its convenient form, and its clear and handsome type, as well as by some special features, among which is the alphabetical index to all the characters in the plays in each volume."—*Daily News*.

"It combines, as far as possible, the requirements of a library and popular edition."—*Literary World*.

"There is certainly no edition of Shakespeare in the market which is more prettily got up or better printed. . . . One of the best editions for the general reader that have ever appeared in this country."—*Scottish Leader*.

"Paper, print, and binding leave little to be desired."—*Standard*.

WESTMINSTER: ARCHIBALD CONSTABLE & CO., 14, PARLIAMENT STREET.